The Making of English Towns

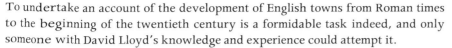

To undertake an account of the development of English towns from Roman times to the beginning of the twentieth century is a formidable task indeed, and only someone with David Lloyd's knowledge and experience could attempt it.

Those fortunate enough to have accompanied the author on one of his celebrated Town Walks will know his gift for bringing the ancient history of a town to life by focusing attention on the significant details in streets and buildings and explaining them in terms of the town's social and economic development. David Lloyd has now brought this skill to examining the overall pattern of townscapes in England and Wales showing, for example, what can still be seen of a Saxon town, how feudalism affected the early growth of settlements and their relation to castles, why boroughs evolved and what was the function of markets and fairs, all of which have left permanent features in towns. He follows this with an intriguing section on the development of medieval streets and houses many of which are seen in the plans of our towns today, and demonstrates the enormous influence of the medieval church on secular as well as ecclesiastical planning, building and institutions.

The dramatic effects of the Industrial Revolution are thoroughly investigated – a number of popular misconceptions are put right for good measure – and there are very different chapters on Georgian London and the development of country towns. To many who may have felt hitherto a lack of enthusiasm for Victorian building and town planning, David Lloyd's summary of the nineteenth century will prove a revelation – the achievements and failures of this dynamic period, the evidence of much of which is still with us, makes compulsive reading and gives an invaluable background to the problems of many towns today. The story ends with the social and economic threads drawn together in the planning and building of Letchworth, the first Garden City.

This is a book to treasure, for it will be read and referred to innumerable times, and there will be few readers whose understanding and enjoyment of English towns will not be immeasurably enhanced.

'Written by a recognised authority, this is an outstanding treatment of its subject.'
– *Library Journal (USA)*

Also by David Lloyd

Historic Towns of East Anglia
Historic Towns of Kent and Sussex
Historic Towns of Hampshire and Surrey
The Buildings of Portsmouth and its Environs
Save the City: A Conservation Study of the City of London (*General Editor*)
with Nikolaus Pevsner – Hampshire (*Buildings of England* series)
with Donald Insall – Railway Station Architecture

The Making of

English Towns

2000 years of evolution

David W. Lloyd

Victor Gollancz Ltd
in association with
Peter Crawley

First published in Great Britain
in association with Peter Crawley
by Victor Gollancz Ltd,
14 Henrietta Street, London WC2E 8QJ
First published in paperback August 1992

© David W. Lloyd 1984, 1992

A catalogue record for this book is available
from the British Library

ISBN 0-575-05311-9

Designed by Harold Bartram

Filmset and Printed in Great Britain
by BAS Printers Limited,
Over Wallop, Hampshire

Contents

List of Photographs

List of maps

Acknowledgments for photographs

All the photographs are the copyright of Peter Crawley except:

Copyright, National Monuments Record
Nos. 103 (Albert Dock, Liverpool); 127 (Liverpool Waterfront); 137 (former Watts Warehouse, Manchester); 139 (Lime Street Chambers, Liverpool)

Copyright, Keith Parkinson
Nos. 64 (sorting wool, Bradford); 92 (view of Todmorden); 128 (Clocktower Mill, Burnley); 151 (housing, Copley, Halifax)

Copyright, The Headmistress, Kettlebridge School, Sheffield
Nos. 147 and 148 (Hammerton School, now Kettlebridge School)

Copyright, David Lloyd
Nos. 61 (Western Walls, Southampton); 68 (Wool House, Southampton); 138 (Theatre Royal, Portsmouth); 145 (The Vale, Portsmouth); 146 (Sussex Terrace, Portsmouth)

Acknowledgements are made to Guildhall Library, City of London, for Map XVII, and to the British Library for the remainder of the maps

Introduction to the first edition

This is a history of towns and cities in England and Wales from Roman times to the beginning of this century, followed by an Epilogue which brings the story to the present day. It explains why they developed and how they obtained their present forms. The scope is enormous, so that the material has to be highly selective. London and the principal cities are covered, to varying degrees of detail. Smaller towns are selected because they provide examples of patterns and tendencies, or because they are specially interesting in themselves.

It is impossible to define a town as distinct from a village. Generally the existence of a successful market provided a criterion before the Industrial Revolution. In more recent periods, industrial developments of great significance have sometimes taken place in quite small places, and it would have been foolish, for instance, to omit mention of Cromford, the site of the first cotton mill, just because it never grew from a village into a town.

Studies of urban history have increased enormously in scope, depth and number over the last thirty years. Some studies, general or particular, relate to the plan forms of towns, others to their buildings, others to their social life, or to their economic activities. Many are confined to particular periods. This book attempts to cover all these aspects—physical, architectural, social and commercial—over two millennia. As a writer whose basic expertise is in architectural history and the problems of modern town planning, I have read and referred to an enormous number of publications in much wider fields. Many of these are listed in the Bibliography. In short, I owe debts, sometimes great, to hundreds of writers and scholars whose works have helped in the compilation of this selective history of a large part of our British civilization. This Bibliography has been omitted in the present edition, for reasons set out in the Introduction to the paperback edition overleaf.

Most of the maps are reproductions of the Victorian editions of the Ordnance Survey six-inch-to-one-mile maps, which have a degree of detail far greater than their modern equivalents. One map, illustrating Georgian London, is to a larger scale, and there is a reproducion of Wenceslaus Hollar's map of the City of London after the Great Fire. (Not all the maps are reproduced to their original scales). There is a small-scale map indicating places mentioned in the text, and also a population table showing how selected regions of Great Britain developed after 1800.

The majority of the photographs were taken by Peter Crawley, without whose drive, inspiration and encouragement this book would never have been achieved. Acknowledgements for the rest of the photographs are indicated on page 12.

DAVID W. LLOYD, Old Harlow, Essex, 1983

Introduction to the paperback edition

This is a reprint of my book published in 1984, with a few corrections but no major alterations. Although knowledge of towns and cities has generally increased, I do not think that the book would have been very different if I had written it seven years later. Perhaps the most relevant discovery since 1983 is that the main part of early Saxon London, was in the Aldwych–Charing Cross area west of the present and original Roman City, the site of which remained largely vacant – although it contained the first St Paul's Cathedral – till later Saxon times.

More is known about medieval timber-framed buildings, especially those that began as hall-houses. More early timber buildings survive in towns in some measure than was previously thought, though they may have been repeatedly altered and adapted so that little of their origin is revealed outside. However their distribution is uneven; most survive in East Anglia, the South-East, the West Midlands and the Welsh Border and parts of the Pennines, together with a few towns elsewhere like York, Salisbury and Exeter.

The relationship of landscape to buildings deserves further study. In Bath, the Royal and Lansdown Crescents confront romantic scenery, much like classical mansions in Capability Brown parks. Georgian squares in London were planted like pieces of rural parkland within the urban framework. Victorian garden suburbs – the idea was developed long before the term was coined – fused buildings and domestic landscape in romantically irregular layouts. Raymond Unwin and his associates developed the pattern more formally. A house in a generally green setting with its own little plot is still the ideal for most British people.

'Tourism' has expanded enormously in recent years, but is far too frequently scorned. To the writer, walking round a fine town is a most pleasurable experience. Of course a few places have too many visitors at certain times. But medieval streets and market places were often thronged, and cathedrals were built (for one among many reasons) to impress occasional crowds. Bath was built to accommodate visitors. I hope that this book will indicate that, for instance, Norwich, Shrewsbury and Stamford are comparable to Canterbury and York, and that Newcastle, Halifax or Liverpool can seem as interesting as many cities which are dominantly medieval or Georgian.

The Bibliography in the first edition was a detailed list of relevant books published up to 1983. Updating this list would have been a major task – and in any case the new inclusions could not have been consulted while writing the book. Rather than reprinting what is now, inevitably, an outdated list it was decided, with great regret, to omit the Bibliography in the present edition. Reference to it can, of course, be made in copies of the first edition in libraries or elsewhere.

DAVID W. LLOYD, March 1992

1
The Roman Beginnings

The Romans invaded Britain in AD 43. By the end of the first century they had conquered what we now know as England and Wales, and established towns and military bases, many of them predecessors of present-day cities and towns.

Archaeologists and historians are not agreed as to whether there were any pre-Roman settlements which could have been called towns as we understand the term. The relatively civilized *Belgae* from Northern Europe had settled for about a hundred years in South-East England; they had important settlements near present-day Colchester and St Albans, and others at Canterbury, Winchester and Silchester. There were numerous hill-forts with earthen ramparts, particularly in the South-West—the best-known is Maiden Castle outside Dorchester in Dorset. Excavations have recently shown that there was an important early trading settlement on Christchurch Harbour in Hampshire. Other significant pre-Roman settlements are known to have existed on the sites of later towns and villages such as Leicester, Worcester and Dorchester-on-Thames, as well as near Cirencester.

The Romans quickly established military bases; the earliest in Britain was at Richborough, near Sandwich, where they first landed. Their first major military centre, where a whole legion was stationed, was at Colchester, adjoining the conquered Belgic settlement. This was soon abandoned as a major base as the Romans advanced into Britain, in favour of new legionary fortresses at Lincoln, Wroxeter (Shropshire) and Gloucester. As the conquerors penetrated still further, these were in turn superseded, before the end of the first century, by legionary bases at York, Chester, and Caerleon in South Wales.

The typical Roman military base, or *castrum*, was laid out to a standard plan. It was a rectangle with external ramparts or walls—usually of earth and timber at first, later often in stone—and gates at the centres of the sides. Streets led in from the gates to form a cross or T pattern. Adjoining the central street junction was the headquarters building, usually set back behind a courtyard flanked by wings. The rest of the *castrum* would contain barrack blocks and ancilliary buildings on a grid of thoroughfares. The outlines of such a plan can be detected at

1. Bridge Street, Chester follows the line of the main street of Roman *Deva*. The *principium*, or headquarters, was where the church is.

Note the Rows, or first-floor walkways, unique to the city (**21**). Buildings date from the 17th century (white gabled range on left) to the early 20th (mock Tudor on right). The tower in the background is the Victorian Town Hall.

both Chester (1) and York, where present-day streets follow the courses of the main Roman thoroughfares—Watergate, Eastgate and Bridge Streets in Chester; Stonegate, and, with some deviation, Petergate in York—and where the medieval city walls partly overlay the Roman defences. At York the remains of the Multangular Tower which stood at one corner of the Roman defences can still be seen, while the Minster is built on the site of the headquarters building. (The place name elements 'chester', 'caster' and 'cester', together with other variants, result from the Anglo-Saxons' corruption of *castrum*, but they used the terms to apply to the remains of any Roman settlements, whether military or not. The Welsh equivalent is 'caer'.)

In AD 49 the first legionary fortress at Colchester was replaced by a *colonia*—a planned town where retired soldiers would settle, providing a model of Roman civilization for the conquered people. It had a grid of streets, preserved to some extent in the present town, and was dominated by a great temple of Claudius, the reigning Emperor treated as a god in his lifetime. This, rebuilt after the city was sacked by the rebel Celtic Queen Boadicea in AD 60, was probably the grandest religious building in Roman Britain; the base survives under the present Colchester Castle. Later, Lincoln (2) and Gloucester, having also ceased to be legionary fortresses, were refounded as *colonia*.

London was established by the Romans just before AD 50 where as far as is known there had previously been no significant settlement. The site—that of the present City—was on relatively high, dry ground adjoining the river, where ships could be moored. The Roman bridge, a few yards downstream from the present London Bridge, became the focal point for newly constructed roads from several Channel ports (at Richborough, Dover, Pevensey, Chichester and elsewhere) and from the rest of Britain. Tacitus, writing in AD 60, called London an important trading city. Immediately after then it was sacked by Queen Boadicea, along with Colchester and St Albans, but like them it was quickly rebuilt.

Outside London, the *coloniae* and the military bases, the Romans developed a series of towns which were the focal points of *civitates*, or civil regions which often corresponded, as nearly as possible, with Celtic tribal areas. These were the centres of administration, justice, commerce and culture through which the Romans sought to impart the supposed benefits of their civilization to the people of the conquered lands. Among the largest were Cirencester, at the heart of a region which came to have numerous *villae*, or Roman agricultural estates; St Albans (*Verulamium*), which succeeded an important pre-Roman settlement; and Wroxeter, established first as a legionary fortress, and then re-founded as a civilian town, where there developed an iron industry. This, interestingly, adjoined the part of Shropshire where methods of processing iron were revolutionized many centuries later. Other Roman regional capitals were at Silchester, like Wroxeter, now a deserted site (I, p. 20), Canterbury, Leicester, Dorchester (Dorset), Chichester (3), Winchester, and Exeter—the last three preserve Roman alignments in their main streets and city walls. Caerwent in South Wales, and Caistor, near Norwich, were smaller towns with similar status.

York was unusually complex. As often happened, a civilian settlement grew up outside the original military base, mainly on the south-eastern side of the River Ouse. This settlement developed into a *colonia*, distinct from the legionary fortress, by the early third century, and became the main administrative centre for the

North of Britain. Two Emperors, Severus and Constantius Chlorus, visited and died in York—in 211 and 306 respectively, and Hadrian had probably been based there when he initiated the building of his famous Wall further north about 122.

As well as the *coloniae* and regional centres, there were numerous lesser towns, which we would now call market towns, in Roman Britain. The sites of some of these are covered by modern cities like Manchester, Worcester, Rochester and Cambridge; others by smaller present-day places such as Dorchester-on-Thames, Towcester, Dunstable and Baldock—the last two were deliberately founded as medieval market towns on former Roman sites which had been abandoned for several centuries. Many of the sites of smaller Roman towns are now deserted, like that of *Durobrivae*, once a brick and pottery making centre, near Peterborough.

The centre of every important Roman town was the *forum*, or civic square, which usually adjoined the *basilica*, or public hall, used as a law court and meeting place—the civilian equivalent of the headquarters building in a military base.

2. Newport Arch, Lincoln, one of the few Roman structures to survive above ground in a British town, is the outer arch of the once elaborate north gate of the *colonia*. The rough hard limestone came from nearby.

3. *Right* **City Wall, Chichester**, originally late second century AD; an earth bank faced in flint and stone, which has been repeatedly repaired and renewed.

The garden behind is of the Bishop's Palace; the Cathedral was started in the 1080s (44).

4. *Below right* **St Albans Abbey**, a spiritual link with Roman Britain, is supposedly where Albanus, a soldier, was martyred in AD 209, just outside the city of *Verulamium*. The view is taken from the grassed-over site of the city. The later town developed beyond the Abbey (7).

The present Abbey, started 1077, with tower of re-used Roman bricks, was a place of pilgrimage (page 77). It became a Cathedral in 1877.

The *forum* was periodically used as a market place and, typically, was flanked by single-storeyed buildings with small rooms set behind colonnade façades, used variously as shops, offices or meeting rooms. The ground plan is known, from excavation, of the *forum* and *basilica* at St Albans, where the Saxon church of St Michael occupies part of the site of the *basilica*; at Wroxeter, where an inscription records a dedication to the Emperor Hadrian in 129; and at Silchester, Caerwent and elsewhere. London had the largest *forum* and *basilica* known north of the Alps, rebuilt in time for Hadrian's visit to the city in 122. It lay on the sites of the present Leadenhall Market and the buildings south of Cornhill.

Leisure was well provided for in Roman towns. Public baths, where people immersed themselves in complex successions of cold, tepid and hot water, were found in quite small towns as well as military establishments. They contained other amenities besides actual baths, and were really public 'clubs' open to the free populace. Foundations of several bath buildings have been excavated, including those at Leicester and Wroxeter; in both places single gaunt stretches of ruined wall survive above ground—the one in the heart of a big modern city, the other on a deserted site, both equally poignant. But the greatest baths in Roman Britain were those at Bath, or *Aquae Sulis*, fed by the remarkable series of natural springs which caused the city to develop again as a watering place in Georgian times. The main bath essentially survives, in the midst of a group of eighteenth- and nineteenth-century structures which include the present Pump Room. Current archaeological investigation is revealing more and more of the original Roman complex.

The more important towns had theatres, built on the classical model with rounded, tiered auditorium, partly open to the sky; the most substantial remains are at St Albans. Amphitheatres were larger, intended for big spectacles and popular gatherings; they were circular or oval, with tiered seats or stands usually on earthen banks, and were usually situated just outside the towns or army bases. Appreciable remains survive at Dorchester, adapted from a prehistoric earthwork, Silchester, Chester and Caerleon.

In religion, the Roman Empire, before Constantine, was polytheistic, with numerous cults, so that towns often had several temples. Perhaps no other was as grand as that of Claudius at Colchester, except possibly that at Bath, dedicated to Sul and Minerva—a characteristic Roman adaptation of a Celtic cult, Sul having been the local Celtic deity of the waters (hence *Aquae Sulis*), linked by the Romans with their goddess Minerva. Entirely Roman was the dedication to Neptune and Minerva of a temple at Chichester, which, as a surviving inscription records, was built in the first century by Cogidubnus. This Celtic 'client king' was allowed to rule locally from his sumptuous palace at nearby Fishbourne, the remains of which are now skilfully displayed. The actual site of the Chichester temple is not known.

The Christians were one sect among many, until the Emperor Constantine made Christianity the official religion of the Empire in 312. The only known remains in a Roman town of what was probably a church are at Silchester, buried under a field. Perhaps the most tangible link with Roman Christianity is provided by St Albans Cathedral (4). This stands on the supposed site of the martyrdom of the soldier Albanus, which took place in 209 just outside the Roman city of *Verulamium*, during a persecution initiated by the Emperor Severus, then in York. Interestingly, the oldest parts of the present cathedral, built in about 1080, are partly constructed of re-used bricks from the then abandoned Roman city.

Although Roman towns in Britain had regular street plans, there seems to have been little attempt to create formal groupings of buildings in relation to streets and spaces, except around the *forum*. Evidence from excavation indicates that buildings of grand and smaller scales were disposed piecemeal within the street patterns. Shop premises often occupied long plots with short street frontages—like medieval town plots—with the retail space in front, stores or workshops behind and, in many instances, living accommodation above. Grander houses were often set round courtyards, and usually had mosaic floors and elaborate heating systems. Little is known of the less substantial dwellings of humbler townspeople.

Most Roman towns were defended with ramparts or walls. At least at first, these would often be of earth, augmented by wooden palisades, with external ditches. Walls of masonry, either revetments to earth ramparts or free-standing, became more general towards the end of the Roman occupation. Materials would be those easily available. Flint or rubble might be used, bonded at intervals by bands of Roman bricks, as in the eroded but still fairly substantial Roman walls at Colchester, and the much more fragmentary ones at St Albans. Substantial remains of Roman stone walls can be seen at Caerwent, Caistor near Norwich, Rochester, and Lincoln where the original *colonia*, set on the hill, was later extended downhill with new lengths of wall. At Winchester, Exeter and Chichester (3) the Roman walls were rebuilt or restored as the medieval city walls, which still partly survive. The same happened in London, and fine stretches of City wall, displaying both Roman and medieval masonry, have been revealed north of the Tower and at the Barbican. At Chester, parts of the city walls still show Roman masonry (60). Lincoln retains the outer arch of one of its Roman town gates (2); Colchester has the remains, and St Albans the foundations, of more impressive gates which, standing at the approaches from London to both cities, were testimonies of civic pride as well as defensive structures. However, none of the surviving pieces of Roman city wall in Britain are as impressive as those of some of the forts built along the south and east coasts in the third and fourth centuries as defences against the threatening Saxons, notably at Pevensey and Portchester. These, together with parts of Hadrian's Wall, are the most impressive Roman structures surviving above ground in Britain. Most of the evidence for Roman towns in Britain is known through excavation, the results of which are sometimes on public display, either on the sites themselves, or in museums such as those at St Albans, Bath, York, Reading (with material from Silchester), Chester, Cirencester, Caerleon, Colchester and London.

Map I Silchester, Hampshire is the deserted site of *Calleva Attrebatum*. This map of 1874 shows the street pattern, the outline of the central *Forum*, of which archaeological excavation had started in 1864, and the remains of the city wall.

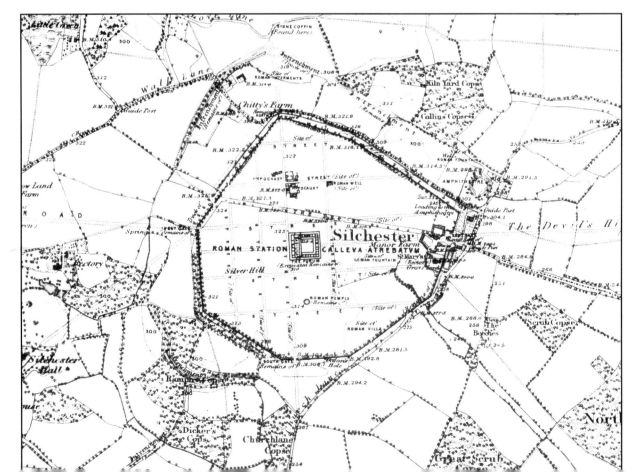

2
The Saxon Settlement

The Roman forces in Britain were recalled by the Emperor Honorius in 410. Urban life continued in some civilian towns, notably St Albans, for a time, but not after the middle of the fifth century. Money was no longer minted; even worn Roman coins ceased to circulate after about 450, indicating that sophisticated commerce had ended. But some, at least, of the Roman towns continued to be occupied on a much reduced, village, scale. Possibly London, York, Bath, Winchester and a few other places had some sort of continuing life until they developed again into important towns.

The first Saxons in Britain were mercenary soldiers under Roman command. Saxons, Angles and Jutes migrated from Northern Europe and spread over eastern and central England by 500; by 600 they had reached nearly every part of England except the far South-West and Cumbria. The extent to which they mingled with, enslaved, or displaced the native people in different areas is in dispute by historians and archaeologists. They lived, at first, almost entirely in villages or farms.

Numerous Saxon kingdoms emerged with fluid boundaries and frequently warring rulers. Of these Kent reached some degree of civilization by the late sixth and seventh centuries, and East Anglia by the seventh – to judge by the artistic quality of jewellery and other artefacts found in graves of the period.

Christianity flourished in Ireland, Wales and the Celtic South-West in the fifth and sixth centuries, but it became almost extinct over most of England under the early pagan Saxons, except, probably, in a few enclaves like St Albans (4). It was brought back at the instigation of Pope Gregory to Canterbury, seat of the King of Kent and his already Christian wife Bertha, in 597 when Augustine was installed as the first Archbishop. By 604 there were bishops' churches in Rochester and London – the first primitive St Paul's. There was a church in York by 627, but the bishopric was not firmly established there for several decades. Meanwhile Celtic missionaries from Scotland founded Lindisfarne monastery on an island off the Northumbrian coast, which became a great centre of evangelism, and of the illustrative arts associated with manuscripts. Many other monasteries were set up under its influence, as at Whitby, Hexham, Hartlepool and, especially, Jarrow, where Bede wrote the first history of the English people in the early eighth century. Jarrow, like its brother monastery at Monkwearmouth, was remotely set beside a swampy estuary, which even then must have been bleak; Whitby and Hartlepool were on exposed coastal sites. It was to be many centuries before towns developed at any of these places. Amazingly, something survives of the churches Bede used, in totally transformed surroundings, at both Jarrow and Monkwearmouth, which is now part of Sunderland.

Eighth-century Northumbria was, because of the culture of its monasteries, one of the few parts of northern Europe with a glimmer of civilization between the collapse of the western Roman Empire and the beginning of the Middle Ages. The capital of the kingdom—which stretched south to the Humber—was York, which regained, or retained, something of its Roman importance. Its school, or seminary, gained some fame; the best known teacher there was Alcuin, who had trained under Bede and was invited by Charlemagne to set up a similar school in Tours, as a centre of cultural enlightenment in his deeply barbaric empire.

Bede records that in his time London was once more a place of trade with continental Europe. It was not the only English trading centre of the period. The royal dynasty of East Anglia, associated with the Sutton Hoo ship burial and its associated treasures, established Ipswich as a port and trading town in the mid seventh century—one of the earliest English towns to develop on a non-Roman site. Canterbury had an outport at Fordwich, and there was overseas trade at Rochester and Dover. Most remarkable of the early Saxon ports was *Hamwic*, the precursor of Southampton, where the outline of a regularly planned town with a grid of streets, and evidence of metal and pottery crafts, has lately been revealed. All these ports traded with northern Europe, especially the Rhine delta, the Somme estuary, and the Seine up to Rouen, from which wine was shipped to England. Once again there was organized coinage.

The Vikings attacked Lindisfarne in 793, and Jarrow in the following year. Attacks on other monasteries followed, and in the mid ninth century there were large-scale invasions. The term 'Vikings' embraces both Norsemen and Danes. At first they were mainly Norse from Norway, who also occupied the Scottish Islands, the Isle of Man and much of Ireland, from which they reached north-western England. The main invasions of England were, however, by Danes, who settled thickly in and around Yorkshire and Lincolnshire where the ending -*by* indicates a Viking settlement. They soon controlled all eastern and much of southern England until King Alfred of Wessex rallied against them and drove them out of his south-western kingdom. At the treaty of Wedmore in 886, it was agreed that the Danes would control all England east of the River Lea and Watling Street, the surviving Roman highway from London to Chester, and Alfred the rest. After Alfred's death his daughter Ethelfleda and son Edward fought on and, by stages, recovered the eastern Midlands and East Anglia. In these conflicts a number of defended settlements were established, some of which have developed into present-day towns.

Alfred instituted in his kingdom a system of *burhs*, or strongholds—the word is related to the German *burg*, originally meaning a defended place. Some were Roman towns whose defences were repaired—Winchester, Chichester, Exeter, Bath. Some were established monastic centres, in good defensive positions, like Malmesbury, in a bend of a river, and Wilton, within a confluence—since rivers provided defensive barriers. Some were on steep-sided hills, like Lewes (**26, 28**) and Shaftesbury. When natural features were not sufficient, earthen ramparts were formed, the most impressive partly surviving being at Wareham and Wallingford.

Most of these *burhs* developed as trading towns (**II**)—though some did not, and are now deserted sites, or small villages like Burpham in Sussex. Many of the *burhs* which developed as towns have regular street patterns which were clearly laid out in the time of Alfred or his successors. The most striking example is Winchester. The Roman city, like others, was largely abandoned after the Romans left, leaving perhaps a small residual settlement beside which the first cathedral was built in the seventh century, and a royal palace established. Except for the main thoroughfare—the present High Street—the lines of the Roman streets were lost. Within the newly strengthened Roman walls, King Alfred (almost certainly) laid out a new pattern of regular parallel streets running north and south off the High Street. Archaeological investigations have indicated that these did not correspond to the older Roman streets, which were covered by the buildings and plots fronting the Saxon thoroughfares. The lines of most of these Saxon streets survive in present-day Winchester. At Wareham, the Saxon *burh* was laid out within the earthen ramparts with four regular streets, and there is a similar pattern at Wallingford. Interestingly, both at Wareham and Wallingford the regular Saxon plan form was overlaid in one corner by a Norman castle of which, in each case, earthworks survive. Oxford is another town which originated as a *burh* of Alfred's time; here the Saxon ramparts were replaced by later stone walls, parts of which survive. The cross pattern of High Street, Cornmarket, Queen Street and St Aldate's, together with some of the lesser streets like Ship Street and the Turl, perpetuate the regular planning of Saxon times. Some of the smaller *burhs*, like Bridport, probably consisted of single streets (5).

Alfred's system of *burhs* was extended into the Midlands by his daughter and son. Roman Chester and Manchester were re-fortified; new *burhs* were established as at Stafford, Warwick and Shrewsbury, the last two on notably good defensive sites. At the same time the Danes developed in the eastern Midlands a system of towns including the 'Five Boroughs' of Leicester, Lincoln—these two were Roman cities revived—Nottingham, Derby and Stamford, each a stronghold and a trading centre; Northampton was another. All in turn fell into the hands of the Saxons, who developed other *burhs*, including Bedford and Hertford, further south.

York had another remarkable phase in its eventful history between 876 and 937, when it was the capital of a distinct Viking kingdom. It was then an important trading city, as recent excavations have revealed, with its commercial heart near

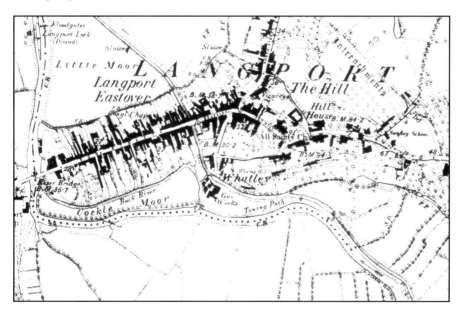

Map II Langport, Somerset, a Saxon *burh* (stronghold) and *port* (trading town), shown on a map of 1891. King Alfred's *burh* was on a bluff (marked as 'The Hill'); the long street extends into low-lying land, defended by artificial water-courses.

5. *Right* **Bridport, Dorset** was a Saxon *burh*, probably of one thoroughfare on the line of South Street, seen in this photograph, with an early church on the site of the present one with its 15th century tower. Opposite (right) are the tall windows of a simple Quaker meeting house, 1697, set in a row of houses.

6. *Below right* **South Street, Bridport**, further north. The Town Hall of 1786, of brick with stone dressings, the stone-faced Tudor building on the right, and the plain late Georgian house fronts mainly of brick, illustrate the contrasts seen in a town on a 'borderline' site, where both stone and good clay for brick are available (page 56).

7. *Opposite* **Market Place, St Albans**, laid out *c* 950 beside the Abbey (**4**). The original space extended from the site of the gabled building on the left to beyond those on the right, which are the results of early encroachments replacing market stalls (page 47).

The tower, *c* 1410, was the town belfry, a rarity in England; the gabled building, left, is 15th century with central hall, subdivided, and wings.

the navigable River Ouse and its tributary the Foss. Many of the city's street names probably originated in this period, particularly those ending in *-gate*, deriving from a Scandinavian word meaning not 'gate' but 'street'. Other towns in northern and eastern England retain street names ending in *-gate*, of similar derivation.

After the capture by the Saxon King Athelstan of Viking York in 937, England had a period of unified government. Athelstan reformed the coinage; he named specific towns where coins could be minted under ultimate royal control. The more important towns were allocated several mints—London eight, Canterbury seven and Winchester six; at the other end of the scale Lewes was allowed two and Chichester one. By this time, towns had become primarily trading centres rather than defensive strongholds.

The Vikings were at first heathen, but when they settled they soon adopted Christianity, and the Church recovered from their earlier, terrible, depredations. The tenth century was a period of European monastic revival, stimulated by the great abbey of Cluny, in Burgundy, founded in 910. In England new monasteries were established and old ones revived; among the greatest were Glastonbury, (claiming its origin in the early days of Christianity), Peterborough and Ely in the Fens, Evesham and Winchcombe in the Severn Valley, Abingdon, St Albans, and, for nuns, Barking, Shaftesbury and Wilton. Towns developed beside these monasteries; perhaps the most remarkable was St Albans. The decayed Roman city was succeeded by a Saxon *burh* nearby (**8, 9**); King Offa endowed a monastery on the supposed site of Albanus's martyrdom (**4**). About 950 Abbot Wulsin laid out a new town north of the abbey, away both from the Roman city and the Saxon *burh*. This was based on a long tapering market place, still evident in the modern city, though partly infilled at its widest end (**7**). He also built three parish churches, including St Michael's on the site of the basilica (page 18).

Some of the Saxon cathedrals were located, following Continental practice, in cities of Roman origin, such as Canterbury, York, London, Winchester, Worcester and Rochester, but many were in small and otherwise unimportant places, like Wells, Lichfield, Sherborne, Crediton and North Elmham—where, for a time, the East Anglian see was located. Many were associated with monasteries. At Canterbury there was a second great monastery, St Augustine's, as well as that related to the cathedral. Winchester must have seemed particularly impressive in late

8. Fishpool Street, St Albans runs along the edge of the site of an early Saxon *burh* which was intermediate, in time and place, between Roman *Verulamium* and the later Saxon town (7). The houses are built on the line of the worn-down earthen ramparts of the *burh*, and so are above the level of the street.

Saxon times, for, beside the original cathedral, which stood just to the north-west of the present cathedral, and its associated monastery, there were a second monastery, a nunnery, and the royal palace. In the tenth century Winchester was famous for manuscript illustration, as Lindisfarne had been earlier.

Apart from cathedrals, there were in early Saxon times other major churches called *monasteria* or minsters, not necessarily monastic as we understand the term, which were centres of worship and evangelism for their surrounding areas. The seventh-century church at Brixworth, Northamptonshire, one of the largest pre-Conquest churches remaining, probably had this status and indicates how relatively grand the more important early Saxon churches might be. Later in the Saxon period, more and more churches were built in the outlying areas originally served

26

by the minsters, most of them eventually becoming parish churches in their own right; by the eleventh century a high proportion of villages in southern and eastern England had their own churches. In the more important towns, churches similarly multiplied; London, Norwich, Ipswich, Lincoln, York, Oxford, Wareham and other towns had several churches even before the Norman Conquest. Among Saxon churches partly surviving in towns, several retain impressive towers including St Benet, Cambridge, St Michael, Oxford, and Holy Trinity, Colchester (10). The tower of the last is built of rough stone laced with re-used Roman bricks. St Martin, Wareham survives substantially intact, a simple two-cell building with nave and chancel, to which a north aisle and lower tower were added later. Fairly similar, but more elaborate, is the Saxon church at Bradford-on-Avon which, having

9. **Fishpool Street, St Albans**, further east. The older houses are timber-framed, often plastered over; many have Georgian brick fronts, and there are a few small former shop fronts.

27

10. Holy Trinity, Colchester
preserves the tower of a Saxon
parish church, laced with re-
used Roman bricks.

The tower in the background
is that of the Town Hall,
c 1900, topped by a statue of St
Helena, the Roman empress
who by long but impossible
local tradition was born in the
Roman town.

ceased to be a church at an early date, was secularized, altered, and embedded in later buildings, to be rediscovered and restored about a hundred years ago. Churches such as these are the only Saxon structures, apart from earthworks, which survive above ground in English towns.

Saxon street patterns often survive, as in towns already mentioned, and also, even, in the City of London. Here, as in many other English cities and towns, there was no large open market place; markets were held along the streets, like Cheapside, Poultry and Cornhill, whose names commemorate a series of early markets, either general ("cheapen"—buying and selling), or specialized (poultry or corn). These were supplemented by side streets whose names still commemorate the commodities originally sold there—Bread Street, Milk Street, Wood Street and also Coleman Street (the street of the charcoal men). There was another market street further east—Eastcheap.

The counties of middle and western England were mostly formed in, or by, the tenth century. Typically each was based on a *burh*—Stafford, Warwick, Lincoln, Shrewsbury and Hertford are obvious examples—to the defence of which landholders might be expected to contribute when needed, and where the shire reeve (sheriff), the king's representative, held his court. Other counties, like Kent and Sussex, were based on earlier Saxon kingdoms.

Two cities became prominent by the end of the Saxon period, Bristol and Norwich. Bristol was probably established in the late tenth century beside a bridge over the River Avon (Bridge-stow, the place of the bridge), on an easily defended site between the Avon and its tributary the Frome. It had a regular cross of streets, represented by the present High, Wine, Broad and Corn Streets in the heart of the modern city. It inevitably became a major route centre, a sort of western counterpart of London, but with its tidal port facing west, which was to be very significant in later centuries. Norwich grew at the expense of Thetford, which for a time had been the principal town in East Anglia.

Vikings harassed England again in the late tenth and early eleventh centuries, until the Danish Canute became king of a once more peaceful England in 1016. Some towns were re-fortified during this period, but one of the most notable events of this unsettled age, in terms of urban history, was the foundation of Durham—by the religious community based originally on Lindisfarne, and displaced by the first Viking raid in 793. In 995 they selected a new site for their monastery, on a steep-sided peninsula almost encircled by the River Wear. The story of Durham is taken further in Chapter Seven. (**XIV**, p. 78)

By the time of the Norman Conquest there were dozens of places, varying in size from London, York and Winchester down to minor market centres, which could be recognized as towns, however small by modern standards. Many were recorded, twenty years after the Conquest, in Domesday Book as having the status of *burgus*—the Latin form of *burh* (the modern form is 'borough')—which by that time had evolved from meaning simply a fortified place to signifying a community with a definite, specifically urban, status where trade was encouraged. The characteristics of medieval boroughs are described in Chapter Four.

3
Feudalism –
Castles and Manors

Within twenty years of the Norman Conquest, Norman barons, Norman bishops and Norman royal officials replaced nearly all their Saxon counterparts. Nearly every piece of cultivable land in England became part of a feudal manor, controlled by a Norman overlord, or sometimes a hierarchy of overlords. Domesday Book, compiled in 1086, shows how completely and consistently William the Conqueror pursued his policy of bringing England under Norman control, through the feudal system.

Feudalism was a pattern of land tenure related to military service, which had developed in northern Europe in the ninth and tenth centuries. All land in a feudal state was held ultimately by the king or equivalent ruler. Under him were powerful magnates, or 'barons', who controlled territories and were obliged to provide him with armed men when required. Ecclesiastical bodies, such as bishoprics and abbeys, could also hold land in this way. Often these landholders, whether lay or ecclesiastic, would grant parts of their territories to lesser lords, in return again for military support. The basic unit of territory in the feudal system was the manor, the organization of which is described later.

Castles

Castles were the most obvious manifestations of feudal power. The first castles were built when the feudal system started to develop, especially in the Duchy of Normandy, which had been conquered and settled by Vikings, or 'Northmen', early in the tenth century. There were none in England until just before the Norman Conquest, when three or four are known to have been built, including that at Hereford. After the Conquest hundreds of castles were built, by the King himself, by his magnates, by churchmen, or by lesser lords.

Castles were more than military strongholds; they were focal points of feudal power. They were the residences, even if only occasional, of the kings or lords who held them, and who might possess several others, or of their tenants and officials. They were garrisoned, regularly or according to need, as bases for campaigns and forays, or as strongholds for defence, and were often used partly as prisons. They were the real and symbolic centres of control over the populace, and were often the administrative and judicial centres of surrounding lands.

The simplest type of castle was a ring of earthworks with outer ditch, enclosing a space, or bailey, within which were buildings for military, domestic or storage use. A typical Norman castle usually had a keep, or broad tower-like structure, within or on the edge of the bailey; this might be on a prominent natural site or, more often, on an artificial mound or *motte*. Important castles usually had two or more baileys. Most early castles were constructed of earth and timber—a strongly built wooden keep, and outer earthworks topped by wooden palisades, could provide effective defence. However, stone was used from the start in some of the more important castles; in many others, timber work was replaced by stone (11). Stone keeps became dominant features in many medieval towns. They were often divided into several storeys, with domestic accommodation on the first and second floors, and space for soldiers, prisoners or storage on the ground floor or in the basement (the term 'dungeon' or *donjon* strictly applied to the whole keep, but has become popularly associated specifically with dank inner rooms). In later times, keeps were often omitted, as the outer defences of castles became

11. **Launceston Castle, Cornwall**, built of timber by the first Norman Earl of Cornwall, and reconstructed in stone 13th–14th centuries, with a circular keep, and a large bailey which extended to the left of the photograph.
   The Saxon village, St Stephen's was north of (beyond) the castle; the medieval town developed mainly to the south (63).

more and more elaborate, with frequent perimeter towers and bastions, and complex gateways. The larger castles, belonging to the king or to major magnates, might contain elaborate domestic accommodation within the baileys, with halls, chambers and kitchens; sometimes there were chapels.

Many of the first castles built by William and his magnates were in the major towns. Two of the more important had great stone keeps from the start; both partly survive. The Tower of London was built on the eastern side of the City, astride its Roman and Saxon wall, to overawe its citizens, and guard the river approach; the present White Tower is essentially the original keep, but the rest of the fortress has gradually expanded and changed over succeeding centuries. At Colchester, the platform of the Temple of Claudius (page 19) was used as the base for the keep, explaining its great width—it has the largest ground area of any surviving castle keep in Europe, but is now only half of its original height. It is built of rough stone and Roman brick, probably all taken from ruined Roman buildings.

Castles were built in all the county towns as the bases for local administration through the Norman sheriffs, or king's representatives, who displaced their Saxon predecessors. Often, large numbers of houses were destroyed to make way for castles, as at Oxford, Lincoln and Huntingdon. At Lincoln, the Norman and later castle partly survives, facing, across a small square, the entrance to the cathedral

12. *Opposite* **Richmond Castle, Yorkshire**, built by Alan of Brittany from 1071 on a dramatic site, one of the earliest to be partly of stone. The keep, unusually slender, was started *c* 1150. The town developed north (right) of the castle; see page 70.

precinct, all within the area of the Roman *colonia* in the highest part of the city. At Norwich, the Norman keep remains, though entirely refaced in Victorian times, rearing, at a distance, over the large market place which the Normans laid out adjoining the Saxon town (**III**); it is now the city's Art Gallery. Among other castles in county towns, some were rebuilt grandly in later medieval times, as at Warwick; some have left only earthworks, as at Huntingdon and Bedford; others have been replaced by later county buildings, as at Chester (**117**).

Many castles were originally built away from pre-existing towns, as at Windsor, where William I chose the top of a chalk cliff by the Thames for his fortress and residence, instead of rebuilding the low-lying Saxon palace at Old Windsor two miles downstream. The first Windsor Castle was entirely of earth and timber, but it covered the same ground as today, with two large baileys on either side of a central keep. The keep was replaced by a stone one—the lower part of the present

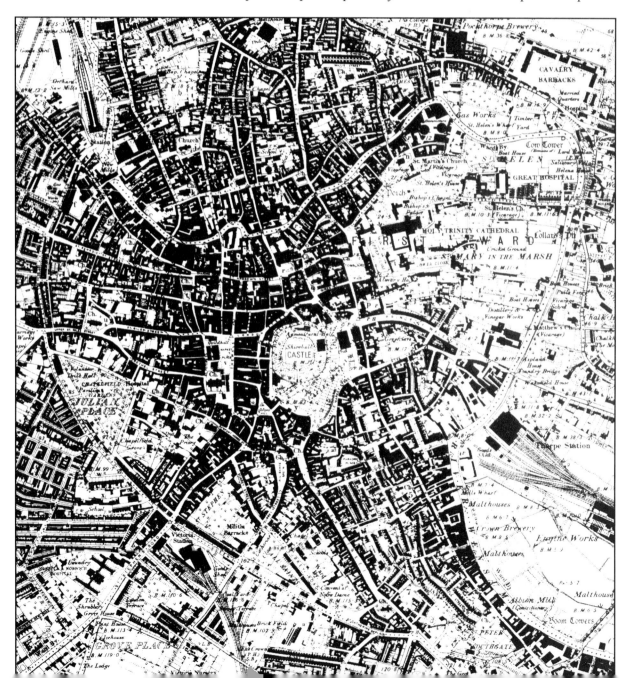

Round Tower—in the 1170s. The rest of the castle was gradually renewed and embellished, not least by George IV who gave it most of its present dramatic sky-line. The town was first established, with its market outside the castle gate, in the early twelfth century, one of many founded beside castles by medieval kings and magnates. Richmond, Yorkshire, is another castle site selected for strategic reasons, beside which a town subsequently grew (12).

The history of two families, Montgomery and Clare, illustrates well the relation-ships between feudal magnates, castles and towns. Roger de Montgomery, who, like so many barons who came with the Conqueror, had taken his name from a Norman village, was made Earl of Arundel. Here he built a castle and probably laid out the town beside it—superseding, as the centre for the surrounding area, the old Saxon *burh* at Burpham nearby. Later he was made of Earl of Shrewsbury, with special responsibility, together with his neighbouring Earls of Chester and Hereford, for defending the borderland against the still unconquered Welsh. He took over a castle which the Conqueror had already built on the isthmus of the Severn loop in which Shrewsbury is set. From there he forayed into Wales, and by 1086 built a castle just inside the present Welsh border, which he named after himself. (This was superseded in 1223 by a new castle built two miles away by Henry III, together with a new town alongside, to which the name Montgomery was transferred.) Arnulf de Montgomery, Roger's son, swept across Wales and established the first castle at Pembroke in 1093.

The first Richard de Clare was a Norman baron who took his name from the small Suffolk town of which he became lord. He built a castle there, displacing many dwellings. The family extended its territory and power, obtaining, through

Map III Norwich. This map of 1887 shows the tight-knit medieval streets centred on the Castle—the circular area in the middle. Because the Castle was then partly a prison, the building was not shown on the Ordnance map for 'security' reasons, but the Norman keep, now a museum, stands in this circular area. To the west, the Normans laid out a nearly rectangular market place which by the 19th century had become partly infilled by buildings. (Most of these intrusive buildings have been removed since the date of the map, so that the market place is once more at nearly its original extent.)

The Cathedral stands in its large, clearly defined Close (page 206). The curved line of the city wall is marked by roads on the west and south-west.

marriage, the earldom of Gloucester, which included the lordship of Glamorgan, centred on Cardiff. This part of Wales had been settled by the Normans soon after their conquest of England. About 1080 Robert Fitzhamon, the new Norman overlord, had built a castle on the site of a ruined Roman fort, and laid out the original town of Cardiff outside its gate. The Clares rebuilt part of Cardiff Castle (141), including the present gateway. More spectacularly, they built another castle at Caerphilly a few miles to the north, one of the largest, and even in its present ruined state, one of the grandest medieval fortresses in Europe. Its basic defensive role was against the truculent Welshmen in the surrounding hills who resented the alien intrusion, but its scale and grandeur exceeded military needs. Overwhelmingly, Caerphilly Castle was an architectural expression of feudal power, pomp and pride. Meanwhile, a younger branch of the Clare family had established itself in another part of Wales; Gilbert de Clare became Earl of Pembroke in 1110, rebuilt Arnulf de Montgomery's castle there, and founded the present town of Pembroke along the ridge to the east. From there, the Clares adventured into Ireland—hence the Irish castle and county bearing their name. It was perhaps 'poetic justice' that the last male member of the senior branch of the Clare family died fighting the Scots at Bannockburn. His daughter, Elizabeth de Burgh, lived in state for several more decades at Clare Castle in Suffolk—of which nothing is left but massive earthworks and a fragment of masonry—and gave the family's name to the college in Cambridge which she founded.

The adventures of the Montgomerys and Clares indicate the ways in which much of Wales was overrun by Norman-English magnates, often against spirited resistance (13, 14, IV). Gwynedd, in the North-West, was the last substantial part of Wales to hold out against the English, until Edward I conquered it in the late thirteenth century. Like the Normans in England two centuries before, he built castles as strongpoints—Flint, Conwy, Caernarfon, Harlech and Beaumaris were the most impressive—and founded towns beside them. Caernarfon Castle (page 71), started in 1283, magnificent architecturally as well as formidable militarily, was intended, like the others, to impress as well as to overawe the Welsh.

Through most of the Middle Ages the Welsh Border was parcelled out between

Map IV Newport, Pembrokeshire. This map of 1891 shows the planned medieval town laid out by Robert of Tours north of the castle (13, 14), with a slightly bent grid and a clear pattern of rectangular house plots.

13. *Opposite* **Newport, Pembrokeshire** grew beside a castle first built *c* 1190 by Robert of Tours, a Norman adventurer, on conquered Welsh territory. To the left of the surviving castle fragment is the 13th–15th century church tower.

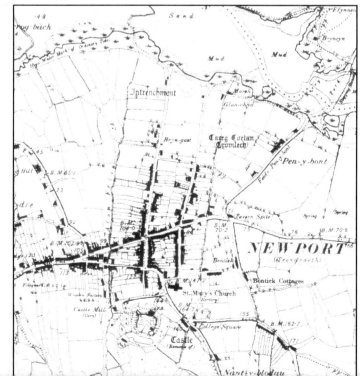

14. Upper St Mary Street, Newport, Pembrokeshire, one of the N. – S. streets of the medieval grid **(VI)**. On the left is the Baptist Chapel of 1789 with simple 'Gothic' windows, one of the oldest surviving of the numerous chapels of Nonconformist Wales. (See also **95, 109**).

numerous 'marcher lords', some powerful, others less so, frequently at odds with each other. All built castles, large and small, and some attempted to establish towns beside their castles. Some of these towns were successful, like Ludlow, Abergavenny and, on a smaller scale, Hay-on-Wye, but many other would-be towns simply receded to the status of villages, or disappeared altogether, when their castles were abandoned and fell to ruin. Examples are Painscastle in Radnorshire, Wigmore in Herefordshire, and, an extreme case, Caus, west of Shrewsbury, where the site of the castle and adjoining small settlement is simply abandoned and overgrown.

Manors

While castles were the architectural expressions of feudal magnates' power, the magnates drew their sustenance from the manors which they held. The manorial system had its roots in Saxon England, and the normal manor was based on a single village with the fields round it, taken over after the Conquest by a new Norman overlord. However, there was enormous variation in the size of manors. Some might embrace a group of villages or farmsteads; others might consist only of part of a village and of its related farmlands. The forms and shapes of villages, the patterns of farming, and the rights and customs of villagers varied greatly over different parts of the country, and even locally within small areas. But, before discussing those variations, it is a good idea to describe the 'typical' medieval feudal village, comprising, with its surrounding lands, a single manor. Such a 'typical' village was encompassed by arable fields, normally three, which were split into individual strips but farmed communally with crop rotations, each field lying fallow every third year. Each villager possessed several strips scattered over the three fields; the lord himself held some strips directly, as part of his demesne, or personal estate. There were communal meadows and pasture, usually beside a stream, and, on the fringes, manorial 'waste', partly wooded, used for rough grazing, and for the gathering of materials for building, tools and fuel. Each ordinary villager lived in a primitive cottage set in its own plot, used for small-scale private cultivation and the keeping of some livestock – for which he would have defined grazing rights in the pasture and on the waste. If there were a resident lord—who might be the tenant of some greater magnate – he would live in a manor house, built with stone or timber-framing; if not, there would be a house for the absentee lord's bailiff or agent; beside either would be the manor farmstead, with barns and other buildings. The lord's own demesne usually consisted of land adjoining the manor farmstead, as well as his strips in the arable fields mingled with those of the ordinary villagers. The villagers normally held their cottages and cottage plots, their strips in the fields, and their grazing and other rights from the overlord in return for requirements to work at specified times on the lord's demesne, and for obligations such as the surrender of beasts or other possessions before land or rights could be inherited. The management of the farming system, and the enforcement of the rights and obligations, were controlled through the manorial courts.

However, this 'normal' manorial system had endless variations. Large parts of England, like Kent, the Sussex Weald, Essex, much of East Anglia, a great deal of the West, and mountain and moorland fringe areas, had different farming systems. Such areas were often, even in the Middle Ages, divided into compact farms, each consisting of hedged fields. The 'typical' feudal village with its communal farming system was specially characteristic of the eastern and southern Midlands, much of Yorkshire, parts of the southern chalklands, and sections of East Anglia. Degrees of feudal obligation varied from place to place; some people had 'free', or almost free, status; some overlords were strict, others easy-going. Nevertheless feudal control, however infinitely varied in form and degree, operated at least in some form over most of England for two or three centuries following the Norman Conquest, after which it quickly weakened. It is against such a background that the nature and status of medieval towns must be understood.

4
Boroughs, Markets and Trade

What distinguished a town from a village in the Middle Ages? It was not simply a matter of size. Basically, a town was a place where a significant amount of trade took place, and where there was a concentration of traders and craftsmen. Most ordinary buying and selling was done in local markets, where the surplus produce from the surrounding areas could be sold, and goods not obtainable in the adjoining villages could be bought. Larger markets, and annual fairs, dealt with a wider range of merchandise.

Burgage holdings
In a feudal village, the only people not primarily concerned with farming, apart from the priest, would normally have been a few basic specialists such as a miller, a blacksmith, a carpenter, and possibly one or more people concerned with the production of clothing; any of these occupations could be carried on part-time together with agriculture. A town would have a far greater number of specialists, mostly full-time, in a wider variety of crafts and trades. It would have been impossible, or very difficult, for such people to pursue their occupations if they were subject to the obligations and constraints associated with the normal feudal village. To allow for, and encourage, such specifically urban activities, there was a special form of land holding, called burgage tenure, through which the tenant was free, or partly free, from feudal obligations, especially those requiring him to work on his lord's land.

Burgage tenure evolved in Saxon times, and was associated with places which had the status of boroughs. Numerous boroughs existed in late Saxon times and were recorded in Domesday Book (page 28), and the number increased through the Middle Ages. A borough, during the early medieval period, was a place where plots of land could be held on burgage tenure. They were called 'burgage plots' and were often long and narrow, with a frontage to a street or market place (36, XI, p. 60). They were subject to fixed annual rents which were paid to the overlord of the borough, who might be the king himself, a baron, or a churchman. Burgage tenancies could normally be bought or sold, subject to the annual rents, very much as in the free market today. The people holding these plots were able to carry on trades and crafts independently of agriculture, though they often cultivated parts of their plots and kept livestock in outhouses, for which they might have rights on the common pasture. Many boroughs were established directly by the king, others by magnates (15) or church dignitaries, such as bishops or abbots. Some borough overlords, particularly ecclesiastical ones, retained, or tried to impose, certain obligations of a feudal nature which restricted the freedom of the townspeople, and this on occasions led to friction.

The term 'burgess', of which the French equivalent is *bourgeois*, originally ap-

plied to the inhabitants of boroughs holding land in burgage tenure. If they were commercially successful, they would constitute an urban middle class, neither peasants nor lords, such as is implied by the modern French word *bourgeoisie*. While feudalism lasted, borough status and burgage tenure provided conditions under which such a class could become established

Markets and fairs

Markets were held weekly or more often, in and around stalls which were normally set up only on market days and removed afterwards. Fairs were less frequent. There were many markets in Saxon times, and their numbers increased greatly in the two and half centuries following the Norman Conquest. This was a period during which population and agricultural production increased as more land was taken into cultivation, before the plagues of the fourteenth century checked both population growth and agricultural expansion.

A new market could be set up only with royal consent, which was not always readily obtainable if there was an existing market near the proposed site. There could be a great incentive for an overlord to establish a market on his territory, since it might become extremely profitable. He would charge rents for setting up stalls in the defined market area, and tolls on goods brought in to sell. Local agriculture would be stimulated, as would crafts in the town itself. Ideally, a market town should also have been a borough with burgage tenure, so that merchants

15. Dunster, Somerset. The first castle was built by the Norman Mohuns, who founded a borough, with a wide street to accommodate a market; the present castle is mainly 17th century and later. Dunster became a weaving centre; the octagonal Yarn Market was built *c* 1590. The Luttrell Arms, left, was adapted as an inn *c* 1650 from a medieval house.

39

Map V *Right* **Blandford Forum, Dorset** grew where routes converged to cross the River Stour. Although nearly all rebuilt, splendidly, after a fire in 1731 (page 199) it retains its medieval layout, with long burgage plots stretching towards the river.

Map VI *Below right* **St Neots, Huntingdonshire** has an almost rectangular market place probably laid out in the twelfth century to the south of a priory (which has vanished), adjoining a crossing of the River Ouse. The plots on the south back on to a stream which was probably accessible to small boats entering from the river. The looser-knit village of Eynesbury, of earlier origin, contrasts with the regularity of the town.

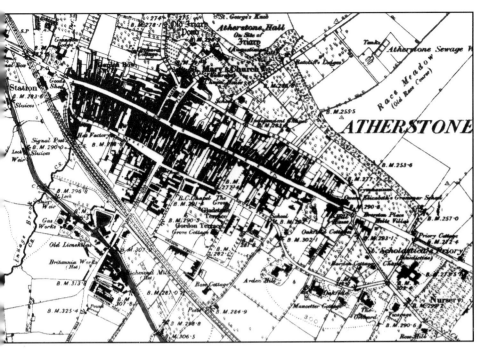

Map VII Atherstone, Warwickshire was a medieval highway town on Watling Street, with a small market place to the north, where Leicester cheese was once sold. In later times the Coventry Canal, which winds to the west, attracted some industry, but the railway (London to Crewe) did not cause much development; it killed the trade of the inns on many of the close-built plots shown on this map of 1890.

Curiously the church, north of the market place, was once a friary—unusual for a small town (page 88).

and craftsmen could live in suitable conditions near the outlets for their goods. Hence the conferring of borough status and the granting of market rights often went together. However, many medieval markets were held in places which did not have borough status or burgage tenure, and some of these grew quite important.

Medieval markets competed with each other. Some were very successful; others did not develop at all; others declined after a period. The most successful were usually well placed on traffic routes, by land or water (**V, VI**). Such towns might draw goods for their markets from wide areas, and some had several markets on different days, perhaps in different places, and for different commodities—grain, livestock, meat, fish, wool and many other categories of goods. Some towns became particularly noted for certain products; Salisbury and Chipping Campden for wool, Chester, Atherstone (**VII**) and Wells for cheese, and so on.

Fairs were normally held annually, for several days in succession. They were both festivals, frequently starting on the feast days of locally commemorated saints, and trade marts; in the most important fairs the latter element normally prevailed. Most towns that had markets also had fairs, and most of these were of purely local significance. Some fairs, however, achieved wider fame, and a few had international celebrity, drawing merchants from the Continent. One such was at St Ives in Huntingdonshire, a small town well situated at the navigable head of the River Ouse, reached by boat from the port of King's Lynn, and near to important land routes (**16**). Other major medieval fairs were those of St Botolph at Boston, for a time a great port; St Giles at Winchester, again near an important port, Southampton; and Sturbridge at Cambridge, which later came to overshadow that of nearby St Ives. Specialized goods of high value and wide variety were brought to, and distributed from, such fairs.

16. St Ives, Huntingdonshire. The Bridge, *c* 1415, built of stone brought by water from Northamptonshire (page 54), is one of the few to retain a midstream chapel (page 88). It and its predecessor hindered river traffic upstream, making the town an important inland port, with a fair that achieved international fame.

Medieval traffic

Medieval traffic was slow and cumbersome. Goods were sent over long distances by packhorse or primitive cart, if they could not go by river barge or coastal vessel. Valuable loads had to be protected by what we now call 'security guards'. Long-distance travellers walked or rode on horseback – anything resembling the coaches and carriages of a later age did not exist in the Middle Ages. If the king or important magnates travelled, they had large retinues. Travel at men's and horses' pace meant frequent stops for refreshment and accommodation. Towns on important routes could enjoy considerable, if erratic, prosperity from this source. A whole series developed along Watling Street, the Roman highway which retained, or regained, its importance in medieval times; examples are Dunstable, Stony Stratford (**120**) and Atherstone (**VII**).

Most goods were sent by river, or coastwise, where practicable. Rivers were variably and sometimes unreliably navigable in the Middle Ages. Bridges, weirs and milldams provided frequent obstacles in addition to natural hazards. Nevertheless, the lower parts of the main river systems were in general use, such as those of the Severn, the Trent, both the Yorkshire and the Fenland Ouses (the latter subject to periodic realignments in conjunction with Fenland drainage), and the Thames, together with quite small rivers such as the Witham from Boston to Lincoln, and the Lea up to Ware (**35**). Towns at the furthest points of navigation were well placed, especially if they were also bridging places and hence centres of local routes.

Corporate status

After about 1200 most of the larger, and some of the smaller, cities and towns obtained corporate status, which was conferred by royal charter and allowed varying degrees of self-government. London was naturally the first city to have such a status, and was always the most important and the most powerful. Corporate cities had bodies of citizens, or corporations, which varied in size, form and constitution. Often they were closely connected with local guilds (page 98) of merchants and craftsmen. These corporations were usually empowered to set up courts to try all but the most serious crimes; they appointed local officials, and they often obtained the right to collect local taxes, in return for paying fixed annual sums ('fee-farm') to the king. Such bodies often developed later into oligarchic, self-perpetuating borough councils.

By the end of the Middle Ages, the meaning of the word 'borough' was changing again. It had begun by signifying a fortified place (*burh*), then a place with a special form of land holding, and finally a place with a municipal corporation with powers defined by charter or custom. Many of the places which were boroughs of the second type—towns with burgage tenure—never became corporate boroughs in the final sense.

Burgage tenure gradually lost its significance as feudalism weakened, and feudal obligations no longer operated, so that it ceased to have any distinguishing characteristics. But there was one curious and significant way in which burgage holdings were still important right up to the nineteenth century. Certain boroughs—not always among the most important—were entitled to send members to Parliament, and in some of these, though by no means all, the right to vote was conferred on the occupants of recognized burgage plots. In a few places which were parliamentary boroughs—including Shaftesbury in Dorset, Westbury in Wiltshire, and Haslemere in Surrey—this led in later times to buying and selling of plots which carried voting rights by people who wanted to control the results of elections. This practice was, of course, ended with the first Reform Act of 1832.

5
Medieval and Tudor Streets and Houses

We have seen how numerous new markets were founded, and many places given the status of boroughs, between the Norman Conquest and the fourteenth century, a period of population increase and economic growth.

Medieval towns—apart from those which had a Roman or Saxon background—can be divided into three broad categories. Firstly, there were those which were deliberately established on new sites. Secondly, those which were deliberate extensions of existing villages, or of much smaller towns. Thirdly, those which simply developed piecemeal, either from established villages or on sites where there were no previous settlements. The third category is far less common than might be thought, since in a feudal age building development on any scale could not easily have taken place without an overlord's control. Most towns of medieval origins came into the first two categories. Some were associated with castles (**17, VIII**), some with monasteries or cathedrals, but most were established simply in the hope that they would develop into trading centres. Some were hardly more than single streets; others had complex patterns of thoroughfares and spaces. Some had regular plans, perhaps grids of streets; others had irregular forms, often constrained by natural or defensive features; many had combinations of regular and irregular elements.

Streets and squares
The basic element in any medieval town was the street. The word is derived from the Latin *strata*, meaning a paved road, and was adapted in Saxon England to refer, at first, to long-distance Roman roads, like Watling Street and Ermine Street. (Places called Stratford or Stretford were where Roman roads crossed rivers.) Later,

17. Kimbolton, Huntingdonshire, laid out as a planned town *c* 1200 adjoining a small castle, with a wide main street and narrower back street. Some of the dominantly Georgian house fronts conceal older structures behind. The church spire is *c* 1300.

it came to mean a thoroughfare lined with buildings.

Buildings in smaller villages were usually loosely disposed, each cottage in its plot, separate from its neighbours, often set back from the frontage to the thoroughfare. In towns, building plots were more valuable, and houses normally fronted streets directly. Typical house plots in medieval towns had frontages from around eighteen to forty feet wide, occasionally less, sometimes more. Plot depths might be anything from about forty-five feet to 200 feet or more. Such plots are often generally called 'burgage plots', because they frequently carried burgage

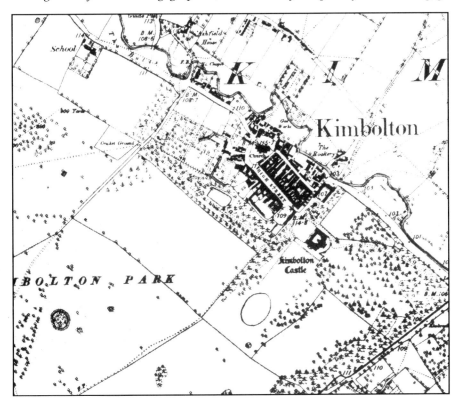

Map VIII Kimbolton. This map of 1890 shows the regular medieval town, with a suggestion of the form of the earlier, more irregular, village near the church (**17, 18**). It is half-enveloped by the grounds of the castle, landscaped in the 18th century.

18. Kimbolton Castle, rebuilt 1707-14 by Sir John Vanbrugh for the Duke of Manchester, dominates the end of the street; the classical entrance is by Robert Adam, *c* 1765. (see also **XIX**, p. 136)

tenure but this was not always so. Even where a street, or a whole town, was laid out by an overlord, he did not actually build the houses; he conveyed the plots to tenants who themselves erected the buildings, so that there were, from the start, variations in detail between adjoining buildings. In subsequent periods, buildings in originally medieval towns were reconstructed or altered piecemeal, often resulting, in time, in great variations in building form, age and materials along particular streets. However, the frontage lines of streets, once established, generally remained the same through piecemeal changes in the structures abutting on to them—apart from encroachments which occurred when market stalls became permanent. To take extreme examples, many streets in the City of London retain their medieval alignments, despite total reconstruction after the Great Fire of 1666, and subsequent piecemeal replacement of buildings sometimes several times over.

Medieval streets are seldom quite straight, except in the most rigidly planned towns. Nearly always there are changes of alignment, or variations in width, subtle or bold. Such irregularities are often related to the courses of rivers—Fleet Street in London, parallel with the Thames, and Coney Street in York are examples; to natural slopes and valleys; or to the fact that the streets follow the lines of pre-existing trackways, like High Street, Chipping Campden (XI, p. 60). Other street alignments were related to defensive features which may have disappeared. For instance, the main street of Trowbridge runs outside the line of the outer defences of the castle, which has vanished, while the eastern part of Oxford High Street takes its majestic curve because this was the alignment of the track between the gate of the original Saxon *burh* and the crossing of the River Cherwell, where Magdalen Bridge is now. Curvatures, whether subtle or bold, nearly always contribute to the visual effect; buildings on alignments at different angles partly close the vistas, which gradually unfold as one proceeds along the street.

Every medieval town had at least one street, but not every town in England had anything recognizable as a central 'square'. In this respect English medieval towns were, on the whole, different from their counterparts in Continental countries, where a *piazza*, *plaza*, *place*, or *plaz* was normally the accepted focal point of any city or town. The English language has no real equivalent to any of these words apart from market *place*, which has a narrower connotation, or *square*, which is not really satisfactory, especially as the term acquired a rather different association during the eighteenth century. The lack of a proper English word for *piazza* and its equivalents reflects the fact that the earlier Saxon towns did not normally have wide market places; the markets were held along the streets, like Cheapside (page 28) in London, Cornmarket in Oxford, and High Street in Lewes (26). Towns which developed later were usually provided with recognizable market places, or with stretches of street wide enough to accommodate several rows of stalls. In Norwich the market place was laid out by the Normans near the castle (III, p. 32); at Nottingham a new, very large market place was provided outside the original Viking and Saxon borough; at Stamford, both a new market place, since reduced by infilling, and a Broad Street, well named, developed outside the pre-Conquest town. In the new city of Salisbury a great market place was a central feature. Some medieval market places were rectangular, like those at Newark and St Neots (VI, p. 40); some were triangular (X, p. 47) or wedge-shaped; many had no regular form; some, as at Richmond in Yorkshire had curved edges related to the town's defences. But in many medieval towns the markets were held in exceptionally wide streets — those of Stockton-on-Tees, neighbouring Yarm (122), Appleby (37), Farnham (XIII, p. 72), Marlborough and Moreton-in-Marsh are notable examples.

Market stalls were normally, as now, temporary structures which were set up on prescribed market days, either immediately in front of buildings facing the streets or squares or, more often, in rows with passageways in between. Normally they were removed after every market day. However, stalls were sometimes allowed to remain from one market day to the next. They might then be replaced by permanent, timber-built booths; this was especially common with butchers' stalls which were usually more substantial than most others. (The medieval name for meat stalls was 'Shambles'; wherever this name, or 'Butcher Row', occurs, such stalls originally stood.) The next stage would be a range of more substantial structures, perhaps with living accommodation above. In this way, what were originally spacious market places or wide streets often became partly encroached by island blocks of permanent buildings, sometimes threaded by alleys. Such encroachments would, of course, take place with the permission, or at least the connivance, of the overlord, or corporate body which controlled the market, generally in return for higher ground rents.

There are many obvious examples of infilling of original market places and wide streets with permanent encroachments; among the most striking are St Albans and Salisbury. At St Albans the long tapering market place, originally laid out about 950 (7), was encroached on at its wider end, by the fifteenth century, with irregular groups of buildings whose present day successors are bordered and threaded by lanes and alleys. The original extent of the market place, between Chequer Street and French Row, can be detected, and the remaining open area is still crowded with stalls on market days. At Salisbury the very large market

Map IX *Below left* **Shifnal, Shropshire** was a medieval market town with a wide street. This map of 1890 shows a long islanded block, representing an early encroachment, replacing market stalls, on the street—a pattern still seen in many towns. (At Shifnal, however, the encroaching block has since been demolished.) The church is on the S.W. edge of the town, indicating the site of the original village before the market was established.

Note also typical features of a Victorian market town— Union Workhouse (page 254), Cattle Market (page 236), two Methodist Chapels, a tannery and a gas works.

Map X *Below* **Swaffham, Norfolk** had a huge triangular market place, encroached on by an island block of buildings, creating an intricate circuit of spaces. The main landmark is a circular open-columned Georgian 'Market Cross' with a domed roof which stands under the word 'PLACE' in this map of 1889.

place, laid out by the bishop when he founded the city in the thirteenth century, was reduced in area by blocks of buildings whose successors still bear names like Butcher Row, Oatmeal Row and Fish Row, indicating the commodities sold there. Other places with infilling on once open areas or wide streets are Ware (34), Ashbourne (XII, p. 68), Lichfield, Bury St. Edmunds, Bishop Auckland, Saffron Walden, Maidstone, Thame and East Grinstead. At Shifnal, a former encroachment has been demolished re-opening the street to its original width. (IX, p. 47)

Besides the main thoroughfares and market places, most medieval towns had narrower streets, or lanes, perhaps wide enough for a single cart (27, 31), together with still narrower alleys or footways. The latter might have resulted from the sort of encroachment on market places already described, or from infilling of the back parts of originally private plots, to which they provided access. Such tight-knit patterns of buildings and spaces are often thought to be specially characteristic of medieval towns. It must be emphasized, however, that large market places like that at Newark, or wide streets as at Marlborough and Ludlow, are at least as characteristic of medieval towns and cities as tightly packed lanes and alleys like those round the Shambles at York or Butcher Row at Shrewsbury.

Houses and house plots

House plots in medieval towns were usually long and narrow, with varying dimensions (page 45). Houses usually fronted the streets directly and abutted on to their neighbours, unless the frontage was exceptionally wide. Behind the house the rest of the plot would normally be open except for outbuildings, and might be used for such purposes as growing fruit or vegetables, keeping livestock, storing merchandise, and domestic recreation—a possible combination, in modern terms, of garden, smallholding, paddock, orchard and service yard. However, if the occupant was a merchant, craftsman or innkeeper, additions to the original buildings as workshops, storehouses or stables might encroach over much of the plot.

Medieval town houses were usually timber-framed, though some were at least partly of stone, and the poorest might be of less durable materials. Not many remain, even in part, from before the fifteenth century, and very few from before the fourteenth. The oldest which survive substantially above ground are stone-built structures of the late twelfth and early thirteenth centuries, which were exceptional even at the time when they were built. There are two well-known examples in Lincoln (19), popularly, though not necessarily correctly, associated with Jewish financiers, and another, Moyses Hall, fronting the market place in Bury St Edmunds (20). The latter shows an arrangement which was fairly common in medieval merchants' houses. The living quarters were on the first floor, with storage or shop space on the ground floor, opening directly on to the market place.

Medieval merchants' houses, even if built mainly of timber, often had stone-vaulted undercrofts, at ground or basement level, which were used for storage, and which sometimes remain when the house above has disappeared or been rebuilt. Examples are at Southampton, which has the remains of many stone-built houses, Stamford and the one-time port of Winchelsea. At Chester, a few such undercrofts survive at ground and semi-basement level, reached directly from the street, while the principal floors of the buildings above are approached from the 'Rows', or public passageways inset in the buildings at first-floor level (1, 21). This arrangement is unique in Britain and probably in Europe, apart from one street in Berne.

The standard form of house in country or town from the thirteenth into the early sixteenth century was the 'hall house'. This had a central hall of one tall storey, with open hearth in the middle of the floor, the smoke from which rose through a louvre, or ventilation turret, set on the roof. At one end was the solar, or domestic quarters, usually two-storeyed, at the other end the service quarters, with kitchen and store space. The whole might be contained in a single rectangular structure, or the solar or kitchen quarters, or both, might be contained in distinct wings, perhaps at right angles to the hall. In narrow town plots it was usual for the medieval hall house to be end-on to the street, with the solar quarters on the frontage, perhaps incorporating a shop, and the kitchen quarters at the rear, perhaps prolonged by a narrower range of outbuildings extending into the plot behind. Where such buildings survive in any measure they have usually been greatly altered and the hall subdivided, but two examples where the hall is open to the roof are Leche House in Chester and what is now the Red Lion in Southampton. In the former the hall is at first floor level and is reached from the Row. The Red Lion has a (modernized) two-storey solar frontage, with the hall rising behind; the original kitchen quarters were at the rear. On a smaller scale is a row of fourteenth-century houses, recently partly restored, in Spon Street, Coventry, where the small halls rose behind a two-storey frontage—these were the homes of weavers, and originally had workshops behind. On wider town plots, the hall might be parallel with the street, with wings at either end, or else a wing at one end only, forming an L plan. Houses of these types, usually much altered and with the halls subdivided, survive in such places as Saffron Walden (**22**),

19. *Above left* **Aaron the Jew's house, Lincoln** (a modern, unauthentic name), one of two stone-built late 12th century houses in the city. The doorway is partly original, the arched window much restored; the brick extensions, like the sash windows, are Georgian modifications. The cathedral towers behind were completed over 200 years after the house.

20. *Above* **Moyses Hall, Bury St Edmunds,** facing the market place (page 77), is a late 12th century merchant's house restored, with the turret added, in the 19th century. The ground floor was used for merchandise; the upper floor, with two main rooms, was the living accommodation.

21. *Right* **Watergate Street, Chester** is at right angles to Bridge Street (1), on a Roman line. Note the Row, above a ground floor which is really an elevated basement. Bishop Lloyd's House, right, is early 17th century, restored; then there is an early Georgian house, with quoins and keystones; then mock Tudor, followed by a frankly modern building.

22. *Below right* **Bridge Street, Saffron Walden, Essex** has medieval hall houses where the central hall was divided into two floors in the 17th century; that on the left is of the 'Wealden' type with continuous roof line (page 53). The town ends suddenly, as it did in the Middle Ages.

St Albans (7) and East Grinstead. The most developed type of medieval town house, needing a plot of some width, was the courtyard house, with front range parallel to the street, containing an arched entrance, sometimes a distinct gatehouse, and ranges behind forming a three-sided or complete courtyard, any one of which might contain the hall. This was a characteristic layout for rural manor houses, and was adapted for colleges, but was probably less common for town houses in England than it was on the Continent. Merchants' courtyard houses are known to have existed in the City of London—the hall of one, Crosby Hall, survived *in situ* until the beginning of this century and has been re-erected in Chelsea. The vestiges of another survive in a mainly later hall at Barnard's Inn off Holborn, where the original louvre remains on the roof. In Salisbury there are impressive remains of two courtyard houses which were the homes of fifteenth-century merchants. One, now Church House, retains its hall and adjoining gateway; the other, called the Hall of John Hall, retains a hall with impressive roof, which was restored by Pugin and is now, extraordinarily but effectively, the foyer of a cinema.

Great changes in the typical form and layout of houses took place in the fifteenth and sixteenth centuries, resulting partly from the use, which became universal in this period in all but the poorest houses, of fireplaces and chimneys, instead of open hearths in the middle of halls. Chimneys and fireplaces had previously been found in castles and in a few stone-built houses, but they were exceptional until the development of brickmaking made them more widely practicable. Fireplaces and chimneys of brick, or fire-resistant stone, were often built into, or added to, timber-framed houses during this period. They were associated with higher aspirations to comfort and, to some extent, with the growing use of coal as a domestic fuel, shipped in increasing quantities from the Tyne to London and other ports.

However, until the major advances in the glass industry, associated with coal, from the later sixteenth century (page 112), glass was still expensive and was used in any quantity only in the more opulent houses. Until about 1600, windows in medium-sized and small houses were usually protected by sacking or shutters. After then, glass became much more easily obtainable, though still only in small panes which had to be bound together with lead.

With the disappearance of open hearths, there was no longer need for tall, open-roofed, multi-purpose halls. Houses were henceforth built to two or three storeys throughout plus, sometimes, attic or roof space, and cellar, with varied room sizes and uses, much as today. In towns, traders or craftsmen might use ground floor space, plus rear wings or outbuildings as shops, stores or workshops, the domestic accommodation being all, or mainly, on upper floors. Access from the streets to the back parts of plots—where there were no back lanes to enable them to be reached from the rear—had to be through passageways within the buildings, either of pedestrian width or wide enough for carts. Wider passageways of this sort were often associated with inns, which often had a courtyard plan, and might extend over two or more original plots. Among very many towns where there are numerous passageways leading to yards are Ware (36), Ashbourne (page 66), Tewkesbury, Totnes and St Albans.

Tens of thousands of houses survive, in towns as well as the country, from the late fifteenth, sixteenth and early seventeenth centuries, the majority of them timber-framed. The framing was usually of oak, though other hardwoods were used; the infill within the wall framework was usually of wattle—strong, small, interwoven branches, often hazel, which was covered with daub, a form of plaster. Upper floors, especially on street frontages, frequently overhung the floors below—for a variety of possible reasons relating to stresses and strains in the structure; to the difficulty of finding timber for corner posts long and strong enough to rise through two or three storeys; to the desirability of sheltering, in some measure, the storeys below, especially when there were unglazed openings; and to the significant extra space which could be obtained by projecting upper storeys without encroaching on the public ground below (22, 24, 32).

Older hall houses were often adapted in this period by having their halls divided into two floors, with new fireplaces and chimneys. Sometimes their roofs had to be raised to accommodate the new upper rooms, but often the old roof timbers were retained *in situ*, though frequently concealed by ceilings or partitions. Many medieval houses altered in this way have had their true age demonstrated when ceilings or partitions have been removed or repaired, exposing the timbers of the original hall roofs.

Houses of the types so far described, which varied in size from large to medium-small, were the homes of merchants, substantial craftsmen or prosperous artisans. Where the poorest lived is not now evident. Some occupied hovels, often on the edges of towns, or down alleys or side lanes. Some lived in large houses that had become subdivided, or in cottages crowded into their former plots. Many lived, as employees, apprentices or servants, in the houses of the more wealthy.

Until the later sixteenth century, the external framing of most timber-framed houses was left exposed, with the wattle panels within the framework being outwardly finished with plaster. Around that time, good timber began to be scarce in eastern England—due to increasing demands for building, for ships, and for fuel, as well as to the advances of agriculture. Pieces of timber came to be used for building which, though sound, might have irregular outlines or surfaces, and they were often more widely spaced than formerly, leaving larger panels to be filled with wattle and plaster. For both aesthetic and structural reasons—to conceal irregular timber and to protect large infill panels—it became the normal practice from the late sixteenth century, on the eastern side of England, to plaster over all the exteriors of timber-framed houses, apart from window and door frames and, often, bressumers (the horizontal beams at the angles of overhanging storeys). Even older houses where the timber had previously been exposed were often plastered over, in the east of England, to conform with this fashion. Most plasterwork was simply and smoothly finished—in colours which ranged from deep blood-red through various ochres and buffs to white. But, in East Anglia, there developed a tradition of pargetting—finishing plasterwork with patterns, or with elaborate detail in relief which might include figures of people or animals. The most spectacular examples are Sparrowe's House in Ipswich, an older merchant's house externally remodelled in the 1670s, late for the tradition, and the former Sun Inn in Saffron Walden, a structural amalgam from the fourteenth to sixteenth centuries plastered over in the seventeenth with varied patterns and scenes. The practice extended as far west as Hertford (23).

In the western part of England from Gloucestershire to Lancashire, and along the Welsh Border, it was not normal for timber-framed houses to be wholly plastered over, though this was sometimes done. Oak remained plentiful for longer in the West than in the East, so houses in the West were built with, generally speaking, better, thicker and closer-spaced timber than those in the East, right up to the end of the seventeeth century. There was therefore no structural or aesthetic need to plaster over. There developed in the West a tradition of elaborate, if naive, timber patterning, often using curved wooden members decoratively within the rectangular or square panels of the timber-framing. Many late sixteenth- and seventeenth-century houses in this tradition survive in towns such as Shrewsbury (24), Ludlow, Ledbury, Chester and as far east as Stratford-on-Avon and Stafford. At some time—no one knows when—the practice of rendering the external timbering and plaster respectively black and white developed in this region, giving vivid visual effects which used to be peculiar to the area; it is only recently that the practice of painting half-timbered houses, original or copyist, in black and white in other regions has gained ground.

The southern parts of England had varied traditions of timber-framing. The 'Wealden' type of house, common in, but not peculiar to, Kent and Sussex, has an inset centre part between slightly projecting wings under continuous eaves (22). In later times, many timber-framed houses in the South-East, and also in Wiltshire, were clad with tile-hanging (50). In parts of the South-West, as at Totnes, houses were sometimes clad in local slate.

Brickmaking, which lapsed after the departure of the Romans, was revived in the Middle Ages. Brick was much used in Flanders in the fourteenth century, as can be seen in Bruges, and, until brickmaking was well established in England, many bricks were imported from Flanders. The earliest extensive use of brick in surviving English buildings is in Holy Trinity Church, Hull and in unseen parts of the vaulting of Beverley Minster nave, both dating from the fourteenth century.

23. Houses in Fore Street, Hertford, mid 17th century, with remains of pargetting, or plaster decoration, in the East Anglian tradition. The windows have been altered to Georgian sashes.

24. **Houses in Frankwell, Shrewsbury** are typical of the elaborate western tradition of timber-framing in the late 16th and early 17th centuries (**30**, **32**).

Brick was used more in the fifteenth century, as at Cambridge. By the middle of the sixteenth century it was extensively used in palaces, as at Hampton Court and in the gateway to St James's Palace, as well as in numerous manor houses and churches, principally in eastern England. In medium-sized and smaller houses the use of brick was at first confined mainly to fireplaces and chimneys, in cases where the rest of the structure was timber-framed. Brick nogging, or infilling the external framework of timber-framed buildings with brick, was practised in parts of southern England by about 1600. Brick came into general use for medium-sized houses in the early to mid seventeenth century over large parts of England, especially where fine stone was not readily available.

The use of stone was restricted by geographical considerations. Most of the finest limestone came from the 'oolite' belt which stretches from Yorkshire through Lincoln and Stamford to the Cotswolds and Somerset. Some of the quarries were near navigable rivers, so that Northamptonshire stone could be shipped to Ely, Cambridge and St Ives (**16**); and Tadcaster stone over the shorter distances to York and Beverley. But, because of the cost of transport, stone sent thus far was used only for important buildings, especially churches and defensive works. York used limestone for its Minster, parish churches and city walls, but nearly all its medieval houses were of timber. Beverley used stone and some concealed brick in its Minster, but brick in its town gates (**62**), and presumably timber in its medieval houses of which hardly any remain. Cambridge used, variously, fine stone brought up river as in King's College Chapel; local clunch, or hard chalk, for some of the colleges and churches; and, increasingly, brick from the fifteenth century. The earlier houses were mostly of timber. Over much of Norfolk and Suffolk the innumerable parish churches, in town and country, were built of local flint, with fine stone from the eastern Midlands, brought as far as possible by water, used for dressings—corners, window frames and parapets. Sometimes stone and flint were used in conjunction to form spectacular Gothic patterns on flat wall surfaces (flush-work). But in Norwich and other eastern towns the houses were, again, mostly of timber, though occasionally partly of flint. In the South-East there were many local materials, including sandstone as well as clunch and flint; for some of the major buildings, like Canterbury Cathedral, stone was imported from Caen. In Winchester and Southampton, limestone from the Isle of Wight, obtainable in fine and coarse varieties, was used in the Cathedral and town walls respectively (61).

In the West and North of England, and throughout Wales, there are many varieties of stone with widely differing qualities and disadvantages as building materials. Some are coarse but long-lasting, incapable of being finely carved. Others, like the brown-red sandstones of the north-western Midlands, are soft and relatively easy to carve, but weather badly. Even the same locality might have two or more different sources of stone (25). At Coventry, the late medieval Guildhall and its associated buildings are partly of soft red sandstone, partly of a harder, whiter stone, both quarried locally, and partly, like most of the medieval domestic architecture of the city, timber-framed. At Exeter, the numerous small churches and other lesser medieval buildings are partly of the rich red local sandstone, and partly of a lighter, harder, stone of volcanic origin from a few miles away. But the Cathedral was built of soft Beer limestone brought coastwise, capable of being exquisitely carved as the interior shows but, alas, weathering badly on the exterior (45). At Bristol, the city's own varied coarse stones are seen in conjunction with fine limestone from Somerset in the churches. Both in Bristol and Exeter, as in Totnes, Dartmouth, Plymouth, Sherborne and Chester, some of the fifteenth-to seventeenth-century houses have party walls of local stone but timber-framed frontages. Timber was more flexible than stone for façades; it enabled overhangs to be built, was easier to use for window frames, and lent itself to decorative display—while stone provided solid insulation and fire protection in party walls.

25. Somerton, Somerset is built of local soft grey-blue lias stone, with dressings of finer golden stone from Ham Hill. The Market Cross, 1673, is a late version of a medieval type (49, 59). In the background a 17th century oriel window (page 191).

Even on the fine limestone belt, many medieval town houses were at least partly timber-framed, as surviving examples at Stamford and Chipping Campden show, but the important wool merchants' houses in the latter town are of stone. In Oxford, all the medieval college buildings are of stone, but the medieval and Tudor houses that survive in High Street and elsewhere are largely timber-framed.

The seventeeth century was a period of transition in domestic architecture. Timber-framing remained a common method of building well into the second half of the century, even in—perhaps especially in—the larger towns and cities. Some of the most elaborate of the timber-framed houses in Chester, among the relatively few that date from before the Victorian period, are of the early or mid seventeenth century (21), while in Bristol an entirely new street, King Street, was developed in the 1650s and 1660s in the medieval manner, with gabled overhanging timber-framed houses; several survive (104). Newcastle, then a notable port, flourishing with the coal trade and growing industries, had a highly individual building tradition in the early seventeenth century. This is exemplified in the four- and five-storeyed former merchants' houses fronting the quayside, with long ranges of mullioned windows on each floor (70). They illustrate, in a special way, how windows in medium-sized houses were becoming larger in the early seventeenth century with advances in the glass industry—of which Newcastle was then the main centre.

During the middle and later seventeenth century brick steadily supplanted timber as the main building material for houses in non-stone-bearing areas. In areas where good stone was readily available, like the Cotswolds, nearly all houses were built of it from the early seventeenth century onwards, as towns like Chipping Campden, Painswick (113), Sherborne, Bradford-on-Avon (96), and Stamford amply show. In parts of Wales, and of northern England, stone was often plastered over, especially where it would have produced a rough or badly weathering surface, while in parts of the South-West, rough stone walls as well as timber-framed frontages were sometimes slate-hung.

Some towns are on geological borderlines, with adjacent sources both of building stone and of clay suitable for bricks. Examples are Devizes, Ashbourne, Stony Stratford (120, 121), Bridport (6) and Tiverton, where stone façades are varied with others in brick, sometimes with stone dressings. Survivals from earlier periods in timber-framing add further to variety; in Salisbury for instance there are buildings of stone, flint, brick, and timber-framing, often tile-hung, sometimes in combinations of two or more of these materials (50).

It must be remembered that surviving old houses have been altered, adapted, or enlarged, in many instances repeatedly, to satisfy changing standards and needs. We have seen how hall houses were subdivided, with new floors and chimneys, in the sixteenth and seventeenth centuries (page 52). Larger windows might be inserted in the seventeenth with the greater availability of glass, and in the eighteenth these might be replaced by sashes, following the then almost universal British fashion. Very often entirely new façades in brick, stone, plaster, or even tile feigning brick (mathematical tiling, 112) would be added to older timber-framed houses in the Georgian period. Innumerable houses in town streets are older internally, or at the back, than they appear from the front. Uses have changed too; a shop may have been inserted in the ground floor of a house, or the whole building may be put to commercial uses.

A typical town street of medieval origin is likely to be an amalgam of building work of many centuries, each plot having its own building history (26), (28). The oldest feature is likely to be the alignment of the street, which usually remains through piecemeal rebuildings of the structures fronting it. Some medieval fabric may survive, sometimes concealed by later accretions. Obviously, the proportion of surviving structures from later periods is normally likely to be larger the nearer one approaches the present day. But this will depend partly on the history of the town; a place which was rich in the sixteenth century but had a slump in the eighteenth is likely to have more Tudor buildings than one which was very prosperous in the eighteenth. Ipswich and Bury St Edmunds illustrate this. Ipswich flourished in late medieval and Tudor times but slumped in the eighteenth century, so that it retains—despite later prosperity—a large number of fifteenth-to seventeenth-century timber-framed buildings, but has relatively few from Georgian times. Bury St Edmunds, on the other hand, was particularly prosperous

26. **Lewes, Sussex** was a Saxon town based on the long High Street descending to a river crossing in a gap of the South Downs, seen in the distance. Buildings are of all dates; the stucco houses, left, are by Amon Wilds, father and son, who worked in Brighton (88).

in the eighteenth century and looks outwardly a largely Georgian town (even though many of the houses are older behind their Georgianized fronts), despite its earlier importance and its Norman street pattern.

The effect of fires must also be considered. Whole towns, or substantial parts of them, were destroyed by fire in the seventeenth century, including Dorchester, Warwick, and Northampton as well as the City of London. More were devastated in the eighteenth century, including Blandford Forum and Buckingham. They were usually rebuilt to the old street plans, with perhaps some straightening, as at Warwick. Fires spread rapidly not just because the houses were of timber, but also because many roofs were thatched. Tile making developed rapidly, however, in the seventeenth century, and by the eighteenth most town houses were either tiled or slated—the latter near where slates were quarried (in Devon, Cornwall, Wales and Cumbria), or where they could easily be shipped. In a few areas, like the Pennines, the Peak (100), the Cotswolds, Dorset and the Horsham area of Sussex, hard stone slabs were used like slates.

Historic streets are often varied in their building materials and styles, and in the shapes and skylines of their buildings. Many pre-seventeenth century houses have gables fronting the streets, but with the onset of the Classical tradition (page 188), façades usually ended horizontally, with cornices, eaves or parapets, although attic windows and chimneys provided variety in the skylines. Heights of buildings often differ considerably in old streets. Not only does the number of storeys vary between two and three (and occasionally four), with or without attics, but room heights in individual houses differ greatly. Prosperous merchants' houses may adjoin humble cottages. Not until the early seventeenth century in London, or the end of the century elsewhere, were streets ever designed as architectual wholes.

27. Keere Street, Lewes plunges downhill from High Street—the timber-framed building in **28** is seen at the top. The brick paving sloping to a cobbled central gully is a restored version of the traditional arrangement in such a street.

We have seen how burgage plots often became largely covered by buildings associated with the trades of the occupants (36). In larger cities, or towns with restricted sites, there was sometimes such pressure on space that the process went further, parts of original house plots being used for smaller dwellings, or by other occupants. This process probably started very early in the City of London, where what may have originally been fairly large house plots became densely developed in late medieval and Tudor times. Access to premises on the 'backland' was often obtained by narrow passages leading from the streets, through the frontage buildings, into small, often irregular, courtyards which were the last remains of the original open areas of the plots. In the City such courtyards still survive, though in diminishing numbers, despite repeated replacement of the buildings round them. Much the same happened in other large cities such as Bristol, Norwich and Newcastle; in towns which were beginning to grow fast, such as Leeds; and in numerous smaller towns, especially those hemmed in by natural or man-made features, such as Tewkesbury, which lay between the abbey and the converging Rivers Avon and Severn. In many other towns, where there was less pressure for infilling, much of the early medieval pattern of long plots, still largely open, survives behind the frontage buildings, as at Chipping Campden, Blandford Forum (V, p.40), Fareham (118), Yarm (122) and Cullompton. In Shrewsbury, the area round the market places became densely developed, but nearby there were more spacious areas where large gardens remained till modern times behind the houses fronting the streets. The same contrast between crowded buildings and low-density development in close proximity was found in many other medium-sized historic towns, such as Chichester, Winchester, Norwich (III, p.32) and Durham (XIV, p.78).

28. High Street, Lewes, looking west. The nearer house, 15th century timber-framed with a later wing, and 17th century leaded windows, may have been for a time tile-hung in the local tradition (page 191). Beyond are typical Georgian fronts with doorcases. Keere Street (27) leads down to the left.

6
Some Medieval Towns

This chapter deals with a selection of towns of medieval origin and layout—though not necessarily with many medieval buildings. Most, though not all, of the examples were, even by medieval standards, quite small towns. They are chosen to illustrate typical elements in medieval town form, particularly in relation to streets and market places and, in some cases, castles and harbours.

The simplest form of medieval market town is one which consists largely of a single main street. A splendid example is Chipping Campden (**XI**), high on the Cotswold Hills. Here there was a small original village whose lord, Hugh de Gondeville, obtained a charter for a market in about 1180. He laid out the High Street, with fronting house plots, along the line of an important established route over the Cotswolds, which here followed a slightly curving shallow valley. The street widens as it curves in its central part, to accommodate market stalls. The market became exceptionally important for wool—not only for the medium quality wool from the Cotswolds themselves but also for wool from the Midlands, including the exceptionally fine product of Herefordshire and the Welsh borderland. Two splendid stone-built wool merchants' houses of the fourteenth and fifteenth cen-

Map XI Chipping Campden. The original village was around the church, to the north-east. The medieval main street, with its irregular curve, has continuous buildings along the frontages, but there were long plots behind which, in this map of 1891, are shown still to be largely open, some containing orchards (page 48).

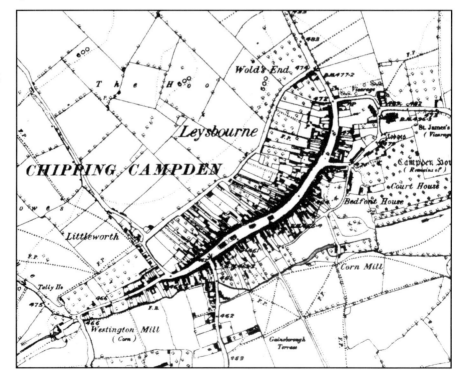

turies testify to the town's medieval wealth, but other buildings fronting the street are of various later dates up to the eighteenth and nineteenth centuries. Almost all are of the abundant local stone, though a few, of late medieval or Tudor origin, have timber-framed upper storeys. The pattern of burgage plots laid out by Gonde-ville, some of them exceptionally long, survives nearly complete; many are still gardens or open yards behind the buildings fronting the street. A series of islanded buildings in what was the widest part of the street are typical encroachments replacing original market stalls that became permanent. The single-storeyed open-sided Yarn Market in the middle of the street dates from 1627, after the town's heyday (29). It was built by Sir Baptist Hicks, who bought the manorial estate in 1610, rebuilt the manor house grandly (its lodges and gateway survive), and built a range of almshouses. The site of the manor house, together with the alms-houses and church, form a group away from the High Street, marking the location of the pre-urban village—the church was rebuilt to a magnificent scale on the original site during the town's mercantile heyday in the fifteenth century. Chip-ping Campden became a backwater by the nineteenth century, and today it has the status of a village, but the architectural character and scale of a town. The magnificent main street, with its buildings of various dates unfolding on the curve, has few rivals in England.

Ledbury, in Herefordshire, contrasts with Chipping Campden in its building materials—timber-framing in the lavish tradition of the western counties, inter-mixed with Georgian red brick façades, often hiding older structures behind. Only

29. Chipping Campden, Gloucestershire. The wide High Street with its medieval curve, and stone buildings of all periods, is one of the finest in England. The arched building is the Yarn Market, 1627.

30. *Above* **Ledbury,
Herefordshire**. The wide
tapering High Street is seen
from the Market Hall (**32**). To
the right is the 14th century
building of St Catherine's
Hospital (page 97), shaped like
a church, with a central turret.

31. *Opposite* **Church Lane,
Ledbury**, leading off the High
Street behind the Market Hall,
contrasts in scale. The church
spire of local sandstone is an
18th century replacement on a
medieval base. The traditional
cobbled surface is retained.

the church and medieval hospital building are of the local sandstone (**30**). The
wide, slightly tapering street may have been laid out by one of the bishops of
Hereford, who were lords. The most striking feature is the black and white timber-
framed open-arched market hall of 1617 and later, one of the best of its kind (**32**).
The narrow, slightly curving lane leading to the church, with timber buildings
framing the view of the tall and slender spire, makes an interesting contrast with
the wide main street (**31**).

Penryn has a dour Cornish character, in contrast to the lushness of the Cotswold
and Herefordshire towns. It was founded in 1236 by a Bishop of Exeter on a pro-
montory between creeks at the head of the Fal estuary, with a single long climbing
street, broadening in the centre where an islanded Georgian Town Hall stands.
There is still a pattern of long narrow plots sloping down to the original shorelines,
now receded through reclamation, on either side. Penryn declined after Falmouth
developed in the seventeenth century; nevertheless it was largely rebuilt or
refronted in the Georgian period, with façades either in exposed coarse local stone
or, more often, plastered over; roofs are of local slate. But behind some of the
classical façades are older, partly timber framed structures.

Ware, in Hertfordshire, was a river port and highway town. It was where the main medieval road north from London crossed the River Lea, navigable up to here, about twenty miles from the capital. The first bridge was built about 1190, and the High Street developed, parallel with the river, between the original village to the west, around the church, and the turning to the bridge. The street was of varying width; the broader parts accommodated the market stalls but, as elsewhere, they became permanent, and are now represented by intermittent blocks of buildings which divide the main carriageway from a series of parallel lanes (33), (34). Long burgage plots extended on either side, those to the south abutting on to the river. Many sixteenth- and early seventeen-century timber-framed buildings, plastered externally, survive on the street frontage, several with passageways wide enough for waggons to enter the plots behind. Some were obviously inns, benefitting from travellers on one of England's busiest roads, a long day's walk or a hard ride from London, but many were merchants' premises. Corn from a wide hinterland was marketed in Ware, and much was shipped by the local merchants to London—or at least to the Stratford area near the mouth of the Lea, where there were many mills supplying the capital with flour. Barley likewise was brought into Ware from the surrounding area, and, from at least Tudor times onwards, was processed into malt, which was sent downstream for the London brewers. Many former malting buildings remain in the town, though none now survive that date from before the nineteenth century; some are on the plots between the High Street and the river. The merchants and maltsters would live on the upper floors of the houses fronting the street; the ground floors and attached outbuildings would be used as shops, offices and stores. Wheat or barley was brought through the passageways from the street; the barley might be processed in maltings behind; the grain or malt would be loaded into barges at the ends of the plots (**36**). To add domestic touches, there were, beside many of the loading places, gazebos or summer houses overlooking the river, where the merchants and their families could enjoy a little relaxation—since the rest of their plots were given over to business. Many of these gazebos, dating from the Georgian period, survive, and some have been recently restored after neglect (**35**).

Stony Stratford in Buckinghamshire is a town whose existence and prosperity depended on transport. Roman Watling Street revived as a major highway early in the Middle Ages, and linear towns and large villages developed along it. Stratford was where it crossed the River Ouse—the ford was stony, unlike that of Fenny Stratford further south—and it is recorded as a town in 1202. It is mainly

33. *Left* **Ware, Hertfordshire**. Originally there was a wide street between the lines of the frontages on either side. The island block in the middle is the result of early encroachment (page 48). The foreground building, now carpet shop, was built as the Town Hall in 1827. Behind the frontages on the left are long plots extending back to the River Lea, many of them entered through passageways (**36**.).

34. *Below left* **Ware, Hertfordshire**. Looking in the opposite direction from the previous photograph, with an originally 17th century plastered building at the end of the island block; the arched facade to the right is the side of the former Town Hall (**33**). The Old Punch House on the left has an early Georgian front with carved brickwork (page 191).

65

35. *Below* **The River Lea at Ware**, where grain and malt were landed on barges for London. Long plots, as shown in **36**, extended from the houses fronting the main street back to the river. The gazebos, or summer houses, overlooking the river were built as domestic amenities.

a long street, bordered by burgage plots whose boundaries are still evident, but with a large market place, now partly encroached on, behind the buildings on the north-western side. Like many highway towns, it grew up astride two older-established manors and parishes, whose common boundary ran along the street; the lord of one of these, Calverton, obtained a charter for a market and fair in 1257, presumably in the present market place, since this was on his side of the street. The present church began as a chapelry, or dependency, of Calverton parish; there was once a chapel on the other side of the street—the tower survives—

36. *Opposite* **Burgage Plot at Ware**. One of the long plots, typical of a medieval town (page 48), entered through a passageway in the 16th century timber-framed house fronting the street. Later outbuildings extend along the side of the plot, culminating in a 19th century malting. Barley was brought in from the street and processed in the malting; the malt was loaded on to barges in the river at the end of the plot, as shown in **35**.

which was attached to the other parish, Wolverton. Stony Stratford is an example, among many, of a town where the street and spatial pattern remain essentially medieval but the buildings are almost all later—due partly to two serious fires in the eighteenth century and also to Georgian prosperity, to which reference is made later **(120)**, **(121)**.

Ashbourne, in Derbyshire, was a Saxon village which seems to have been extended into a market town by its overlords, the Ferrers, in the thirteenth century. Presumably they laid out the burgage plots beside the long main street leading east from the church, where the older village lay, to the originally triangular market place, which characteristically, has been partly infilled by irregular blocks of buildings threaded by alleys **(XII)**. The thriving weekly market is still held on the remaining open parts of the triangle. Many of the burgage plots became infilled in post-medieval times, and some have groups of cottages and other buildings round small courtyards entered through passageways from the street. The fine Elizabethan Grammar School is, like the nearby church, of local sandstone, but the few surviving Tudor houses are timber-framed; later houses are of brick or stone.

66

Wymondham, in Norfolk, is another town with a triangular market place. Its growth was more complicated than Ashbourne's. There was a Saxon village, near which William d'Albini, or William of Albany, founded a priory in 1107. A market charter was obtained in 1202, and it may have been then that the market place was laid out, well away from the priory and original village. It is an elongated space extending, unusually, over a hillbrow, which, unlike many other market places described, has never been encroached on, except for the octagonal market hall on the brow. This was built after much of the town was destroyed by fire

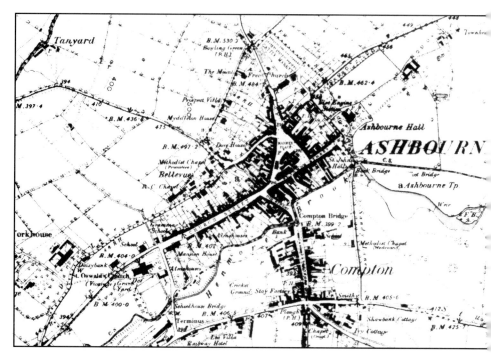

Map XII Ashbourne, Derbyshire was developed as a market town in the 13th century, with a long street leading to a triangular market place, since reduced by building encroachment. The long house plots to the left are still largely open behind the houses on this map of 1887, but those round the market place have become more densely developed (page 202). Note the church at the west end, marking the site of the original village, and, slightly to the right, the Grammar School (page 96).

37. *Opposite top* **Appleby, Westmorland** was laid out by a Norman baron below his castle, with the church at the bottom. The buildings, mainly 18th-19th centuries, are in the austere classical tradition of the North.

38. *Opposite bottom* **Appleby, Westmorland**. The weekly market is still held in the wide street. The white painted building, right, seen also from the opposite direction in 37, is the Moot Hall of 1596, refaced in the 18th century, with Westmorland slate roof.

in 1615; the rebuilt houses were, like the market hall, timber-framed, but many have since been refronted in brick. An interesting survival is a former chapel of about 1400 in flint and stone, like most of the churches in the area; it originally served a guild or religious fraternity, was converted into a Grammar School in Elizabethan times, and is now a social hall.

New Buckenham, also in Norfolk, was an entirely new medieval town, founded later in life by the same William of Albany who established Wymondham Priory. The family castle had been at nearby Old Buckenham; about 1145 William built a new castle about a mile away and laid out the new town adjoining. It had a grid plan, with three parallel east-west thoroughfares, cross streets and a large market place. The layout survives, but the former market place, slightly encroached on, has become a village green, with a diminutive former town hall. The change from market place to village green is symbolic of the fact that New Buckenham, after flourishing moderately for a time, declined by the eighteenth century to the status of a village. The present-day houses are largely of cottage scale; only the parish church indicates late medieval prosperity. The castle is represented by overgrown, but still impressive, earthworks.

Appleby, the old county town of Westmorland, is another town established by a castle. The first castle was built by a Norman baron about 1110, on high ground overlooking a bend of the River Eden. Perhaps at about the same time the present wide main street was laid out inside the bend, with the church closing the view at the bottom, just as the present castle does at the top (37), (38). Borough privileges were granted (or perhaps existing ones were confirmed) in 1179. There was an older village—with the Norse name meaning 'village of the apple trees'—east of the river, represented today by a small irregular green and a church, still with Saxon features, which preceded the one in the medieval town. Interestingly,

68

this area is now called Bongate; the street of the bondmen, or peasants—presumably they were distinct from the burgesses, who would have occupied the plots in the planned town under the castle.

Bishop Auckland developed beside the castle, really a fortified palace, built in the twelfth century by the politically powerful Bishops of Durham, on a site where the hunting facilities were probably a major attraction. The town was originally built round a long, wide and tapering space extending west of the castle— analogous to many of the huge greens which are characteristic of the medieval County Durham villages. Part became a borough, under the control of the bishops; the rest, towards the west, remained a peasant community withoug burgage tenure; this area is significantly called Bondgate—the name is identical in meaning to Bongate in Appleby. Infilling has greatly reduced the original space; there is a substantial island block at the Bondgate end, and a more irregular group of encroaching buildings in the wide market place within the original borough; this now includes a Victorian Town Hall and church—a chapelry of the distant parish church outside the town. The houses fronting the market place are dominantly dour Georgian; in contrast is the light-hearted Georgian Gothic of the entrance to the castle grounds at the end of the square. The castle retains a superb late twelfth-century former Great Hall, one of the finest of its kind, converted to a chapel in the seventeenth century; the park, now public, still has the character of a historic deer park. Bishop Auckland boomed as a mining centre and iron town in the nineteenth century; this prosperity has now receded but the market element remains; the central space is crowded with stalls and people on market days.

Richmond, in Yorkshire, is much more complex and dramatically sited than either Appleby or Auckland. The castle (12) was started in 1071 by Alan the Red, the Norman lord of Swaledale, on a splendid defensible site, partly cliff-bound, within a bend of the River Swale. The town was established then or soon after. At first it was mainly confined to a horseshoe-shaped market place north of the castle, contained on the outer side by a curving town wall—in effect an outer bailey of the castle. This is still the heart of the town, with mainly Georgian buildings occupying the radiating burgage plots, and an irregular encroaching block including a small former church. But the medieval town extended outside the inner walled area. One street, Frenchgate, long and tapering, may represent the original Saxon village which had a different name; it passes the parish church to which the small church in the walled town was a chapelry. Other streets plunge dramatically to the riverside or, like Newbiggin ('new buildings'), run fairly regularly along the hillside. There was a Franciscan friary—an indication of the town's relative importance—of which only the elegant tower survives. It groups on the skyline with the lower towers of the other churches and, supremely, the surprisingly slender though powerful Norman keep which stands on the perimeter of the castle bailey on the town side.

Pembroke was one of the first of the many towns established in Wales by Norman and English conquerors. It was founded about 1110 by Gilbert de Clare, when he rebuilt the castle he had taken over (page 33). It consists essentially of a single street extending eastwards from the castle along an undulating ridge whose sides sloped down, originally, to two tidal inlets, the southern of which is now dried up. The street broadens and narrows intermittently, and there is an island block, now containing a big Methodist chapel, in its originally widest part. Long burgage plots, many now domestic gardens or yards, descend behind the frontages on either side; they ended at the town wall which bordered the creeks—of which most of the line is still apparent, and a few turrets and stretches of masonry survive. Except for the superb castle, and a very modest church, all the buildings in the town are outwardly eighteenth- or nineteenth-century with dour stone or stuccoed fronts, but some are older behind the façades.

Caernarfon Castle was begun in 1282, immediately after the death of the Welsh Prince Llywelyn. The locality had a long history; the Romans had a fort near, and the Norman Earl of Chester had penetrated as far by 1090, when he built an earthen castle, occupied for only a few years, on the site of the present one. It was re-taken by the Welsh, and became the site of a princely palace, till finally captured by Edward I. Beside Edward's magnificent castle (page 34), the new town the King established seems small and very straightforward, a simple grid of one street by three, none of them wide, set within the impressive surviving town wall which was an extension of the perimeter of the castle. There are two town gates, at either end of the axial main street, one opening on to the quay. There was no internal market place; the markets have for centuries been held on the irregular space outside the castle and town walls which is the hub of the present town. As in other towns which the English planted in Wales, the burgage plots within the walls were at first available to English settlers only, but the Welsh would have lived and traded around the market place outside the walls.

Winchelsea, another town newly established by Edward I, contrasts in many ways with Caernarfon. It was not primarily a defensive stronghold, but a commercial port. The earlier town, for long subject to erosion, was finally swamped in a storm of 1287 (see Chapter Eleven). Work had already started on a successor town about two miles away, set on a plateau beside what was then the tidal estuary of the River Brede. The street plan was a rigid, unimaginative grid, with two wider sections of street intended for market stalls, and a single block allocated for the principal church. But before the new town was fully built or settled, the sea retreated, leaving the site high and dry. Now only a small part of the originally planned grid is occupied by houses, mostly Georgian and later, though some incorporate medieval stone vaulted undercrofts (page 48). Only the eastern part of the church stands, though this has a splendid scale. The straight streets, which would probably have had few interesting vistas, would surely have resulted in a far duller place—had it developed fully and survived—than most other medieval English towns and cities, with their characteristically curving or sinuous thoroughfares of varying widths. It would also, almost certainly, have been less interesting than other major planned medieval cities, such as Salisbury, Lichfield and Bury St Edmunds (all described in Chapter Seven), which too were laid out with grids, but with more subtleties and irregularities than in Winchelsea.

Newtown, in the Isle of Wight, was another planned town which finally came to almost nothing. It was first established beside a navigable creek by Bishop Aymer of Winchester in 1256 but, because of its potential strategic importance, was taken over as a royal borough by Edward I in 1284. But the town suffered, like other southern ports, from French raids in the fourteenth century, and never properly recovered. It declined to a shrunken hamlet, which it remains. The basis of the street plan can still be traced—two parallel and slightly curving main streets,

Map XIII Farnham, Surrey was laid out by a Norman bishop, with a wide street for a market, leading south from the castle, and an east–west thoroughfare along the route from London to Winchester. The map of 1873 shows the ancient deer park, and fields still coming to the ends of the plots of the houses fronting the streets.

and two wider cross streets, where markets were held. Parts of these are metalled; the rest are grassy tracks. Along one of the original streets is now a scatter of rural cottages, and a small Gothic Revival church on the site of the medieval one, always a chapelry to the mother parish of Calbourne, a village two miles away. The most remarkable building of all is the early eighteenth-century Town Hall, of brick and local stone in simple classical style, which stands in the wide grassy space that must have been the principal market place. The setting was nearly as deserted when the Town Hall was built, but the building had a purpose. For Newtown was still nominally a borough, with two seats in Parliament and the few who qualified for votes gathered there on husting days—until, like other 'rotten boroughs', it lost its Members of Parliament in 1832. The hamlet today, by the seemingly remote creeks, used only by small pleasure vessels, is evocative and delightful.

Newtown was only one of several towns established by medieval Bishops of Winchester on their widespread estates, not all in their diocese. Some of these were entirely new towns; others were enlargements of existing villages. Some have prospered, others have declined to villages. Farnham in Surrey, was a Saxon village on the very important route—partly of prehistoric origin—between Winchester and London. A Norman bishop built a castle on a strategic site overlooking it, and probably laid out the present wide Castle Street, leading southward from the castle which dominates it, at right angles to the main highway, along which the town also developed. Farnham prospered, notably in the eighteenth century, and is now well known as a substantially Georgian town, but its street and plot pattern is medieval (**XIII**). Similarly Fareham in Hampshire, another village extended by the bishops into a town, became prosperous in the eighteenth century (**118**). Witney, in Oxfordshire, was laid out by an early bishop on one of the outly

ing episcopal manors around a very large, tapering space, flanked by burgage plots, the church standing at the wider end. The northern, narrower, part of the space developed as the market place, with some islanded buildings; otherwise the town grew northward along fairly narrow streets. The southern, wider, part of the original space became a large green, which it remains today. Witney developed a textile industry, and came to specialize in blankets. New Alresford was an entirely new town, laid out by the bishop in 1200 on the London road six miles out of Winchester, partly along the highway and partly along a wide street leading north, forming a T pattern like Farnham, but without a castle. The town prospered with traffic, markets, especially for wool, and to some extent cloth weaving, but in later times declined. It was largely rebuilt, to the old plan, after a seventeenth-century fire, and there was much Georgian refurbishment. Today it is of little commercial importance, but still a town in character. Hindon in Wiltshire was another entirely new town of one wide street laid out by the bishop in 1220; it prospered in a modest way, especially in the coaching era, but receded to the status of a village in the nineteenth century. Its architectural character is largely Georgian, in local stone, thanks to a fire in 1754 and subsequent rebuilding. Downton, south of Salisbury, was an important Saxon and Norman village east of the River Avon. In 1208 the Bishop of Winchester established a new borough, consisting of burgage plots on either side of a wide street leading west from the river; the street may have been based on a pre-existing causeway across the valley floor. Downton did not develop as a trading centre, probably because it was, very soon after its foundation, eclipsed by the new city of Salisbury. Today the wide street is partly a long green, bordered by houses, mainly in eighteenth- and nineteenth-century brick, which are predominantly of cottage scale (**39**)—although the older part of the village, east of the river, possesses a more urban character.

39. The Borough, Downton, Wiltshire, laid out by a bishop along a wide street adjoining an older village, did not develop as hoped, owing to competition from neighbouring Salisbury (page 83), and the intended urban street is now a village green.

40. Godalming, Surrey grew gradually from a village, and has a tight-knit character different from that of planned medieval towns. Many of the buildings are timber-framed, with local tiles and brick infill, but the once colourful effect has been muted by too much white paint, not traditional to the area.

Like neighbouring Hindon, and also Newtown, Downton returned two Members of Parliament until 1832.

Finally, Godalming is selected because it can still give an impression of a small town in an immediate rural setting which is recognizably medieval (**40, 41**). It was a Saxon village which obtained a market charter as late as 1300, when the Bishop of Salisbury was lord of the manor—indicating, like some of the previous examples, how far from his diocesan centre a bishop's lands might extend. The town is particularly tight-knit, with narrow streets converging on a small space now occupied by a late Georgian market hall, lined by buildings in varied materials including decorative seventeenth-century brickwork, timber-framing with curved members almost as on the Welsh border, and the local sandstone. It was a cloth-making centre by the sixteenth century. To the north, by the River Wey, are the Lammas Lands. These are ancient pastures, part of the original village's medieval economy, perpetuated in the later market town, which were divided in springtime into sections, each held by a particular inhabitant for the growing of hay. At Lammas, the first of August, when the hay would have been harvested, the whole fields were thrown open to those inhabitants who had the requisite

rights for pasture, till the following spring. There was something similar in many medieval villages (see Chapter Three), and even in quite large towns—such as Southampton, where the Lammas Lands were turned in the nineteenth century into city centre parks. Godalming is one of the relatively few towns which retain such common meadows as pasture, even though they are no longer managed to quite the same system as originally. They provide a stretch of rough, old-fashioned grazing land, extending to the river, beyond which rise the church with its fine spire and the roofs of the tight-knit original town, all seen against the backcloth of a wooded slope which is today only partly dotted with houses. Although the town has spread in many directions, this short-distance view across fields to the historic town centre is much as it was in the Middle Ages. An even more impressive view, giving a similar effect, is seen at Stamford (55).

41. Godalming, looking in the opposite direction from **40**. The medieval spire is of timber, covered in lead (page 94).

7
Monasteries, Cathedrals and Churches

There were many wealthy and important monasteries, some of them also cathedrals, at the time of the Norman Conquest. Most were rebuilt more grandly than before in the century or so after the Conquest; the Norman parts of Durham, Ely, Peterborough, St Albans (4), Romsey and other great churches remain as testimony to this. All these old-established monasteries were Benedictine. Many new monasteries were founded in Norman times. A few of these were associated with Cluny, the great French Benedictine abbey which placed special emphasis on elaborate ritual in grand and artistically rich surroundings. One such was Lewes Priory, founded in 1077 by William de Warenne, a member of a militant but pious Norman family and builder of Lewes Castle. The site was below and outside the Saxon hill-town, now dominated by Warenne's castle, but nothing but a few pitiful fragments survived the Reformation. The same fate befell Reading Abbey, founded by Henry I with monks from Lewes, on the outskirts of a well-established town. Other monasteries followed the Augustinian rule, which was a little less strict than that of the Benedictines; examples were St Bartholomew's in London, founded in 1132 with the adjoining hospital, on the edge of the City where part of the original church survives, and St Augustine's in Bristol, established in 1140, the forerunner of what is now Bristol Cathedral. The latter retains a fine chapter house from soon after the foundation. In contrast to the Benedictines and Augustinians, whose monasteries were usually in towns, the Cistercians sought solitude and natural beauty, as is shown by the setting of Fountains and Rievaulx Abbeys in Yorkshire. They had little influence on the development of towns.

Monasteries were essentially inward-looking; the monks' lives were centred on the churches with their frequent services, and on the cloisters round which their domestic accommodation was built. Only the heads of the monasteries—abbots or priors—and those concerned with the administration of the usually extensive monastic estates normally had much direct contact with the outside world. So a typical Benedictine or Augustinian monastery in a city or town would stand within its own precinct, often walled-off from the rest of the town, and entered through gatehouses, such as survive at Bury St Edmunds and Abingdon, where little else of the abbeys remain. The abbey churches were often, at first, also the parish churches of the neighbouring towns, but this led to difficulties due to the different nature of the monastic and popular services. Parish churches for the people were therefore sometimes built alongside abbeys; the most famous is St Margaret's at Westminster, where the present early sixteenth-century church replaced one first built in the eleventh century. At Evesham, two parish churches were built outside the monastery; these survive while the abbey itself has all but disappeared.

Many monastic churches were centres of pilgrimage. They might have relics of their own saints, such as St Alban; St Edward (King Edward the Confessor) at Westminster; and St Cuthbert at Durham. Or there might be holy objects associated with miracles, like the crucifix at Waltham Abbey. Already famous churches might acquire additional fame through martyrdoms like that of St Thomas in Canterbury Cathedral. The pilgrims, many of whom would have travelled far, would pray at the shrines and leave offerings, which helped to enrich the monasteries. In this way many great churches became centres of popular attraction and veneration—it is a mistake to assume that the large numbers of tourists who visit many of the same churches today had no predecessors in the Middle Ages.

Monastic towns

Two outstanding towns which were centred on monasteries are Bury St Edmunds and Durham—the latter, of course, also a bishopric. The first church at what is now Bury St Edmunds was established in the seventh century; it became famous when the body of King Edmund of East Anglia, killed by the Danes in 869, was interred there; a Benedictine monastery was established in 1020. A great abbot, Baldwin, from St Denis near Paris, ruled from 1065 (he survived the upheavals of the Conquest because of his French background). He rebuilt the abbey on a grand scale and greatly enlarged the small town. His is the layout of the present town, a grid of streets, originally with two large rectangular market places, one of which, Angel Hill, remains an impressive space outside the surviving gateway to the abbey (42). The other market place became encroached on through market stalls becoming permanent, and by civic buildings represented by the Georgian Town Hall and Victorian Corn Exchange. Now this market place, as at St Albans, is an irregular series of interconnected spaces, where stalls are still set up on market days. The Norman Moyses Hall (20) is still a dominant feature. Like most medieval towns laid out on grids, the streets are not very rigidly aligned or spaced. But one of them, Churchgate Street, was axial to the great west door of the abbey (43). If this alignment was deliberate, it was very unusual, perhaps unique, for a medieval town. The axiality was emphasized when, in the middle of the twelfth

42. Angel Hill, Bury St Edmunds was one of the central spaces of the town laid out by Abbot Baldwin adjoining the monastery. The 14th century gateway led into the domestic and administrative quarters of the Abbey.

Map XIV Durham. The Cathedral is set on a cliff-bound peninsula (page 28), with the Castle on its isthmus. The city developed where it could—a long street east of the Cathedral; a market place north of the Castle; a street along the ridge beyond; suburbs across the medieval bridges. The railways had recently been built when this map was printed in 1861, but the city never grew much, apart from the University, first based on the Castle (pages 209, 253). Note the monastic buildings, largely intact, round the cloister south of the Cathedral.

century, an abbot built the present magnificent bell tower above an archway on the same alignment, so closing the present view down Churchgate Street. The bell tower now serves the adjoining church of St James, the present Anglican cathedral, one of the two parish churches, grandly rebuilt in late medieval times, which were established by the Abbey on the edge of its precinct to serve the townspeople. Alas, the abbey church itself is a shattered remnant; only the hulk of the lower part of the west front, quaintly converted to houses, and a few fragments of rubble-core masonry remain of one of the greatest churches of medieval England.

Durham is totally different from Bury St Edmunds in history, topography and character. Here the story goes back to the bringing of Christianity to the island of Lindisfarne in the seventh century, and to the sacking of Lindisfarne by the Vikings in 793. The monks then carried away for protection the remains of their patron saint Cuthbert who had been Bishop and Abbot of Lindisfarne. Eventually (page 28) the monastic community re-settled on a cliff-girt peninsula within the bend of the River Wear, which could be made nearly impregnable. The cathedral-monastery they established was rebuilt on a grand scale by Norman bishops, who also built a castle on the neck of the peninsula. This is essentially the Durham

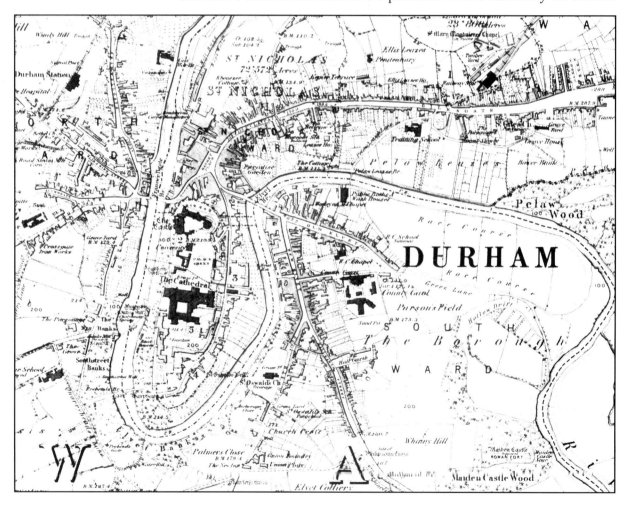

78

43. *Previous page* **Churchgate Street, Bury St Edmunds**, one of the main streets of the town laid out by Abbot Baldwin in the eleventh century (page 77). It was axial to the abbey church; the present bell tower with gateway underneath was built on the axis *c* 1140. The Georgian houses are characteristic of what became an elegant county town in the 18th century (page 207).

44. *Opposite* **The Close, Chichester**, in the S.W. corner of the Roman walled city (**3**), has no wide space, but a network of lanes bounded by garden walls of clergy houses in local flint and brick. The original cathedral spire, 13th century, collapsed in 1861; its successor, a replica, is shown undergoing repair in 1981.

of today; the cathedral and castle on their magnificent sites, with the steep slopes to the river planted with trees in the eighteenth century; the town crowding in wherever this was possible. A long narrow street curves round the eastern edge of the peninsula outside the monastic precinct; a small triangular market place lies to the north of the castle; and streets descend to bridges leading to old suburbs on either side of the river loop. The architecture of the city, apart from the cathedral, its appendages, and the castle, is mainly Georgian and later, but the form and outline are superbly medieval. The former monastic buildings, centred on the cloister to the south of the cathedral, are perhaps more nearly complete than anywhere else in England except at what his now Chester Cathedral. The tradition of the monastery is partly perpetuated by the University, which was founded by a bishop in 1832 in the cathedral precinct, using the episcopal castle as its first college.

Cathedral cities

Durham was one of the monasteries which were also cathedrals—an arrangement which was common in the British Isles but unusual on the Continent. A cathedral is a church which contains a *cathedra*, or bishop's seat; it need not necessarily be large—though in medieval England it usually was. Some of the Saxon cathedrals had been in important towns, others in quite small villages (page 26), but many of the latter were replaced by cathedrals in larger places; for instance the first cathedral at Exeter superseded that at Crediton in 1030. After the Conquest the present Chichester Cathedral replaced that at Selsey, which was affected by erosion; its site has since been submerged. The first cathedral at Lincoln replaced that at Dorchester-on-Thames, in another part of a very large diocese, and for a time the Norman Bath Abbey replaced Wells as the cathedral for Somerset, although Wells later regained its old status.

In Wales, the loosely organized but vital and vigorous Celtic Church was re-organized in the twelfth century, with cathedrals at St David's—associated with Wales' patron saint—Llandaff, St Asaph and Bangor. All these places were and, apart from Bangor, remain villages, even Llandaff, on the fringes of modern Cardiff.

About half of the English cathedrals, including Canterbury and Winchester, were monastic; the rest, including York, Lincoln and St Paul's in London followed the more normal European practice in having a hierarchy of clergy who were not monks. The bishop was responsible for the whole diocese; the dean for the cathedral itself and its organization, as head of the chapter of cathedral canons—some of whom had special duties, such as the precentor, in charge of music and singing. There were also, usually, priests who were full-time choristers (vicars choral). These clergy usually lived in a distinct precinct adjoining the cathedral—the bishop in his palace, the dean and canons in separate dwellings, the vicars choral collectively in a small group of buildings. Where cathedrals were founded in already established cities like York, Exeter, Chichester and Lincoln, adjoining areas were defined as precincts at an early date; they were usually entered from the rest of the cities through gates and were often, in later times, walled. Usually a large space was left on one or more sides of the cathedral, with clerics' houses facing it, an arrangement very clearly seen at Exeter, where some of the medieval canons' houses, variously altered, survive on the eastern side (**45**). At Lincoln the Exchequer Gate, opening from the former market place in the upper town,

symbolically separated the cathedral precinct from the town proper, with the castle, the seat of temporal power, situated on the opposite side of the square (page 31). At Chichester no large space was left adjoining the cathedral, but the south-western quarter of the Roman walled town became the cathedral precinct, with its own network of paths and lanes (3, 44).

Lichfield and Salisbury are two cities founded and planned by bishops in conjunction with cathedrals, and are in many ways similar to each other. Lichfield Cathedral was founded in 669 by St Chad, a missionary from Northumbria; its diocese extended from Warwickshire to Lancashire. In 1075 the bishop's seat was moved to Chester, then the most important town in the diocese. About twenty years later it was moved again, to Coventry, where an existing abbey, founded by Earl Leofric and his famed wife Godiva, became a monastic cathedral. In the early twelfth century the church at Lichfield was re-constituted a cathedral, jointly with that at Coventry—but Lichfield was still only a village. Roger Clinton, bishop from 1129 to 1149, laid out an entirely new town to the south of the cathedral (**XV**). It had a simple grid of streets, including the present Bore and Market Streets which led into a rectangular market place, now reduced in area through encroachment. Clinton also laid out a precinct, or Close, round the cathedral, with bishop's palace, clergy houses and College of Vicars Choral; the outline remains, though all the houses are now structurally later. The cathedral itself was rebuilt from the thirteenth century onwards. Clinton built a wall round the Close—fragments survive—which was entered through two gates. The town itself was never walled. Like many basically medieval towns, Lichfield has a largely Georgian and later architectural character, related to an earlier street pattern.

The medieval city of Salisbury was more ambitiously planned than Lichfield. It superseded an old hill town on a site, now called Old Sarum, which was one

45. The Close, Exeter is a typical setting for an English cathedral—a grassy enclave, originally entered through gates, fronted, on the far side, by originally medieval clergy houses variously altered (page 206). The commercial life of the city has spread discreetly into the buildings on the left, without seriously affecting the Close's precinctual quality.

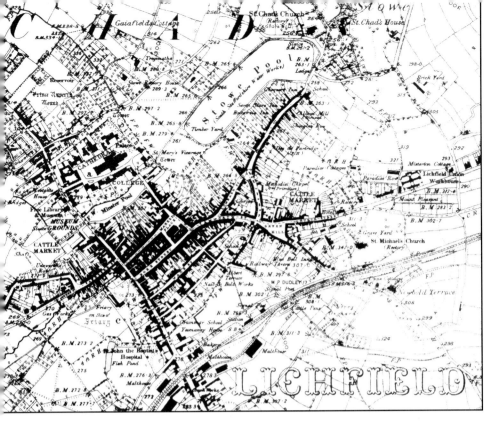

Map XV Lichfield, Staffordshire, in contrast to Durham (XIV) is regularly planned—mainly c 1140 by a bishop. He laid out a grid of streets, a square Market Place, since partly infilled, and, across the Minster Pool, a small precinct round the already existing Cathedral (page 26) which was rebuilt in the 13th century. The city has grown, but not greatly, since this map was printed in 1890.

of the most extraordinary ever to have been occupied by a town in Britain. Old Sarum began as an Iron Age hill-fort with earthen ramparts, near to which there was a small town in Roman times. After that the hill was probably deserted for several centuries, until re-occupied and re-fortified about 1000, when the Danes were marauding England. A town developed within the strengthened ramparts, and a castle was built there after the Conquest. Then, in 1075, the bishop's seat which had been in Sherborne, well to the west, was transferred to a new cathedral, next to the castle, inside the defences. The site proved too cramped for both cathedral and castle, whose activities were incompatible. The town spread outside the ramparts, but water supply was difficult on the chalky ground.

In the early thirteenth century Bishop Richard Poore decided to build a new cathedral and to lay out an entirely new city on a much more convenient site beside a river, south of Old Sarum. The foundation stone of the cathedral was laid in 1220 (48); permission was obtained for a market in the previous year. The city was laid out in an approximate grid—with variations from strict geometry to suit the topography—and included a large, approximately rectangular, market place. The new cathedral was set in a distinct precinct, or Close, following the established precedents elsewhere (46). A very large space was left north and west of the cathedral, which was bordered by individual houses for the dean and principal clergy, each set in a large plot—providing a distant precedent for the 'garden suburbs' of the nineteenth and twentieth centuries. Some of the medieval houses, built originally of stone and flint, survive, though all were modified in later centuries (47). A wall was built around the Close in the fourteenth century, not for military reasons but for protection against malefactors or unruly citizens, and the

83

46. *Right* **The Close, Salisbury** was laid out by Bishop Richard Poore *c* 1220 as the setting for his new cathedral (**48**)—a wide expanse, surrounded by clergy houses, decorously landscaped in the 18th century (page 206).

47. *Below right* **A House in Salisbury Close**. A clergy house built in the 14th century, altered in the 15th and subsequently, built variously of stone, flint, and brick. It retains the fine timber roof of the original hall. See also **124**.

48. *Opposite* **Salisbury Cathedral** was begun in 1220 by Bishop Richard Poore on a new site, with a new city adjoining. The spire, added a century later, is the tallest and finest in England; its design is related to that of the earlier St Mary Redcliffe, Bristol (**69**), which had a Salisbury connection.

Close was entered from the city proper through two gates, which survive. But the town itself, like Lichfield, was never walled. The Close was beautified in Georgian times when what had been rough ground was transformed into lawns, trees planted, and many of the houses were refronted or rebuilt (**124**).

The city proper was always more tightly built than the Close. Plots facing the streets were let off, in the normal manner, by the bishop as overlord. By the early fourteenth century the city was thriving, and parts of several merchants' houses survive from the fourteenth and fifteenth centuries, though often concealed by later alterations (**50**). Most of the medieval houses in the city proper were timber-framed, though a few were of stone and flint, like those in the Close. The market place was partly infilled at an early date (**49**). Salisbury became particularly notable first as a wool marketing centre and then as a weaving town.

49. *Right* **Poultry Cross, Salisbury**, built in the 15th century, of Chilmark stone like the cathedral (compare Chichester Cross, **59**). The site was originally a corner of the city's market place, which was encroached on early by predecessors of the buildings seen behind.

50. *Below right* **High Street, Salisbury**, one of the streets of the 13th century city, though the oldest house, the two-gabled Old George, is 14th, with original timbers exposed. The house to the left is 15th century, tile-hung in the 18th (page 191). The gate into the Close is at the far end.

51. All Saints, Maidstone, Kent was collegiate—served by the priests of a college whose tower is seen far right. In the foreground the former Palace of the Archbishops of Canterbury, mainly 16th century. The buildings are of Kentish ragstone, shipped from here for use in London (71; page 128).

Collegiate churches, chantries and friaries

Comparable to cathedrals in organization and, sometimes, scale were collegiate churches. A collegiate church was served by a group, or college, of priests who were not monks. Often they were termed canons, and sometimes they were headed by a dean, as in a cathedral. They normally lived together in a group of buildings including a hall and individual lodgings, often in courtyard form. (The word 'college' was originally a collective noun, applying to the corporate group; only later was it applied to the buildings which housed them.)

The grandest collegiate churches were at Beverley, Ripon and Southwell, all in the original diocese of York, for which they seem to have been regarded as subsidiary cathedrals. Ripon and Southwell have become Anglican cathedrals in modern times. Wimborne Minster in Dorset and the church at Ottery St Mary in Devon, both collegiate, have the plan form of miniature cathedrals. Many other collegiate churches are, in appearance, like large parish churches, as at Maidstone (51), Wolverhampton and Manchester. The collegiate church at Manchester, now the cathedral, is particularly interesting. Originally the parish church of a small market town near a Roman site, it was re-constituted as a collegiate church in about 1411 by Thomas de la Warre, lord of the manor and himself a priest, and subsequently rebuilt in its present form. It was wholly restored externally in the nineteenth century, but internal features, including the beautiful choir stalls, remain intact. The priests lived in collegiate buildings to the north, which were converted from the medieval manor house. These in turn were converted, after the college was dissolved at the Reformation, into Chetham's Hospital, an endowed school, founded in the seventeenth century by a Manchester merchant who was one of the earliest importers of cotton; the present Chetham's School occupies the site and the partly medieval buildings. The church itself became the cathedral of a new diocese in 1847.

Chantries were common in the later Middle Ages. They were organizations funded by bequests, donations or income from property, devoted wholly or partly to maintaining priests to say—or *chant*—prayers for the souls of departed people. At the least there would be a specific altar in a church where the prayers were regularly offered. Sometimes a chantry chapel, containing such an altar, was added to a church, in which the donor or members of his family were buried. Sometimes a separate chantry chapel was built. Chantries and their endowments were often associated with guilds, charities or schools, parts of the endowments going to support such institutions. They might even be associated with public facilities such as causeways and bridges. An exceptional endowment was that of Thomas Rotherham, Archbishop of York, and minister of state, which he made for the benefit of his native town of Rotherham in Yorkshire. Under this benefaction a chantry chapel was added to the already impressive parish church, where prayers were to be sung, after their deaths, for the souls of the archbishop and members of his family. A college of priests was established near the church, which thereby became collegiate, and a grammar school was founded. The church survives, but not the college or school buildings. Also probably associated with the archbishop's bequest was the medieval bridge at Rotherham of which there are partial remains, including a restored chapel which stood in the middle of one side of the bridge. Such bridge chapels, where passers-by were expected to pray and leave money offerings, were once common, but the only other intact, and restored, ones remaining on existing bridges are at Wakefield in Yorkshire and St Ives in Huntingdonshire **(16)**.

From the early thirteenth century, when two great Orders of Friars were established by St Dominic and St Francis, friaries were characteristic features of important European cities and towns. Friars lived communally, but in poverty, and depended on charity; they preached and ministered to the poor. The Dominicans (Blackfriars) and Franciscans (Greyfriars) were present in most important British towns. Smaller Orders like the Carmelites (Whitefriars) and Austin Friars had establishments in some towns. A typical friars' church had a large nave for preaching to the populace, and a structurally distinct chancel for the friars' own devotions.

52. Former Friary, Chichester. The eastern part of the Franciscan church, established 1269, in simple early Gothic characteristic of the area; one of the few friary buildings to survive in England.

A belfry or steeple often rose above the division between the two parts of the church. The friars' living accommodation was, at least at first, modest and austere. Because friaries were usually in prosperous towns, their sites were often valuable after the Dissolution, so that few substantial parts of friary buildings survive. The most impressive remains are at Norwich, where the Dominican church survives, much restored, as a concert hall, though without the steeple it once had, while to the north are parts of the former domestic buildings. Other friars' churches remain in part at Reading, now a parish church restored outside, at Chichester (52), at Gloucester, and at Atherstone. In Coventry the beautiful, once central, spire remains of the Greyfriars church, which has otherwise disappeared. Parts of friars' domestic buildings, altered for various purposes, remain at Newcastle, Bristol, Coventry (Whitefriars), Ware and elsewhere. In many other places, names like Greyfriars and Austin Friars testify where friaries once stood.

Effects of the Reformation

The effects of the Reformation were literally devastating. Every monastery in England and Wales was dissolved, mostly between 1538 and 1540. Many guilds, colleges and charitable institutions were abolished, but not all; it depended on circumstances. All chantries were suppressed by 1548. Thousands of buildings, including a large proportion of the grandest and most beautiful in the land, suddenly became redundant. Most were sold to private buyers by the royal commissioners, some for the value of the sites and materials, others on nominal terms.

Many monasteries were partly converted into houses. At Wilton, the nunnery, with a history going back to Saxon times, was conveyed to the Earl of Pembroke, who reconstructed it as a country house; later alterations resulted in the present Classical mansion, with no significant trace of the abbey buildings. At Titchfield in Hampshire the small monastery just outside the town was taken by Thomas Wriothesley, later Earl of Southampton, who was closely involved with the dissolution of other monasteries in the area. Wriothesley transformed the abbey buildings into a mansion, with the converted cloister as a courtyard, and built a grand gatehouse across the site of the nave of the church, parts of which were retained in the flanking wings. It was abandoned as a residence by the eighteenth century; ruins survive, mainly the shell of the gatehouse. The different fates of Wilton and Titchfield are both fairly typical. At Westminster many of the monastic buildings were converted for the School. At Malmesbury the abbey buildings were bought by William Stumpe, a cloth manufacturer, who converted some of them into what was, in effect, an early factory. But he gave part of the abbey church to the town as its parish church.

Very often the redundant buildings, especially the churches, were simply dismantled. Lead from the roofs was often the most valuable item; roof timbers were also valuable, so that many churches quickly became open to the sky. The market value of the stonework varied. In areas with no good local stone, such as East Anglia, to which stone had been brought expensively when the churches were built, the fine dressings were quickly plundered, sometimes leaving, as at Bury St Edmunds, parts of the flint or rubble cores of walls and piers. Stone was often re-used in local houses; at Lewes, where the splendid priory church was undermined and demolished by hired Italian engineers, Caen stone from it was re-used in the nearby Southover Grange. Many other great monastic churches, which had dominated their towns physically, spiritually and socially, were similarly reduced to pathetic fragments, as at Reading. Others disappeared altogether above ground, as at Winchcombe and Shaftesbury, or subsidiary features were left intact like the bell tower of Evesham.

A few monastic churches were largely preserved. Apart from those which were already cathedrals, five others became Anglican cathedrals at the Reformation, at Gloucester, Peterborough, Chester, Bristol and Oxford—the last associated with the deposed Cardinal Wolsey's new college of Christ Church, taken over and re-endowed by Henry VIII. Elsewhere, local townspeople bought abandoned churches from the royal commissioners, usually at 'market' prices which covered the value of their materials, and turned them into disproportionate, but magnificent, parish churches. This happened at Romsey, Tewkesbury, Sherborne, Bath and Pershore, though the last lost its nave. Congregations simply moved into the abbey churches from adjoining smaller parish churches which were usually then demolished; at Pershore it survives. At St Albans the abbey church (4) was similarly bought by the local people, even though the town already had, and retains, three parish churches. The abbey church became a cathedral in the nineteenth century. At Waltham Abbey, the Norman nave, which had always been used by the parishioners, was kept. Selby Abbey and Christchurch Priory probably also owe their preservation to the fact that parts were already used by the parishioners, who retained the whole buildings. Christchurch Priory is the most nearly intact of all English monastic churches. It even retains, though not in its original position, what was claimed to be part of a beam touched and miraculously lengthened by Christ who, according to legend, appeared and helped with the building of the first church. This became a goal of pilgrimage, and a source of funds for the church.

Relics such as this and, especially, the bones of saints, together with the often extremely beautiful shrines in which they were contained, were almost all systematically destroyed during the Reformation. Even the shrine of St Thomas at Can-

53. St Mary, Thirsk, Yorkshire. The medieval town of Thirsk developed to the south of the earlier village, whose location is indicated by the church, grandly rebuilt from 1419 through an endowment by Robert Thirsk, who set up a chantry (page 88) in the church. To the left is Thirsk Hall, 18th century successor to the original manor house.

terbury was smashed. Parts of the shrine of St Alban were used to patch up the abbey church, and were recovered in a nineteenth century restoration. Enough of the shrine was then reconstructed in the original position to give a good idea of the destination of many pilgrimages in the Middle Ages, although all the gorgeous embellishments have gone. Other fittings, furnishings and decorative features, including stained glass, in churches all over the country, were damaged or obliterated in waves of iconoclasm from the 1540s to the 1650s.

In one respect, however, the Reformation was not destructive. The reformed Church of England retained the Catholic episcopacy, and with it the cathedral establishments. The hierarchy of deans and canons in the non-monastic cathedrals was preserved, and the constitutions of the cathedrals which had been monasteries were reformed on the same lines. After a time, marriage were permitted for the clergy of the Church of England, even for bishops and canons. The old celibate precincts evolved into domesticated Cathedral Closes—which are described in the context of the eighteenth century (see Chapter Fifteen).

Parish churches

All the churches so far described were cathedral, monastic or collegiate churches, or special chapels. What of the parish churches, where ordinary people worshipped? By the twelfth century there were churches in or near most villages in the East, South and South-West of England, although they were more widely spaced in parts of the North. Several cities and towns which were important early had numerous parish churches (page 27); the medieval City of London had over a hundred; Norwich about fifty; York, Lincoln and Winchester twenty or more; many other towns had large numbers, including Oxford, Cambridge, Canterbury, Colchester, Ipswich, Exeter and Lewes. Smaller market towns normally had only one church.

By around 1200 parish boundaries, in country and city, had become largely established on lines which usually remained fixed until the nineteenth century. During this long period it was difficult for new parishes to be formally constituted, and new churches built after about 1200 usually had the status of chapels (often called 'chapels of ease') dependent on the older parish churches. The distinction is important. Tithes, or proportions of output from land (originally paid in kind, later in money), were, at least at first, payable to parish churches, not dependant chapels. Baptisms and marriages had normally to take place in parish churches, and burials in the churchyards surrounding them (though there were exceptions). Later, as local government developed on a parochial basis, the areas of parishes became units of administration.

Medieval church sites, once established, usually remained fixed, even through successive rebuildings, and despite population movements. Therefore the parish church of a town which developed out of an earlier village is usually located in the original village area, even if the town has grown away from it; Thirsk (53), Chipping Campden, Ashbourne (XII, p.68) and Wymondham with its priory church are examples already cited. Where a town developed on a new site, the church of the original rural parish in which it was located often remained the parish church, even though it might be some distance away from the town. Stevenage in Hertfordshire provided an interesting example. The medieval market town, on the Great North Road, developed nearly a mile away from the original

Saxon village, which became largely depopulated as people moved away to the newer town, leaving the church isolated, apart from a manorial farm, but continuing to serve the adjoining town. It remained in a rural setting until the building of the post-war New Town.

Where a medieval town developed away from an original parish centre, a dependent chapel was often built in the town. Two examples are provided by Uxbridge and Market Harborough. Uxbridge was established as a market town in the thirteenth century, within the parish of Hillingdon, a village two miles away. A chapel dependent on Hillingdon was built in the market place—it remains, partly hemmed in by buildings which later encroached on the market area. Only centuries later did it gain the status of a parish church of its own right; even today the borough centred on Uxbridge is called Hillingdon, not Uxbridge. Market Harborough was a new town founded in the late twelfth century. A chapel was built in the market place, to which the present grand and beautiful spire was added in the thirteenth century. Although a substantial building, its status was that of a chapel dependent on the older parish church in the village of Great Bowden nearby. The originally subservient status of the churches at Uxbridge and Market Harborough is evident today since neither has a large churchyard adjoining— burials took place in the churchyards of Hillingdon and Great Bowden respectively. However, some new medieval towns did obtain parish churches of their own, independent of the original rural parishes; New Buckenham (page 68), and also Baldock in Hertfordshire are examples.

There were many sources of funding through which parish churches might be built. Many were first erected, and afterwards maintained, by lords of manors. Tithes payable to local churches would originally have been used for the maintenance of their fabrics and the sustenance of their rectors. However, tithes often became appropriated by monasteries or other bodies, to which the payments originally due to the individual churches were re-directed. The abbot, or head of the appropriating body, would become nominally the rector of the parish, but would appoint a vicar (the term strictly means 'substitute') who would be supported by a proportion of the tithes. Monasteries, having appropriated tithes, sometimes, but not always, paid fairly generously towards the fabrics of the parish churches in their care. Where a community became particularly wealthy, rich individuals, or groups or merchants or craftsmen, would often pay for grand rebuildings or embellishments of churches, as can be seen in the wool marketing towns of Chipping Campden and Northleach in the Cotswolds, or in weaving towns such as Lavenham and Long Melford in Suffolk.

There was no notable architectural distinction between town churches and those of country parishes, except those resulting from constrictions on urban sites. Whether in town or country, medieval church building was influenced by national stylistic fashions at the time of building; by regional variations which might derive partly from materials locally available; and, where appropriate, by the traditions and practices of monastic or other bodies which sponsored the building operation. From Norman times onwards, churches were almost always built of stone or other quarried material, in contrast to medieval houses which were much more often timber-framed. (There were a few medieval timber-framed churches, but they were exceptional.) Sometimes, fine stone was brought many miles, often by river, for use in churches—frequently in conjunction with local, humbler, materials such as flint, as in the churches of East Anglia.

54. St Mary, Higham Ferrers, Northamptonshire. One of a group of fine medieval spires which soar above towns and villages in the Midland limestone country; others are at Rushden, Kettering and Market Harborough.

Many parish churches date from several successive periods, the results of enlargements, partial rebuildings, and beautifications at different times. However, a high proportion of English town churches date largely or wholly from the late fourteenth, fifteenth and early sixteenth centuries, especially in those areas where the wool trade or weaving flourished. These are in the specifically English Perpendicular style, so different from the flamboyant style of the contemporary churches of France, and of some in Scotland. The names of the designers of these churches are usually anonymous, but are sometimes known through documents, or presumed with high probability through circumstantial evidence. To give two examples, the great parish churches of Saffron Walden and of St James in Bury St Edmunds, now the cathedral, were both probably designed by John Wastell, architect of the central tower of Canterbury Cathedral and of the upper parts of King's College Chapel, Cambridge. Yeovil church in Somerset has been attributed to William Wynford, who worked at Wells, and for William of Wykeham at Winchester.

It was the steeples—the word embraces towers and spires—which were usually the most important features of churches in the visual compositions of towns. Spires are essentially Northern and Central European features. Britain has some of the finest, not only on cathedrals like Salisbury (48) and Norwich, but on hundreds of parish churches. The great period for spires was the thirteenth and fourteenth centuries, although some were built right up to the time of the Reformation and, of course, after. The Midlands are spire country *par excellence*, and among towns still punctuated by major medieval stone spires are Louth, Market Harborough, Grantham, Newark, Oundle, Witney, Leighton Buzzard, Thaxted (an outlier from the stone spire country), Shrewsbury (with two), Higham Ferrers (54), and the otherwise mundane Northamptonshire towns of Kettering, Raunds and Rushden. Even Birmingham has the outlines of a medieval spire, restored but not entirely rebuilt, at St Martin's, the original church of the small medieval town. Coventry has the most spectacular set of spires—those of the parish churches of St Michael, latterly the cathedral, and Holy Trinity, and of the otherwise vanished Greyfriars church. They grouped with the steeples—there were three—of the great monastic cathedral in the city (page 82) which was destroyed at the Reformation; when these stood the skyline must have been fantastic. The church of St Michael, already mentioned, became the cathedral only in the 1930s; its steeple, soaring now from the preserved ruins of the bombed church, is particularly poignant; it is the tallest in England that rises directly from the ground and not from the centre of a cruciform church, as at Salisbury and Norwich Cathedrals.

All these are stone spires. Medieval wooden spires, faced with lead or shingles (small pieces of wood shaped like tiles) were also common, but fewer have survived. The two tallest, which rose from the central towers of Lincoln and Old St Paul's Cathedrals have long since disappeared. The best remaining is at Hemel Hempstead, built in the fourteenth century on to a Norman tower; others are at Godalming (41) and Chesterfield—the latter famous for its weird twist. These are lead-covered; the largest medieval shingled spire is at Horsham in Sussex.

From about 1400, tall towers, often with elaborate crowns and pinnacles, were generally preferred to towers with spires. Somerset is the greatest tower county. Many of its grandest towers are in quite small villages, but the tallest of all, at Taunton, soars in the middle of a town. Bristol retains many fine medieval towers, apart from the spired St Mary Redcliffe (69), and there is another in the Bristol tradition dating from the fifteenth century in Cardiff (142). Other towns, among very many, which retain particularly distinctive medieval towers are Wrexham, Ludlow, St Neots, Derby, (which developers and planners by accident or design still allow to dominate the adjoining part of the city), Ashford, Loughborough, Cirencester and Melton Mowbray. In East Anglia they are numerous; Beccles and Lavenham are just two examples. Devon and Cornwall have many fine, severe towers; in Plymouth the fifteenth-century tower of St Andrew's remains the finest landmark in the reconstructed centre of the city; it is very similar to that of Fowey, which stands in a more traditional setting.

Perhaps the place which gives the most vivid impression of a medieval town when seen from outside is Stamford. This, a major town in the Middle Ages, but a minor one now, nearly all built in the dark brown local limestone, retains five medieval parish churches, two with spires, the rest with pinnacled towers, which

can be seen rising over the old roofs of the town, with no later competitive features, from across the meadows which still come up to the old town on the south-western side (55). Many other towns once looked like this as one approached before the days of sprawling suburbs and intrusive, more bulky, buildings on the skyline.

The naves of parish churches were used for many community purposes, including meetings and even festive occasions, in the earlier Middle Ages. Smaller gatherings might take place in porches, which often had upper stories. However, in the later Middle Ages secular uses of church interiors were increasingly disfavoured, and many naves were filled with pews from the fifteenth century onwards. From then, festive and other secular activities which might previously have happened in the churches were held in 'church houses', often built nearby; in local guildhalls or town halls; or in inns.

Many churchyards were originally places of public assembly; even markets were sometimes held there in early times. But in time their use as burial places almost always became dominant. Today churchyards are often much-appreciated green spaces in the middle of towns; there are many examples, for instance, in Norwich and Ipswich with their numerous surviving churches, and in the City of London.

55. Stamford, Lincolnshire. Many towns looked like this from outside before modern times, with fields stretching to the backs of close-built streets, and skylines of steeples.

8
Institutions and Public Buildings

The idea of a college of priests, described in the previous chapter, developed into that of a college for academic study and training. The University of Paris, established by the twelfth century, contained several quasi-independent colleges, each with its teachers who were in holy orders. The pattern was taken up at Oxford and Cambridge in the thirteenth century, and later, but not permanently, at Stamford and certain other towns. The concept of a college to house students as well as academic 'staff' who were not necessarily priests was effectively established by William of Wykeham, Bishop of Winchester, when he founded New College, Oxford in 1379. From then on, colleges developed at both Oxford and Cambridge in a way that is now unique to England—the collegiate system at Paris and elsewhere on the Continent having long since been superseded. The typical Oxford or Cambridge collegiate plan is analogous to that of many large medieval manor houses and a few town houses, consisting of one or more courtyards, entered through a gateway that is sometimes made a major feature in itself, and containing a chapel, hall, and service and domestic accommodation.

Bishop Wykeham also founded Winchester College in 1382, for boys (as boarders), most of whom, he hoped, would go on to his college at Oxford. It and New College were imitated on a grander scale by Henry VI at Eton College and King's College, Cambridge. It also set the pattern for innumerable more humble grammar schools founded in towns and villages from the fifteenth century onwards, usually for day boys but sometimes—from the start or later—taking boarders as well. The founders were frequently locally-born people who had grown rich or attained high office. Sometimes the founder was, at least nominally, the monarch himself—as with the many grammar schools set up in the reign of Edward VI partly out of the funds of dissolved chantries. Some of these Tudor schools had fairly substantial buildings, as at Berkhamsted (founded in 1544), of brick, with a central hall, or classroom, and accommodation for master and usher— a kind of second master—at either end (**56**). Ashbourne (founded in 1585), is built of stone, looking outwardly like a small manor house of the period, and Guildford (founded in 1509), surrounds a small quadrangle reached off the main street. Other early grammar schools were more modest, at least to begin with, but a few developed, in time, into what we now call public schools; Rugby is an example. Of the three schools mentioned above, Berkhamsted is now a large public school; Ashbourne is a comprehensive school, no longer in the original building; and Guildford an independent day school. In addition, there were the purely charitable schools, originally for orphans or other destitute children, sometimes called Bluecoat Schools, because of the colour of the uniforms. The most famous was Christ's Hospital, founded on the site of the dissolved Franciscan friary in the City of London in 1553.

Hospitals

The old, infirm and poor, including the travelling poor, were served in the Middle Ages by hospitals—the word had a wider meaning than today. They were, at first, usually quasi-monastic, with a master or warden, and a staff of brothers, who might be clerics or laymen. Earlier medieval hospitals were often in the form of churches. The occupants lived in the structural nave, perhaps in lightly partitioned bedspaces or cubicles such as remain in the large fourteenth-century St John's Hospital at Bruges, while the chancel was used for services—the inmates could be given the sacraments in a consecrated building without going outside. St Mary's Hospital at Chichester, built about 1290, retains that form except that miniature one-storey 'houses' of brick, each with a hearth and chimney, were built within the hall in the seventeenth century; they are still occupied by old people. The fourteenth-century building of St Catherine's Hospital at Ledbury, just a 'nave' and chancel, remains (**30**), though superseded by Victorian almshouses nearby. What later became the Royal Garrison Church at Portsmouth, now partly roofless, was originally a hospital, founded in 1215 as a *Domus Dei*, Maison Dieu, or God's House, like several others so called, in whichever language, in ports. There were examples at Dover and Southampton—intended primarily, but not wholly, for poor travellers, especially those on pilgrimage, before joining or after leaving ships.

Other medieval hospitals, especially the later ones, are built in courtyard form. The most splendid is St Cross at Winchester, richly founded in 1136 by a bishop, and augmented in the fifteenth century by another. It has a superb church of the earlier date, and domestic buildings of the latter period. Examples of smaller hospitals, among many, with a courtyard plan are the tiny and delightful Wynard's Hospital at Exeter of 1436 (but embellished by the Victorians), and Ford's Hospital at Coventry, with small timber-framed courtyard, founded by a merchant in 1519. Restored after bomb damage, it continues its original purpose.

Many hospitals were closed at the Reformation because of monastic connections, such as the once large St Leonard's Hospital in York, now a fragmentary ruin. Fortunately St Bartholomew's Hospital in London survived as an institution, despite its monastic association; it is now housed in eighteenth-century and later buildings on the original site. St Thomas's Hospital, originally in Southwark, also survived; it moved to new buildings opposite the Houses of Parliament in the nineteenth century.

56. Berkhamsted School, Hertfordshire, founded, like many in Tudor times, by a local person successful in life—John Incent, Dean of St Paul's—and built *c* 1544. The central hall was the teaching space, the gabled wings the houses of master and usher. The school has expanded greatly since mid Victorian times (page 253).

Hundreds of hospitals and almshouses—in modern terms old people's homes—were founded in Tudor, Stuart and Georgian times. Their buildings, sometimes modernized and still used for their original purpose, sometimes converted to other uses, are found in towns and villages all over the country. The humblest might be a simple row of small dwellings, the larger ones were often in college-like buildings round courtyards, with chapels and wardens' lodgings. Two substantial examples are Abbot's Hospital, founded by an archbishop in his native Guildford in 1619, with a grand gateway in the Tudor tradition, and Whitgift's Hospital in Croydon, founded by another archbishop (together with a school) in 1596. The brick-built courtyard of the latter is still a home for old people, right in the centre of modern Croydon, having survived successions of councillors and developers who threatened it with road schemes and redevelopment. But the school founded at the same time, which was endowed with a piece of agricultural land nearby, is now a wealthy establishment, thanks to the unimaginably increased value of its endowed property when it was sold three and a half centuries later.

Guildhalls, town halls and market crosses

Guildhalls were originally the halls or premises occupied by guilds. A guild was an association of people with a corporate constitution and limited membership, always, in the Middle Ages, with religious affiliations. At its simplest, it might be a fraternity or 'club', associated with a church; at its grandest a body of powerful merchants who might effectively control the economy of a city. Many guilds were associations of people in a particular craft or trade, which strictly controlled entry and practice in that trade, in a particular locality. There were subtle and complex hierarchies within and between the larger guilds. Close relationships often developed between guilds and the governing councils of cities and larger towns, such as remain today between the Livery Companies (successors to the medieval guilds) and the Corporation of the City of London (71). For that reason, the chief civic halls of many important medieval towns were called Guildhalls; medieval examples survive in varying measure in London, York, Norwich, Exeter, King's Lynn and, on a smaller scale, Leicester. Much of the shell, and the fine vaulted undercroft, of the London Guildhall dates from 1410–40, even though the building had to be reconstructed after two fires, in 1666 and during the bombing of 1940. York's fifteenth-century Guildhall was similarly damaged in the Second World War, but the interior with its oak columns has been restored in replica. York retains three other basically medieval guildhalls—those of the Merchant Adventurers, the general merchants' guild; of the Merchant Taylors, an important craft guild; and of St Anthony's, a social and religious fraternity.

At Coventry, St Mary's Hall, which was built in 1340 and enlarged in about 1400 for the city's merchant guild, became the hall of the City Council when the guild was dissolved at the Reformation. It is perhaps the best preserved medieval civic hall in England, and even retains a tapestry made for it at Arras in the fifteenth century. The hall itself stands at first floor level above an undercroft on one side of a courtyard entered through a gateway from the street (page 55). The merchant guild also had its own grand church, St John's, elsewhere in the city, while the craft guilds, which were in many ways subservient to the merchant guild, had their own chapels in the city's two parish churches.

Many guilds were dissolved at the Reformation because of their religious

connections (page 89). Others, particularly craft guilds, were reformed on a secular basis and often became known as companies. Several existed in the seventeenth century and later in such cities as Bristol, Salisbury and Chester, often in modest premises—in Newcastle they occupied various converted towers, some of which survive, of the city wall. In the City of London the Livery Companies, some derived from medieval guilds, others founded after the Reformation, remain important institutions, whether or not they retain close connections with the trades after which they are named. Often they occupy their original medieval sites, although only the Merchant Taylors retain any medieval fabric. A few others, like the Apothecaries and Skinners, occupy premises partly dating from the rebuilding after the Great Fire of 1666; they are grouped round small courtyards entered through passageways from the streets.

Many lesser guilds and fraternities in small towns and villages met in buildings, often quite modest, which are sometimes still called guildhalls, especially in East Anglia. A fine example of a small-town guildhall is at Thaxted in Essex. This was built about 1400, possibly by the Cutlers' Guild when the town was a centre of the knife and blade industry, and was, in effect, the town hall. It has

57. Hungerford almshouses and school, Corsham, Wiltshire, a fairly typical charitable combination for young and old, built 1668 in a 'Gothic Survival' style with rustic Baroque details, characteristic of the time—in the local golden-brown stone which was quarried in huge quantities in Victorian times as Bath stone (page 218).

two timber-framed overhanging storeys, over an open-sided ground floor which accommodated market stalls. It contrasts with the magnificent church, partly of about the same date, whose stone spire soars from higher ground behind (page 94).

Thaxted Guildhall is a fairly elaborate example of a type of building, also called, variously, town hall, market hall or tolbooth (the last is a common Scottish team), which typically stands in the middle of a market place or wide street, usually with a single upper storey over an open-arched or columned space at ground level. Examples among many are at Ledbury (32), which is timber-framed; at Shrewsbury, built about 1596 and of stone; at Tetbury, also of stone (58) and at Faversham, originally of Elizabethan date but with the upper room remodelled in Georgian times. At Chipping Campden the so-called Yarn Market (29) is simply a single-storeyed open-arched shelter, that at Dunster (15) is octagonal. The most splendid of all the earlier market halls is that at Rothwell, in Northamptonshire, erected in 1578 by Sir Thomas Tresham, the eccentric squire of nearby Rushton, where he built an extraordinary Triangular Lodge. The Rothwell market hall is an elaborate piece of Elizabethan architecture in the local stone, with flat roof boldly projecting with eaves, and frieze full of shields. The arched ground storey, now partly blocked, was originally all open. These open-sided ground floors could shelter a small proportion of stalls on market days, perhaps those with the more perishable commodities.

Related to these market halls, but more ornamental than utilitarian, were the octagonal stone Gothic 'Crosses' which survive at Salisbury (49), Chichester (59) and Malmesbury, providing very limited roof shelter, and rising, with elegant curves, to what were originally Gothic turrets. That at Chichester, built by a bishop in 1501, stands at the junction of the four main streets and closes the views along three of them; it is now crowned by a Georgian cupola. Much more common in the Middle Ages were the purely ornamental 'Crosses' which, at their most elaborate, were like large Gothic pinnacles rising in several graceful stages. They were

58. Tetbury Market House, Gloucestershire, a common type of country town building, containing shelter for market stalls on the open ground floor, and a public room above. Built 1665 in local stone with rustic Renaissance details; it contrasts with the slightly earlier, timber-framed one at Ledbury (32) in a very different tradition.

59. Chichester Cross, built by a bishop in 1501, in Caen stone, at the meeting of the city's main streets with their Roman alignments (page 16). The cupola replaced the original pinnacle in 1746. Compare the Poultry Cross, Salisbury (**49**).

usually surmounted by stone crucifixes, and were delicately treated with Gothic cusping and crocketing, including niches which contained small figures of saints or angels. Very few have survived the destruction of the Reformation, the zeal of the Puritans, or the forces of decay. That of Bristol, which stood at the junction of the city's four main streets, was bought by Henry Hoare the banker in the eighteenth century and re-erected as a focal feature in his beautiful park at Stourhead in Wiltshire, where it remains. That at Winchester survived an attempt to remove it similarly to a nearby park and it remains *in situ*, in the widest part of the High Street. The medieval cross at Leighton Buzzard is elegant and twotiered, set, like many crosses were, on a stepped base. These are only a tiny proportion of the crosses that once existed. Banbury Cross, for instance, was destroyed during the Commonwealth (indicating how old the nursery rhyme connected with it must be); the present Gothic cross, on a different site, was built only to commemorate the marriage of Queen Victoria's daughter to the Crown Prince of Prussia.

9
Walls and Gates

On the whole, strongly walled towns were not as characteristic of medieval England as they were of most of the Continent. Because of our island situation, we escaped the continental-scale wars which on occasions resulted in large areas being ravaged. Except near the Scottish and Welsh Borders, and on the vulnerable coasts of the South and East, English towns needed to be defended against nothing worse than dynastic struggles or baronial conflict. In Wales the circumstances were different; almost all the towns there were English plantations, and many were strongly defended against the hostility of the local populace.

Many Roman towns had walls, or ramparts faced in stone or flint; some of these were maintained or augmented intermittently through the Middle Ages, as at Lincoln (2), Chester, Chichester (3) and Colchester. Saxon and Viking towns often had earth ramparts, occasionally strengthened with stone, which sometimes provided the basis for later, stronger defences. The Normans relied overwhelmingly on castles, and built few if any new town walls not directly related to castles,

60. City Wall, Chester, with Roman masonry in its lower courses (page 16), and medieval work above; restored in more recent times. The canal below was constructed by Thomas Telford as part of the link between the Midlands and the Mersey (page 180) and opened in 1795. Tall blocks of flats of the 1960s loom in the distance.

61. Western Walls, Southampton, built in the 14th century in front of a low natural cliff, originally facing open water. The ruined Arundel Tower, left, was the north-west corner of the town; the nearer Catchcold Tower was added in the 15th century.

though they sometimes dug ditches and ramparts, which might have wooden palisades on top.

The great period for building city walls in Britain was from about 1200 to the early fifteenth century. On the whole, outside Wales and the Scottish Border areas, only the most important towns were stone-walled. Even places as important as Cambridge, Ipswich and the new city of Salisbury, apart from the Close (50), never had more than low ramparts, ditches and gates.

City walls sometimes rose straight from the ground; often, as at York, they were built on top of, or against, earlier earthen ramparts. Sometimes they were simply retaining walls set against natural cliffs or steep slopes. Towers or bastions, of varying shapes, sizes and heights, normally projected at intervals. There were usually continuous walkways along the tops of the walls, passing through or behind the towers and bastions, and protected from outside by parapets, often battlemented. Medieval walls belong essentially to the age of bows and arrows, so that towers, gates and sometimes parapets were pierced as appropriate by arrow slits, vertical or cross-shaped. A few later examples had larger slits with round apertures suitable for small guns—the first effective guns dated from the fourteenth century. Wherever practicable, walls were protected externally by ditches or moats.

York and Southampton have the best remaining town walls in England. At York, the earthen ramparts constructed by the Vikings covered the north and east walls of the original Roman legionary fortress and extended in other directions to enclose the rest of the city of the time. Stone gates were built in the twelfth century; something of these survive in the lower parts of Bootham and Micklegate Bars (a 'bar' in York is a gate). The extant, often repaired, walls were built from about 1270 onwards, mainly on top of the older ramparts, and the gates were mostly rebuilt or strengthened in the fourteenth century. At Southampton, the medieval town was away from the earlier Saxon town of Hamwic, and had a frontage to the water. Ramparts and ditches were formed on the landward sides by the early thirteenth century. Perhaps a little earlier, the first stone northern gate was built; it survives as the core of today's Bargate. Stone walls were erected in stages from the mid thirteenth century, but this still left the waterside open, apart from the Castle. A French raid devastated the town in 1338; twenty years later work was under way on a series of massive stone walls along the waterfront, much of which survives today (61). Interestingly, they incorporate parts of earlier stone-built merchants' houses which had faced the open quay (page 48).

At Chester the existing walls incorporate Roman masonry on the east and north sides (60), but are of later origin to the south and west, since the walled area was extended in these directions in the Middle Ages. Large sections are in effect retaining walls, where the ground levels inside the walled city are higher than outside. The Chester walls have been greatly altered and restored, particularly in the eighteenth and nineteenth centuries—all the city gates are Georgian rebuildings—but the walk along them is still a memorable experience.

Elsewhere in England, stretches of city wall remain at Canterbury, Rochester, Chichester, Winchester and Exeter, all following Roman alignments, and at Newcastle, (built during the Anglo-Scottish war), Oxford, Coventry, Norwich, Yarmouth and Hartlepool. In Wales, the splendid walls of Conwy and Caernarfon, constructed under Edward I in conjunction with the castles, survive almost intact, and there are impressive stretches at Tenby and Chepstow. At Denbigh, the town has grown out of its original small walled area, which is now largely deserted,

62. North Bar, Beverley, Yorkshire, built 1410, one of the earliest brick buildings (page 54), is the survivor of four town gates—although Beverley was never properly walled and had only defensive ditches between the gates.

appearing as an outer bailey to the adjoining castle.

Gates were often among the most impressive structures in medieval towns. The earliest were simple archways, sometimes with small rooms above. Later, massive towers were often built to flank the archways, either rounded as at the Landgate in Rye, or polygonal, as at Hotspur Gate, Alnwick. At Canterbury the Westgate, with its great round flanking towers, was rebuilt, with other parts of the wall, in about 1380 under the charge of Henry Yevele, who designed the nave of the cathedral. Similarly William Wynford, William of Wykeham's architect at Winchester and Oxford, may have been concerned with the building of the impressive north front of the Bargate at Southampton, between two earlier round towers, in about 1400. The town's medieval Guildhall was in the room over the arch, with windows facing south down the main street. A few towns which were not fully walled nevertheless had gates—like Beverley with its brick fifteenth-century North Bar (62).

Most walled cities and towns extended beyond their defences even in early times. Bootham was a substantial early suburb of York, along the road leading north-westward from Bootham Bar; there were medieval suburbs outside the other city gates. At Lincoln the suburb of Wigford outside the old south gate became

63. South Gate, Launceston, Cornwall. The town adjoining the castle (11) had its own walls and gates; this is the only survivor, with modern pedestrian arch to its side. In the foreground a (probably) 17th century timber-framed house, hung in local slates (page 191) and with Georgian sash windows.

so important that the gate itself, with the city's Guildhall above, was virtually the centre of the lower, mercantile, part of the city, as distinct from the upper part, round the castle and cathedral. Much the same happened on a smaller scale at Totnes, where what was originally the east gate, much altered and with the Guildhall adjoining, now crosses the main street in the very centre of the town. Even monasteries, or major charitable institutions, often stood outside city walls. At Winchester, the great abbey of Hyde, the College and the Hospital of St Cross were all outside. At Shrewsbury the Abbey was in a suburb across the river. At Oxford both St Giles and Broad Street, and the eastern part of High Street, together with some of the medieval colleges, such as Magdalen, were outside the line of the walls.

Very occasionally areas originally outside the walls were brought into the defended areas of cities by extensions of the walls. This happened early at Chester, as we have seen. Bristol, by the fourteenth century, had far outgrown the original, small, late Saxon *burh* (page 28). New walls were then built to enclose most of the large and populous district across the River Avon, but still left outside the walls the suburban church of St Mary Redcliffe, later to be enlarged into one of the grandest parish churches in the country (**69**). At about the same time a newly developed area just to the south of the original town was also walled. But the monastery of St Augustine, now the Cathedral, together with three major friaries, remained outside Bristol's walls.

London never extended its defences significantly beyond the line of the Roman walls, which were retained and heightened in the Middle Ages, partly to compensate for the raising of ground level within the walls. This can still be seen in the stretches of City wall which remain north of the Tower (page 20)—which was itself built across part of the line of the Roman defences. There were extensive medieval suburbs outside the gates of London, as described in Chapter Twelve.

The facts that smaller English towns were usually unwalled, and that extensive suburbs of London and other cities remained outside the defended areas, indicate how relatively peaceful the country was by medieval European standards, despite dynastic and baronial conflicts. Few English towns were besieged or severely attacked before the Civil War of the seventeenth century, when several places suffered long sieges. Only then were the walls of York, of Chichester, of Colchester and of Gloucester (which have entirely disappeared) put to the test—to some effect—and the suburban areas outside these cities' gates devastated. At Colchester the Norman priory church of St Botolph, which had been partly retained after the Reformation as a parish church, was completely wrecked; the ruins are preserved. At Lichfield the walled-in Close became a battleground. The cathedral spire was hit by cannon fire and crashed into the choir; fortunately both were well repaired afterwards. By then, stone walls were obsolescent; Continental cities were coming to be protected by more sophisticated systems of defence which were seen in England only at Berwick-on-Tweed, Hull (**XVII**, p. 119) and Portsmouth (page 185). In many cities, walls and especially gates were demolished in the eighteenth and early nineteenth centuries in the name of 'improvements'. But at Chester, Chichester, in part, and later, York, they were maintained and restored as agreeable and romantic promenades.

10
Early Industries

Wool and wool products were the main source of incoming wealth in England from the Middle Ages to the mid eighteenth century. At first the wealth came from the export of raw wool, especially to Flanders, when Ghent and neighbouring cities were the greatest weaving centres in northern Europe. Some even went to Italy, where some of the early prosperity of Florence was similarly derived from weaving. But from the fourteenth century onwards, English weaving developed rapidly, and cloth far exceeded raw wool in the export trade.

In the twelfth and thirteenth centuries the English weaving industry, far less significant than it later became, was largely centred on a few important towns, including Lincoln, Winchester, Stamford, Marlborough, Beverley and York. By the late fourteenth and early fifteenth centuries the industry had declined in these places, apart from York, but was developing rapidly in other cities such as Norwich, Coventry and Salisbury. However, most of the huge expansion of English weaving which continued through the fifteenth and early sixteenth centuries took place, not in the larger towns, but in small towns, in villages, and in the open

64. **Sorting wool, Bradford, Yorkshire**. The scene is in 1982 and the building is Victorian, but wool has been sorted, spun and woven in Bradford since the 15th century, even though it was then only a village (page 110).

107

country. For this there were two main reasons. Merchant and craft guilds often controlled the weaving industry strictly in the larger towns, but they did not exist, or were much weaker, in small towns and villages, where the industry could therefore develop more freely. Water, essential for processing, and used to some extent for power, was more likely to be in plentiful supply, and relatively pure, away from large towns. By this time, feudal obligations and controls, which would have hindered the development of the cloth industry in rural areas at an earlier date, were weakening or had disappeared.

One of the most important technological developments of the Middle Ages was the invention of the fulling mill. Woollen cloth production included several successive processes, of which the most important were spinning and weaving. These were done with hand-operated instruments or machinery, which gradually became more sophisticated, right up to the nineteenth century. The heavier types of cloth went through a final process called fulling, or tucking in the West, which turned the fabric from a series of interwoven, but distinguishable, strands into a consolidated piece of cloth, where the separate strands were no longer evident. Originally the fabric was first soaked in liquid, usually urine because of its chemical properties, and then 'walked over' by human feet—hence the surname Walker (identical with Fuller or Tucker, while Webster or Webb signified a weaver). The first fulling mills were recorded in the twelfth century, and they became common from the fourteenth century onwards. They were ordinary water mills where the mill wheels, instead of driving stones to grind flour, powered hammers in repeated action, so that the soaked fabric was beaten more thoroughly than was possible by human feet. This was a major, very early, step towards the full mechanization of the textile industry.

Apart from fulling, and also dyeing, medieval clothmaking was an entirely 'domestic' industry, in the sense that all the operators worked in their own homes, or in workshops close by. Often whole families participated. The first stages, including carding (preparing the raw wool for spinning), were often done by children; the spinning customarily by women; and the weaving by men. But these domestic workers were not necessarily independent. By the fifteenth century, large numbers of textile workers were employed by master clothiers, who might buy the raw wool, and pass it in succession to carders, spinners and weavers, paying them usually on a piecework basis. The clothiers would then arrange for the woven cloth to be fulled—they often owned fulling mills themselves. They might also dye the cloth—which was sometimes marketed after dyeing, sometimes not. Dyestuffs came from various sources; many were imported; others were grown in England, notably saffron—Saffron Walden (22) was a noted centre for this crop.

There was thus a distinctly 'capitalist' system in the medieval weaving industry, with large-scale employers and numerous wage-earners, long before the Industrial Revolution—but the employees worked in, or near, their own homes, not in large factories. However this pattern was not universal. There were many independent weavers, or families of clothworkers, who bought the wool and sold the cloth on their own terms. Some clothiers' dynasties grew fabulously rich, and dominated the economies of their small towns for a generation or two. Examples were the Springs of Lavenham—the most medieval of the former clothing towns in its present-day form—the Terumbers of Trowbridge, and the Hortons of Bradford on

65. *Left* **Bocking, Essex**, near Braintree, one of the richest Eastern weaving centres in the 15th–17th centuries. The near house, possibly 16th century and plastered in the Eastern tradition, has 17th century first-floor windows and Georgian ones below.

66. *Below left* **Bocking, Essex**. The long sinuous street has houses of all periods; sometimes Georgian fronts conceal earlier timber-framed buildings (page 194). After the demise locally of wool weaving (by hand), a silk weaving factory was established nearby in the early 19th century (page 216).

Avon. The clothiers might sell the cloth to merchants for distribution, or might be shippers themselves, like John Greenway of Tiverton, who exported his cloth through Exeter, and added an aisle to Tiverton Church which he embellished with stone carvings of ships.

Not all cloth was fulled. Worsted, named from a Norfolk village, woven from long wool and relatively light, did not go through the fulling process. It remained a speciality of Norfolk and especially Norwich.

By Tudor times there were certain well-defined weaving areas. One of the two most important of these areas extended over southern Suffolk and northern Essex, including among its main centres Sudbury, Long Melford, Lavenham, Hadleigh, Coggeshall, Bocking (65, 66) and Colchester. The other covered western Wiltshire, especially Trowbridge and Bradford-on-Avon; eastern Somerset, especially Frome; and parts of Gloucestershire—where the industry developed in the deep valleys round Stroud, rather than in the northern Cotswolds round Chipping Campden, which was concerned with the marketing of raw wool rather than the production of cloth. There was a separate south-western weaving area extending from Dunster (15) and Taunton to Tiverton and Totnes. Other smaller, but still important, cloth-producing regions in the South of England were in the Kennet valley, including Newbury, and the Weald of Kent, especially round Cranbrook. In the Midlands the industry remained concentrated in Coventry, famous for its 'True Blue' cloth—but it declined there after the Reformation, which affected the city more severely than other important textile centres because of its numerous religious institutions, which, like its guilds, were dissolved. Shrewsbury was the market for cloths woven in Wales.

In the North, changes occurred in the textile industry in the later Middle Ages which, in retrospect, are seen to have been of profound significance. York declined as a major weaving centre from the fifteenth century, while the industry developed in remote Pennine dales to the west, with fast-moving streams and freedom from guild controls. By the sixteenth and seventeenth centuries there were thick scatters of cottages in smallholdings around the developing market towns of Wakefield, Leeds and Halifax and villages such as Bradford (64). Families living there would produce one or two pieces of cloth a week, as well as cultivating their holdings, and bring their pieces to the markets in the towns. West of the Pennines was an originally much less important textile area, centred on the market town of Manchester. Further north, Kendal was an outlying important centre of the weaving industry.

As the medieval and Tudor weaving industry was largely home-based, the physical evidence for it is mainly in the houses of the period which survive in the cloth-producing areas, particularly in East Anglia, and, for instance, in Coventry (p. 49). Paycockes at Coggeshall in Essex is a well-known example of a timber-framed master clothier's house of about 1500. Even in early Tudor times, clothing magnates sometimes moved out of the towns where they made their fortunes, to nearby country estates, as did the Hortons, clothiers of Bradford-on-Avon, who settled in nearby Westwood House in 1515.

Much of the wealth of the wool trade and weaving industry went, before the Reformation, into the rebuilding and embellishment of parish churches. Apart from the well-known churches of East Anglia and the Cotswolds, examples of 'wool' churches include Cullompton in Devon, where an elaborate aisle with fan-

vaulting was added in 1526 by John Lane, a local merchant; Newbury, where the church was rebuilt from 1500 by 'Jack of Newbury', a famous clothier; and Halifax, where the large-scale rebuilding of the church in the fifteenth century indicates how wealthy this still remote Pennine area had already become through weaving—it can have had no other significant source of wealth.

The East Anglian cloth industry began to decline in the mid sixteenth century, but was reinvigorated by an inflow of Protestant refugees from Flanders in the 1570s. They brought with them skills in what were called in England 'New Draperies', fabrics lighter than traditional woollen cloths, but more like the worsteds of Norfolk. They settled in large numbers in Norwich and Colchester, and also in smaller Essex towns, as well as in Sandwich and Canterbury. Colchester still has its so-called 'Dutch Quarter', with late sixteenth-century timber-framed houses which may have been occupied by these Flemings (67). The 'New Draperies' were successful, particularly in the export trade, and their manufacture spread to other regions, notably Devon and West Somerset. Wiltshire, East Somerset and Gloucestershire, continued to manufacture heavy broadcloths of the traditional types, for which they remained famous up to the nineteenth century (page 166).

67. The Dutch Quarter, Colchester, reputedly the area where Flemish refugee weavers settled in the late 16th century (page 126). The timber-framed houses, plastered in the East Anglian tradition, date from about then, with, of course, later windows.

Iron and the early use of coal

Iron ore was laboriously smelted and forged with charcoal in what were called bloomeries, until the invention of the original type of blast furnace in the 1580s. This was operated by bellows, driven by water power, producing pig iron—which in turn was refined and forged partly by means of hammers, also operated by water power. The first blast furnaces were in the Weald of Sussex and Kent, then the main iron-producing area, depending on local supplies of ironstone. Cannon, as well as smaller goods like railings, firebacks, and cooking utensils, were produced there. But it was a rural industry, employing relatively few people; the main physical evidence today is provided by large ponds, formed artificially as heads of water for the furnaces and hammers.

There were also early furnaces and forges in the once heathy and infertile region where Staffordshire, Worcestershire and Warwickshire interlocked, making use of local ore, timber, and, even to a small extent as early as the sixteenth century, coal. The small market town of Birmingham, centred on its triangular market place or Bull Ring, was by the sixteenth century famous for metal products. These included knives and edge tools, forged in local workshops and sometimes sharpened on water-powered grindstones, as well as nails, which were brought in from neighbouring villages to be sold. More famous already for fine cutlery was Sheffield, a small and remote town to which, astonishingly, fine ores from Sweden were imported through Hull, shipped up the Trent and its tributary to Bawtry, and then carried overland. The knives were produced in small workshops depending partly on water power to turn the grindstones. Thaxted (page 100) in Essex was also noted for cutlery, but it is not known where its supplies of iron ore came from. There were beginnings of Welsh metal production from the 1580s onwards round Neath and Swansea, to which copper was shipped from Cornwall for smelting using Welsh coal—long before coal was used successfully to smelt iron (see Chapter Fourteen).

Foreign immigrants, many of them escaping religious persecution, helped to stimulate British industries from the sixteenth century onwards. Among them was glass-making, developed on the Tyne from the early seventeenth century, using chalk from Kent brought as ballast in collier ships returning from the Thames, and local coal. This development increased the supply, and reduced the price, of glass sufficiently to allow its general use in quite modest houses (page 51). The splendid early seventeenth-century houses near the quayside at Newcastle, with their long ranges of windows illustrate early generous use of glass (though still in small panes) at its place of production (70). Coal was also used early in salt production, again on the Tyne, where sea water was boiled in huge metal pans, leaving the salt as sediment; in sugar refining in Bristol, where the sugar was imported from the West Indies; in malting; and, on occasions, in brickmaking. Water power was harnessed for an increasing number of industries—notably paper making which, depending on rags as raw materials, developed under immigrant stimulus; the first successful English paper mill, licensed by Elizabeth I, was established at Dartford, Kent, in 1588.

11
Ports Before 1600

The greatest English port has always been London. There were numerous other ports in medieval and Tudor England. A few became large and relatively powerful corporate cities, like Bristol, Hull and Newcastle, or had special privileges, like the Cinque Ports. Most of the others were small, but some had periods of great prosperity. Internal trade, both coastwise and up navigable rivers, was of comparable importance to overseas trade. The two types of waterborne trade were often interdependent; many cargoes were transferred from overseas ships to coastal or river vessels, and vice versa. Fishing was of special importance in particular ports.

The fortunes of ports could fluctuate, sometimes hugely, due to many possible causes. Harbours could silt; coasts could be eroded; new harbours could be created through natural or human action. Enemies might sack and ravage. Overseas trade could be severely affected by wars and changing political situations. Demands for products rose and fell. The prosperity or otherwise of the hinterland would affect the fortunes of a port.

The ports of medieval and Tudor England and Wales (apart from London) are treated in five regional divisions.

The South-East

The Cinque Ports originated in late Saxon times, and obtained special privileges in return for supplying the king with ships and men, when needed for war. Most declined early. Of the original five, only Sandwich was important through the Middle Ages—largely as an outport to London, and outlet for the fertile Kent coastlands. Its harbour started to silt seriously in the fifteenth century, and its trade was virtually lost by the seventeenth. It remains a very medieval town in feeling, with a close network of streets, numerous timber-framed houses, landward earthen ramparts and one surviving small town gate, Fishergate, opening on to the quayside. Dover had few natural advantages other than its nearness to the Continent and especially Calais, held for a long time by the English and the 'staple' or base for much of the raw wool trade. It is not clear what and where Dover's medieval berthing facilities were. Hythe and New Romney were left high and dry through coastal changes, but their fine churches indicate that they were still wealthy in the twelfth and thirteenth centuries. Due to the action of the sea, the topography of Hastings is very different from that of Norman times; the old town lies in a hollow east of the fragmentary hilltop castle. Rye and Winchelsea joined the Cinque Ports federation in about 1190; Winchelsea (page 71) provides the most dramatic example in Britain of changing fortunes of towns through natural causes; it is now the size of a village. The Cinque Ports had various limbs or associate towns, some of which became specially prosperous, such as Faversham.

68. Wool House, Southampton, built after 1400 of Isle of Wight stone to store wool and other export goods; now the Maritime Museum. There are Georgian alterations, including the hip of the roof, but the main roof timbers inside are original.

Further west, New Shoreham, succeeding an older Saxon port at Old Shoreham to the north, flourished in the twelfth and thirteenth centuries, as its magnificent church testifies, but declined as a long shingle bank built up, blocking the original mouth of the River Adur. Chichester had the status of a port, but its maritime facilities were distributed among a number of small places on the many-branching Chichester and Langstone Harbours. Portsmouth was founded as a town by an Anglo-Norman merchant, John de Gisors, about 1180, but was taken over by Richard I as overlord, and given a royal charter in 1194. Part of a once fine medieval church, the present cathedral, and the former hospital of Domus Dei testify to early prosperity, but the town did not grow substantially until the Dockyard developed in Stuart times.

Southampton was the greatest medieval port on the south coast. It was important as a transit town between England and Normandy when they were in the same realm, and as the port for Winchester in its heyday. As the main English holdings in France moved south-west to Gascony, it developed a wine-importing trade from there, and exported wool and cloth from Wiltshire (there were close links with Salisbury merchants) and even, via the overland route, from the Cotswolds. Southampton was also an outport for London; in the fourteenth and fifteenth centuries the periodic convoys of ships from Venice and Genoa to northern Europe frequently called there, in preference to making the long and often dangerous passage round Kent to the Thames. Their cargoes of silks, spices and other valuable goods from the East were taken overland to London, and in return they loaded with fine cloths or wool. The stone Wool House on the Town Quay, built about 1400 and now a museum (**68**), together with the remains of several merchants' houses dating from the late twelfth to the sixteenth centuries, are testimonies to the town's medieval prosperity, although the finest features from the period are the walls and gates (**61**). Southampton declined drastically from Tudor times, as more and more of the kind of trade that had gone there went directly to London, and the Venetians and Genoese ceased coming to England.

The South-West

South-Western ports benefited especially from the English hold on Gascony in the thirteenth and fourteenth centuries, and many of them resumed their wine trade after Bordeaux fell finally to the French in 1453. Some, especially Bristol, developed trade with Spain and Portugal. As well as wine, raw materials for cloth-making and dyeing, and special goods such as raisins and spices, were imported, and cloth exported. There was also, when political circumstances permitted, much cross-Channel traffic to Brittany, and a great deal of coastal trade.

Poole grew up in the twelfth century, and in the thirteenth must have prospered with the shipment of Purbeck marble, quarried nearby, which was much used in major churches, such as Westminster Abbey, at the time. Its connections with the Newfoundland trade began in the sixteenth century but reached their height in the eighteenth (see Chapter Fourteen). Weymouth was an outlet for cloth, and developed connections with New England in the early seventeenth century (**XVI**). Lyme Regis was, and is, an extraordinary place. It was a village till Edward I created a borough (hence 'Regis') in 1284; it reached the peak of its prosperity in the early seventeenth century, yet its only harbour was the prede-cessor of the present stone-bound Cobb, now largely of the eighteenth and nine-teenth centuries, one of the most oddly shaped and situated artificial harbours in England. It is away from the town proper; it could at some time have replaced a natural harbour beside the town which was eroded away—there is no positive evidence for this, but the coast has always suffered severely from erosion.

Exeter was a considerable estuary port, with its output at Topsham; it was especially prosperous in Tudor and early Stuart times as the outlet for the rich Devon weaving towns like Tiverton and Cullompton. Dartmouth thrived, partly in conjunction with nearby Totnes, which was another important weaving town. Dartmouth was much concerned with early Atlantic voyages, and with coloniza-tion in America; it was closely involved with the early Newfoundland cod trade which first developed in Elizabethan times, but in this was later overtaken by Poole. The town has many timber-framed merchants' houses, mostly dating from after 1600. Plymouth began modestly, but developed rapidly from the fifteenth century, and achieved legendary fame in Tudor times with the exploits of Sir Francis Drake and other great maritime adventurers. By the early seventeenth century it was one of the most important ports in England, and developed its well-known links with early colonial America. Something of the flavour of that period is still apparent in the old harbour quarter. Fowey was by far the most important maritime port in later medieval Cornwall.

Bristol dominated the coasts along its Channel to Cornwall and Pembroke, and river trade far up the Severn. In many ways it was a western London; it grew at the lowest bridging point of its river, where routes had to converge, defended for several centuries by a major castle, now all but vanished. That it developed as a major port seems at first sight extraordinary, since it is approached by ship up several miles of the severely tidal River Avon through the dramatic Clifton Gorge. But there was no possible harbour on the nearby open shore of the Severn estuary, and Bristol, once reached, was a safe anchorage. At first, ships moored at quays alongside the Avon (**69**), but in 1240–50 the city authorities diverted the tributary River Frome from a curved to a straight course, with several hundreds of yards of new quays, which remained at the heart of the port, and the city,

Map XVI Weymouth, Dorset
developed from two originally
separate towns on either side
of the Harbour; it expanded
north in Tudor times with a
tapering grid of streets, clearly
seen on this map of 1868.
Further north are the terraces
of the Georgian royal resort,
facing east over the beach
(page 151), with the Victorian
railway station behind

till partly covered over in the 1930s. Bristol had very strong links with Bordeaux, which survived the cession of Gascony to France, and also, when circumstances permitted, with Spain and Portugal—Bristol is still famous for its imported wines. Inland, Bristol was the base for much of the barge trade up the River Severn. Many goods imported into Bristol were trans-shipped to barges which carried them up to Gloucester, Tewkesbury, Worcester or Bewdley—from which there were overland routes into the Midlands, while goods from there were brought down to Bristol for export. Bristol also had links with numerous small South Wales ports, including Chepstow, Cardiff, Swansea, Tenby and Haverfordwest; produce from Wales was exchanged with manufactured and imported goods from Bristol. There were similar links with Barnstaple and Bideford on the North Devon coast, but these two ports had important trading connections of their own, especially,

69. St Mary Redcliffe, Bristol, seen along the original course of the River Avon (page 106), testifies the wealth of the medieval port. The spire, long truncated, was restored to its full height in the 19th century. On the right are Georgian merchants' houses. This part of the Avon became tideless *c* 1809 when a new course for the river was cut further south (page 181).

from the late sixteenth century, with North America. Bristol also traded with southern Ireland, including Dublin.

The most famous figures connected with late medieval Bristol were John and Sebastian Cabot, Genoese in origin, who sailed across the Atlantic in 1497 and were very probably the first Europeans (unless there were Vikings) to set foot in the North American mainland—it has even been claimed that the continent was named by John Cabot after a contemporary Bristol citizen of Welsh origin called Richard ap Meyric, or Ameryck. This claim, overriding the one that the continent was named by Columbus after Amerigo Vespucci, has never been completely disproved. Bristol merchants, and landowners from the country round, were involved with some of the early American colonization, and, to a much greater degree, with that of the West Indies, but the heyday of the Caribbean connection was the eighteenth century. (See Chapter Fourteen).

Eastern England

London has always overshadowed the many ports of East Anglia. Colchester was an outlet for some of the East Anglian cloth, shipped mainly to London to be handled by merchants there. Ipswich was more important as an overseas port and had wealthy merchants; it retains some late medieval atmosphere with narrow streets, timber-framed houses and many flint churches. Yarmouth was both the port for Norwich, which small ships could reach up the Yare and Wensum, and a very important herring fishing port, which grew up in early medieval times on what had been a shingle spit. Dunwich, an important port in the early Middle Ages, had almost completely disappeared through coastal erosion by Tudor times; the only tangible evidence of the medieval town is the scant remains of a friary which stood on its landward edge. The nearby small town of Southwold was in some measure a successor to Dunwich, and a magnificent church in East Anglian flint with stone dressings testifies to its fifteenth-century prosperity.

King's Lynn was the maritime outlet for a huge area south and south-west of the Wash, including most of the Fens. The town was first founded by a bishop of Norwich in the late eleventh century, and extended rapidly, the king taking over from the bishop as overlord. It is now at the mouth of the River Ouse, which flows from Bedfordshire and Huntingdonshire through the Fens, but the river's present course is the result of a series of major river diversions, connected with drainage schemes, which began in the early Middle Ages and culminated in the seventeenth century. Medieval vessels came up the Ouse as far as St Ives with its famous fair (16) and, most importantly, up the tributary River Cam to Cambridge. King's Lynn had intermittent connections with the Baltic as well as with Holland and Germany, but its overseas trade, like that of many East Coast ports, was much curtailed with the huge development of the port of London, and the increasing power of London merchants, from Tudor times onwards (see Chapter Twelve). King's Lynn retains two magnificent medieval churches, two guildhalls and many late medieval to seventeenth-century timber-framed or early brick houses, several of them set round courtyards. Much fine stone from Northamptonshire and neighbouring counties was shipped down the Rivers Welland and Nene to the Wash, then via King's Lynn up the Ouse and its tributaries (page 54).

Boston was for a time in the thirteenth century the second richest port in England, after London. It was closely connected with Lincoln, which was reached by boat up the River Witham, and was then also in its heyday. It exported much of the wool for which Lincolnshire and the East Midlands were noted, but with the decline of raw wool exports, and of Lincoln, it lost much of its importance as a port. Henceforth much of the local wool was sent across England, by river or road, to weaving centres such as Coventry or to the wool markets of the Cotswolds. Boston is still dominated by its great parish church with its tall tower or 'Stump', so called because the tower was intended as the base for a taller spire, never built. There were close connections with Holland; indeed the people who became the Pilgrim Fathers left Boston for Holland, before returning to England to set sail for America. The town's very name went across the Atlantic.

The North-East
The Humber was one of the most important trading estuaries in medieval Britain. The history of the ports which emerged and declined along its banks is even more complicated than that of the Cinque Ports. The earliest important ports were on the south bank, first at Barton-on-Humber, then at Grimsby. Hedon, east of

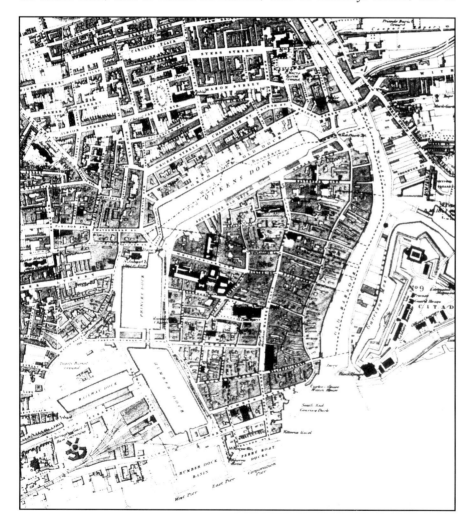

Map XVII The Old Town, Hull. The medieval town wall (page 212) was demolished in stages and replaced by docks from 1778, making the Old Town an island, with the River Hull to the east and the Humber to the south. The first town developed along the very narrow street just west of the River Hull; it was enlarged by Edward I as Kingston-upon-Hull, still the official title. The fortified building shown on the map of c 1855 east of the River Hull was the 16th–17th century Citadel, since demolished (page 185).

modern Hull, was founded as a port in the twelfth century; it still has a magnificent thirteenth-century church. Hedon was soon overshadowed by Ravenser, which developed rapidly on a shingle bank near the Humber mouth, only to sink beneath the waters between 1340 and 1360. By that time another town had risen, at first called Wyke, on the edge of reclaimed marshland by the small River Hull, just above its confluence with the Humber. It was first developed by nearby Meaux Abbey, which owned and drained the marshes, but was taken over in 1293 by Edward I, greatly enlarged, given municipal privileges, and renamed Kingston-upon-Hull—although then, as now, it was commonly known as Hull (XVII). Hull never since ceased to prosper. It commanded the river trade up the Yorkshire Ouse, the Trent and all their tributaries. Most important in the Middle Ages was the connection with York, which had its own quays accessible by small seagoing vessels, but came to be dependent for overseas trade on Hull, where goods were transferred to or from larger ships. Trade up the Trent reached to Gainsborough and, for smaller vessels, Newark, from which there were land routes further into the Midlands; there was also trade up the small river Idle to Bawtry, connecting with Sheffield (page 112). Hull's own overseas connections were with the Baltic, the Hanse cities and the Low Countries, and, of course, it had important coastal links, especially with London, carrying the products of its huge hinterland. The main medieval monument of Hull is its great parish church of Holy Trinity, including some of the earliest brickwork in England. It is one of a series of magnificent churches on and around the Humber estuary including the Minster and St Mary's at Beverley, the parish churches of Grimsby, Hedon and Patrington, and the collegiate church at Howden.

Scarborough was a medieval port of some importance, particularly for fish; it supplied the Yorkshire abbeys—but its dramatically sited castle is its main historic landmark. Whitby has its impressive Gothic abbey ruin, on a clifftop site with long traditions, but the town itself, hemmed in by a hinterland of wild moors, was not very important before the development of the Tyne coal trade, in which many Whitby ships participated.

There was little maritime activity on the Tees estuary in medieval or Tudor times; even the ancient little port of Yarm (122), several miles up the river, did not significantly develop till the seventeenth and eighteenth centuries. But Hartlepool was an important medieval port with a romantic history. The first Saxon monastery on a windswept headland was destroyed by the Vikings. A town developed in Norman times under the lordship of the Bruce family, which had estates in both Scotland and England. They probably built the present magnificent church of St Hilda, possibly on the Saxon monastic site. The Bruces had to forfeit their English lands when Robert Bruce made his eventually successful claim for the Scottish crown; Hartlepool then became a special target for the Scots in the Anglo-Scottish wars. The small harbour, sheltered by the headland, was strongly walled together with the town—the wall even crossed the harbour, leaving a gap through which ships could pass, easily blocked by chains—an arrangement unique in Britain. By Tudor times the town was fast declining, to be revived in the nineteenth century; only the superb church and a stretch of town wall, with a gate, survives from its medieval heyday.

Newcastle grew round the castle first built in the late eleventh century, on the site of a Roman fort on Hadrian's Wall. The present castle keep, dating from

the twelfth century and one of the best preserved of its time, stands at the top of a steep hill overlooking the River Tyne crossing, where there was a bridge in Roman and also in medieval times (70). Its situation—the lowest river crossing, with good anchorage—was analogous to that of London and Bristol. The prosperity of the hinterland was severely affected by Anglo-Scottish wars and skirmishes, but this may have tended to increase the importance of the town itself, within its strong walls built in the thirteenth century, to which many people may have moved from the hinterland. It developed its maritime trade and, in particular, profited from the outcrops of coal in the surrounding area. Coal was extracted on the estates of the Bishop of Durham and the Prior of Tynemouth as early as the thirteenth century. At Tynemouth there were outcrops on the low coastal cliffs, so that coal was gathered from the beach; this may have been the origin of the term 'sea-coal', still used in the North-East for coal washed up on beaches.

70. Newcastle upon Tyne. Eight centuries of history summarized. The Norman castle keep (with 19th century battlemented top) defended a crossing of the River Tyne, which is just out of view on the left. Early 17th century timber-framed houses have long windows originally with locally made glass (pages 51, 112). The Neo-Classical Moot Hall, 1810, replaced the medieval castle hall as a law court. The High Level Bridge in the background, 1850, carries a railway above a road.

By Tudor times coal was sent in ever-increasing quantities by ship from the Tyne to London and other eastern ports. At first it was used mainly for domestic fires (page 51), but its industrial use, particularly on Tyneside, was beginning by the end of the sixteenth century. The pitmen of Northumberland and Durham, the keelmen of the Tyne who carried the coal from riverside pits and quays to the seagoing vessels, and the sailors on the collier ships developed their own very distinctive characteristics. Many of the Tyneside merchants lived around the Newcastle quayside, in tall timber-framed houses, some of which, dating mainly from the early seventeenth century, still survive.

The North-West

This was, in maritime terms, by far the least significant coastal region in the Middle Ages, since it faced nowhere but Northern Ireland—and Ulster was one of the poorest provinces in medieval Ireland. Chester was the chief port; it was active in the time of Edward I's campaigns against the Welsh. Materials and supplies for his castles and garrisons were dispatched from there. In the Middle Ages ships came close outside the city's Watergate, but the River Dee steadily silted and changed its course, making Chester less and less suitable as a port. Liverpool was founded beside a small creek, or pool, of the Mersey by King John in 1207, but it remained very small till the later seventeenth century. There was no significant port on the Cumbrian coast before the development of Whitehaven at the end of the seventeenth century.

12
London – City and Port

Medieval London was essentially the City, with Westminster as a royal and monastic appendage, and Southwark a suburb across the Bridge. Its street pattern bore little relationship to the original Roman layout, but was re-shaped as London recovered from the Dark Age which followed the Roman occupation. There were important west-east streets which had open markets, such as Cheapside, Cornhill and Eastcheap, and numerous lanes or subsidiary streets, many running north-south and showing in places a fairly regular pattern which must date from Saxon times (see page 28).

Some of the medieval City merchants' houses were in courtyard form (p. 51). Others would have conformed to the more normal medieval urban pattern, facing the streets with long, originally open, plots behind. As was usual before modern times, most merchants and craftsmen carried on their trades in or near their own houses and house plots. The open backland behind the houses would become encroached on, and, as pressure on space and property values increased, premises would often be divided among several occupants. In this way, dense patterns of building developed around small courts, often entered through passages or

71. Guildhall, London, built c 1410–40; gutted in the Great Fire of 1666 and later restored; gutted in the 'blitz' of 1941 and again restored. Yet parts of the outside walls of Kentish ragstone (51) and a fine undercroft are original. The three-storey 'Gothic' extension, in Portland stone, is of 1789; the concrete canopies date from c 1970.

under archways, as described on page 59. Many of these courts and passages still survive in the City, despite the devastation of the Great Fire, which was followed by rebuilding to the same layouts, and despite subsequent piecemeal rebuilding often several times over. The present-day City is overwhelmingly commercial, but the medieval and Tudor City was densely populated. Generally, rich and poor lived in close proximity, but there were areas where the poor were tightly packed, especially outside and just inside some of the gates.

Besides Old St Paul's and over a hundred parish churches, many of which were small, there were numerous monastic institutions, particularly on the fringes of the City. Of these, something survives of St Bartholomew's Priory in Smithfield, the Carthusian Priory or Charterhouse, and the Temple—the last the London base of the international Knights Templar before their dissolution in 1308. Other monasteries have disappeared, including all the friaries.

London's medieval City walls overlay, and to some degree incorporated, the Roman defences (page 106). The medieval gates survived, though frequently altered or partly rebuilt, until they were all demolished around 1750–60. Of these, Bishopsgate spanned the street of the same name; Aldgate was east of the junction of Leadenhall and Fenchurch Streets, and Aldersgate spanned the street called St Martins-le-Grand just north of St Paul's. Interestingly, parish churches dedicated to St Botolph, all rebuilt in the eighteenth century, stand outside the sites of these three gates, though it is not known why this East Anglian saint became specially associated with the entrances to the City. The western gates of the walled City were Newgate, later notorious as a prison, and Ludgate, which spanned Ludgate Hill not far west of St Paul's. (XVIII, p. 132)

The medieval City was not confined by its walls; there were dense suburbs along Fleet Street and Holborn, at Smithfield, and outside Aldgate. The City's jurisdiction extended over parts of these areas, as it does today. Its westward limit was Temple Bar, never the site of a defensive gate, but simply an administrative and ceremonial barrier. Just outside was the church of St Clement Danes, later rebuilt by Wren (78).

The Strand, running parallel with the river, linked the City with Westminster. Along it, and specially on the river side, was a series of palaces and large town houses belonging, at various times, to medieval and Tudor magnates, bishops and noblemen. Only a few names now commemorate these; Arundel Great Court is named from the Earls of Arundel, later Dukes of Norfolk; Somerset House is the site of the palace of the Tudor Duke of Somerset; Savoy Hill and the adjoining Hotel commemorate the medieval palace of the Savoy, later replaced by a hospital for the destitute. From Charing Cross—which was an irregular road junction before Trafalgar Square was formed in the nineteenth century—the main thoroughfare now called Whitehall ran into Westminster.

From the time of King Edward the Confessor, just before the Norman Conquest, to the Tudor period, the Palace of Westminster was the chief residence of the Kings of England. Edward re-established Westminster Abbey as a royal monastery, on the site of an older minster; most of the church was rebuilt in the present form in the thirteenth and fourteenth centuries. The town of Westminster developed in the limited space between the Palace, the Abbey, the river and the marshy land to the west; on the City side was what became Whitehall Palace. This was originally the London palace of the Archbishops of York; it was taken over by

Henry VIII from Cardinal Wolsey, who was Archbishop, on his downfall. Henry and his successors enlarged and altered Whitehall Palace piecemeal; it was the chief royal palace until largely destroyed by fire in the late seventeenth century. Meanwhile, the medieval Palace of Westminster became what its successor is now, the Houses of Parliament—it was burnt down, apart from the superlative Westminster Hall, in 1834. Westminster Hall itself was the main seat of the Judiciary until superseded, in that role, by the present Law Courts in the Strand.

Henry VIII also built a new, relatively small, palace on the site of the leper hospital of St James, then on the edge of the country; his fine gateway survives as the entrance to the present St James's Palace.

Across the Thames from the City was Southwark, which was an Anglo-Saxon *burh*, and is even today sometimes called 'The Borough'; Borough High Street still has the form of a medieval street with recognizable burgage plots. Southwark had an Augustinian priory—its church is now the Anglican cathedral—and a bigger Cluniac monastery, now vanished, on its outskirts at Bermondsey. The Bishops of Winchester, whose diocese extended across Surrey to Southwark, had their London palace there; one wall and a fanciful circular window survive among the (now fast-disappearing) Victorian warehouses of Bankside. The Archbishops of Canterbury's London palace was, as now, further upstream, in Lambeth, opposite Westminster; much of the present Lambeth Palace is still medieval.

Overseas trade was concentrated in the Pool of London, the stretch of river between London Bridge and the Tower of London. Quay space was very limited; most ships anchored in the river, men and cargoes being brought ashore on smaller boats. Medieval London Bridge, with its narrow arches and strong currents, was a barrier to all but the smallest vessels, which had to be skilfully handled. Even so, some goods were brought from ships moored downstream to wharves above the Bridge. There was a great deal of local barge traffic on the Thames; it was possible for small vessels to reach upstream as far as Lechlade in Gloucestershire.

Eastward of the City were the Tower Hamlets, so called because they were under the jurisdiction of the Constable of the Tower of London. (The name has been revived for the modern borough.) In Tudor times the hamlets coalesced into continuous maritime settlement for about two miles. Here sailors lodged, and made merry. Here ships were built, maintained and supplied, or lay at anchor when there was insufficient room in the Pool of London. However, port regulations required that goods should be landed only in the City, to which they would be taken by boat. Similar development extended along the south bank to Deptford, which in Tudor times was an important maritime community, adjoining Greenwich with its royal palace.

In 1500 London's population was around 50,000—about four times that of Norwich or Bristol, the next largest English towns, but far less than that of several European cities, including Paris, Lyon, Naples, Venice and Milan, and less than that of the closely related Flemish cities of Antwerp, Ghent and Bruges taken together. But by 1600 the population of the built-up area, including Westminster, Southwark and the Tower Hamlets as well as the City, had reached 250,000, making it one of the largest cities in Europe. Two of its rivals in size were then Lisbon and Seville, which had grown equally rapidly in the previous century. By 1700 London's population was about 675,000, exceeding that of all other European cities.

Overseas trade

London's phenomenal growth in Tudor and early Stuart times was due to two main causes—its development as a port and mercantile centre, and its role as a political and courtly capital. The latter role is described in Chapter Thirteen. During the sixteenth century London captured the greater part of Britain's fast-growing export trade, especially that of cloth—which accounted for about four-fifths of all exports in 1570. Much of this trade was handled by the Merchant Adventurers, an association of London traders. They became specially powerful after the expulsion of the once prominent Hanseatic merchants from London in 1558, and completely overshadowed their similarly named counterparts in York, Bristol and Hull. Most English exported cloth was, for a time, shipped to Antwerp, which in the middle of the sixteenth century was the chief trading centre of Northern Europe—having overtaken the nearby port of Bruges, by then hopelessly silted, and the Hanseatic cities further east. From Antwerp, English cloth was distributed widely over Europe. In return, imports were collected at Antwerp for shipment to London.

Antwerp's trade was, however, fatally affected by religious conflicts, especially in the 1570s when thousands of Protestant clothworkers, craftsmen and traders fled from Flanders, many to England (page 111). Sir Thomas Gresham who, for a time, was the royal agent in Antwerp, foresaw that city's decline—and London's opportunity in taking over its role as a European mercantile centre. In 1566 he built the first Royal Exchange, modelled on its equivalent in Antwerp. It was set round a courtyard, with two tiers of shops, business rooms and places of refreshment, and became the central meeting place for English and overseas merchants. It symbolized London's newly won status as a major centre of world trade.

In the seventeenth century, worldwide commerce increased vastly in scope and extent, and ceased to be dominated, as it had been for a time, by the Spanish and Portuguese. The latter pioneered the route round the Cape of Good Hope, but after 1600 the oriental trade route round the Cape was developed largely by the Dutch and British. The Dutch became a great maritime nation, after breaking away from Spanish control as a Protestant republic, later a kingdom. The rivalry of the British and Dutch was particularly intense around the Indian Ocean, the British concentrating especially on India itself after the formation of the East India Company in 1600, by means of a royal charter which gave it immense powers in the sub-continent. Nearly all the East India Company's shipping was based in London.

Colonization and trade across the Atlantic developed steadily in the seventeenth century. Sugar, timber, cotton and other products came in increasing quantities from the West Indies and the North American mainland, with corresponding exports in the other direction. However, unlike the Eastern trade, transatlantic commerce was not dominated by London. Western ports, most notably Bristol and Plymouth, played major roles.

After the demise of Antwerp as a mercantile centre, London's Continental connections were re-directed. Much trade went through Amsterdam—which took on some of the role of Antwerp but never quite overshadowed London—and there was also a resurgence of trade with Hanseatic cities such as Hamburg. Trade with the Baltic increased; Hull and other eastern ports took some part in this, but London was dominant.

London was always a major centre of coastal trade. Both manufactured goods and farm produce reached London from all round Britain's coasts, and much was redistributed, by water or overland. Shipments of coal from the Tyne were particularly important, as the domestic use of coal increased. In both overseas and coastwise trade, London between about 1550 and 1660 was more dominant over other British ports than it had been before or was to be since.

The fabric of London

At first, the huge increase in London's population in the sixteenth century and afterwards was largely accommodated by intensified building in the City and just outside. The process of infilling on original large house plots has already been described. The sites of some of the dissolved monasteries, like that of the Dominicans or Blackfriars, became tightly filled. In the middle of the seventeenth century the population of the City of London was probably its highest and densest ever. People of all degrees of prosperity and social standing, apart from the aristocracy, lived, traded, worked, worshipped, took refreshment and sought recreation within the approximate square mile of the City or just outside. It is exceedingly difficult to imagine this today, when the City is overwhelmingly commercial— even though it retains a great deal of its intricate medieval, Tudor and early Stuart street pattern (72) amid totally different buildings (see Chapter Seventeen).

There was not much expansion of London outwards till after 1600. Westward,

72. Carter Lane, City of London. The alignment of this medieval lane, south-west of St Paul's has been preserved through centuries of piecemeal rebuilding. Originally people lived here, but most of the present properties were built for commercial purposes in Victorian times. (See pages 134, 217.) On the right was the site of the medieval Dominican Friary, or Blackfriars (page 88).

the Drury Lane and St Martin's Lane areas developed sporadically in the first decades of the seventeenth century, leaving the site of Covent Garden to be built up a little later in quite a different way. Clerkenwell and Shoreditch, north of the City, grew irregularly, partly over the sites of dissolved monasteries, largely as skilled artisans' districts, and the Tower Hamlets riverside continued to consolidate as a maritime area. Southwark developed in various ways—early theatres, including Shakespeare's Globe, were built on Bankside opposite St Paul's, where they were outside City jurisdiction. Islington, Hackney, Stepney, Camberwell and other places further out were separate villages where many merchants already had country homes, which they maintained in conjunction with their more cramped living quarters in the City.

Medieval London was built of timber and of stone. The houses, except a few of the grandest, were timber-framed, but the churches and some of the most important secular buildings were of stone. Stone came from two main sources. There was a hard, lasting sandstone called Kentish ragstone from the Maidstone area (51), unsuitable for fine carving, which was shipped down the Medway and up the Thames, and there was a soft chalky stone called Reigate stone from the Surrey hills, brought overland, which could be delicately carved but which weathered very badly. The internal work of the greater churches, such as Westminster Abbey, was usually of Reigate stone, while ragstone was used for solid walling in buildings such as the Guildhall (71), where it can still be seen, and parish churches.

Brick became the normal building material in and around London for palaces and other important secular buildings by early Tudor times. This can be seen in the Tudor part of Hampton Court, in the great gateway to St James's Palace, and in some of the buildings of the Inns of Court.

After the demise of the Knights Templar, the Temple area became occupied by lawyers who, by Tudor times, formed two distinct collegiate organizations, the Inner and Middle Temple, retaining the Templars' beautiful twelfth-thirteenth-century church as their joint chapel. Concurrently Lincoln's Inn and Gray's Inn, of diverse origins, grew into similar institutions. All four Inns of Court—as they came to be called—developed on the collegiate, courtyard plan, characteristic of the Oxford and Cambridge colleges. The resemblance was more than architectural, for in Tudor and Stuart times the Inns of Court were places of academic study and legal training, which attracted students from all over the country. Today they evoke the atmosphere of sixteenth- and seventeenth-century London more effectively than anywhere else (75).

128

13
The Capital and the Great Resorts, 1630–1830

The pure Classical architecture of the Renaissance was first seen in England in about 1620, when Inigo Jones' Queen's House at Greenwich, now the central part of the National Maritime Museum, had just been built, and work had started on his Banqueting House in Whitehall (74). Both stood in serene contrast to the rambling Tudor palaces beside which they were built and which they have both outlasted. The first piece of town planning on the Renaissance model in England was also designed by Inigo Jones, at Covent Garden, for the Earl of Bedford in 1630.

The Earl was a fairly typical aristocrat of the period, with country estates and a London town house. The former surrounded the sites of three dissolved abbeys, at Woburn (Bedfordshire), Tavistock (Devon) and Thorney (Cambridgeshire); the latter was on the north side of the Strand, with open land, the Covent Garden, which had been monastic property, behind it.

Inigo Jones' design for the development of this open land was influenced by two Continental squares which were well-known at the time. One was the Piazza at Livorno (Leghorn), the port for Florence—a formal town square with regular classical buildings and a church. The other was the Place Royale, now Place des Vosges, in Paris, which was built in 1605–12 by King Henri IV and consisted of four regular rows of grand classical houses, intended for the aristocracy, surrounding a perfectly square space. It must have seemed startling in its classical serenity when first built on the edge of Paris, which, like London at the time, was irregular in its plan and individualistic in its buildings, in the medieval tradition. The Place Royale was not only the forerunner of subsequent classical development in Paris; it was also the prototype of upper-class residential squares which became such distinctive features of London.

The typical Italian *piazza*, and the residential square as pioneered in the Place Royale, were really very different in character and function. The first was a civic, or public, focal point (page 46), the second an exclusive enclave. Jones' Covent Garden had some of the elements of both (73). On its north and east sides were ranges of aristocratic houses, with their ground floor frontages set back behind Italian style arcades. To the west was the severe Tuscan portico of the new St Paul's Church, essentially a temple of the Protestant faith, axial to a street (Russell Street) which came in from the east. On the south side was, at first, the wall of the grounds of Bedford House. The central rectangular area was paved and open, but it soon accommodated a small fruit and vegetable market, which gradually grew until, much later, it dominated the whole area. The streets east and west of the central square, and (after 1700) on the site of Bedford House itself, were developed piecemeal, but fairly regularly, under the control of the Bedford Estate. Little survives of seventeenth-century Covent Garden other than the street layout. St Paul's Church was reconstructed, faithfully, after a fire in 1795. Bedford

Chambers, on the north side, is an 1879 rebuilding of one of Jones' blocks, in much the same style but with an extra storey, and with a replica of Jones' treatment of the ground storey—the arcaded and vaulted passageway still gives an impression of what this corner of the 'Garden' was formerly like. All the other original buildings have gone, and the once open square is occupied by the nineteenth-century buildings of the market, recently refurbished.

Covent Garden was fashionable for a time, but, in the Restoration period and after, the area developed a heterogeneous character as one of the 'lively' parts

73. **Covent Garden** was laid out in 1630 by Inigo Jones, but only St Paul's Church (portico on left) remains of his design. The block in the background (1879) is fairly similar to Jones' original, but with an extra storey. The Market building (right) was built over the once open Piazza in 1830, with iron roof added later (page 224).

of London. The first Drury Lane Theatre was opened in 1663; the precursor of the present Opera House in 1732. Gregarious literary and artistic people came to the numerous coffee houses—which were favourite meeting places in London during this period. There were gaming clubs and night life; Nell Gwynn symbolized an important element of the area's reputation. Shops and small businesses developed, especially after the Great Fire devastated the City. By the beginning of the eighteenth century, high fashion had moved west.

Covent Garden was built in brick and Portland stone. The latter, a particularly fine limestone from Dorset, is said to have been introduced to London by Inigo Jones himself, especially for his extensive work on Old St Paul's Cathedral, before its destruction in the Great Fire. But Portland stone was always expensive, and brick became the normal material for all but the grandest houses in London from Jones' time onwards.

The area between Covent Garden and the City, adjoining Lincoln's Inn, was built in the new manner, with red brick classical houses, from 1638. Inigo Jones was certainly concerned with some of this development, and the one house surviving from the period, Lindsey House, is attributed to him, although his original brick façade was stuccoed over in Regency times. The house is part of a group facing over Lincoln's Inn Fields, the existence of which is due to the protests of the seventeenth-century lawyers of Lincoln's Inn against the original proposal to build over the area entirely. The eventual result was that the central part of the old fields was left open as a rectangular green space which the new houses faced—an early triumph by self-interested conservationists. In this fortuitous way, Lincoln's Inn Fields obtained the form of what later became the typical Georgian square.

74. The Banqueting House, Whitehall, by Inigo Jones, one of the two first pure Renaissance buildings in Britain, built 1619–29 as part of the otherwise rambling Tudor Whitehall Palace which it has outlasted—it is now set amid Government buildings of the last 250 years.

Map XVIII The City of London after the Great Fire

Map XVIII The City of London after the Great Fire of 1666. This map was drawn by Wenceslaus Hollar after the Great Fire, which destroyed about four-fifths of the area within the city wall, which is shown clearly on the map, and part of Fleet Street to the west. Note the close-knit network of

London after the Great Fire

Most of the City was devastated by the Great Fire of 1666 (**XVIII**). Plans by Wren and others to rebuild it in a grand Baroque manner were set aside, and it was reconstructed quickly on the old medieval street pattern with the same property boundaries. But there was stringent control over the nature of the new buildings. Timber was not allowed except in roofs, doors, windows and internal work; all outside walls had to be of brick or stone. The City was rebuilt quickly but individualistically; each property owner built in his own version of the now established

domestic classical style, so that every street had detailed variety in building heights, and window and door treatment, while achieving a general consistency in style. Portland stone became firmly established as the prestigious material for major public buildings and most churches, and made a striking contrast with the brick used generally on private properties. Sir Christopher Wren was the architect not only for the new St Paul's, but also for the numerous City churches which were rebuilt on old sites. It took a few decades for all his works to be completed, but the skyline of the eventually rebuilt City was a fantasy of steeples in endlessly medieval streets and alleys, the numerous small churches destroyed in the Fire, and Old St Paul's, which was left a wreck. By this time the City had spread far beyond the walls, leaving a few spaces, of which some survive, such as Lincoln's Inn Fields on the extreme left of the map.

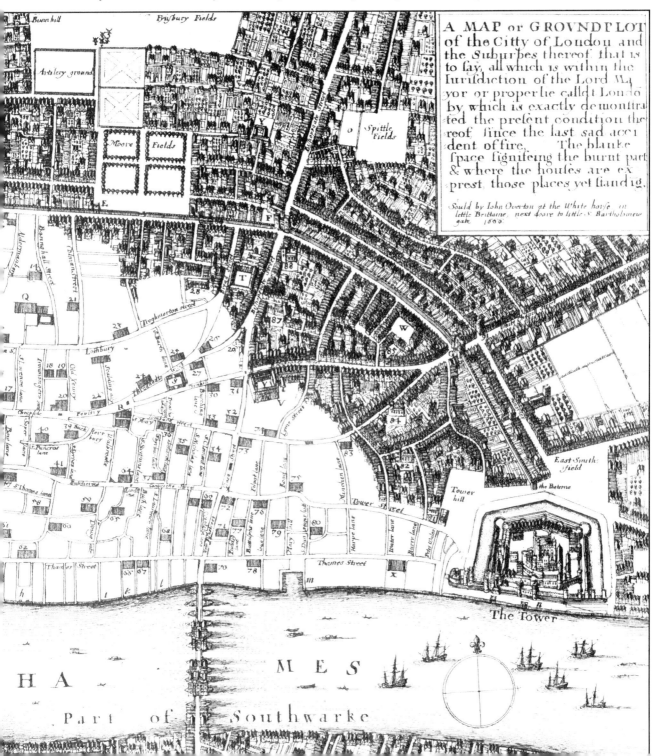

varied Baroque or sometimes Gothic themes, culminating in his great cathedral dome, all rising over the domestic-scale buildings which still formed most of the fabric of the City. Merchants, craftsmen and shopkeepers still normally lived 'over' or near their work; there were no purpose-built offices until those of the East India Company were opened in 1726. Although many of the substantial merchants then had country villas in neighbouring villages, such as survive in Highgate, Hampstead, Clapham, Dulwich and Stoke Newington, they retained living space in or near their business premises in the City.

Not all the City was burnt in the Great Fire. Parts that escaped, mainly on the edges, as around Aldgate, north of Bishopsgate and towards Holborn, became, more than they had been before, densely inhabited by the poor, who crowded into subdivided old houses and infilled yards. Even more noticeable than these areas were the western slum enclaves or 'rookeries', as at Drury Lane and St Giles-in-the-Fields, on two sides of Covent Garden, as well as the Sanctuary at Westminster where Parliament Square now is. The last derived its slum character from the time when, as the sanctuary associated with the medieval Abbey, it harboured thieves and other wrongdoers who could remain there for a time unmolested. The growing East End already had its large enclaves of poverty, particularly around Whitechapel, but it was dominantly an artisan area. Spitalfields had its silk weavers, just as Shoreditch its stocking knitters and wood workers, and Clerkenwell its clock makers. The Tower Hamlets riverside, with the corresponding southern strip through Rotherhithe to Deptford, continued to develop as a crowded maritime area, with shipbuilding and servicing facilities, as well as sailors' haunts. The great Baroque church of St Paul, Deptford, by Thomas Archer; the more modest St Mary, Rotherhithe; and the eccentric St Anne, Limehouse, by Nicholas Hawksmoor, have outlasted their contemporary shipyards and warehouses, crowded lodgings, and with a few exceptions, shipmasters' houses and riverside taverns.

London's westward growth
The pace of westward growth continued after the Great Fire. The first known large-scale speculative builder was Nicholas Barbon, who in the 1670s and 1680s developed large areas north of Holborn and elsewhere, and also built some of the surviving early blocks of lawyers' chambers in the Temple. Some of his houses remain, with varying degrees of alteration or renewal, in and around Great James Street and Bedford Row. They were narrow-fronted, usually of three storeys with basement, with two main rooms on each floor, internally panelled, outwardly of dark red brick with tall rectangular windows, and wooden eaves. They were built for the bourgeoisie.

Higher up the social scale, two of London's squares started to take shape just before the Great Fire—Bloomsbury Square and St James's Square. The fourth Earl of Southampton, son of Shakespeare's patron, whose country estate was at Titchfield (page 89) in Hampshire, built a new town house on the edge of London at Bloomsbury. Soon afterwards, in 1661, he laid out Southampton Square, now Bloomsbury Square, in front. The square was not built in a single operation, but piecemeal through a series of building leases, either direct to intending occupants, or to builders, generally for periods of between forty and seventy years, with the stipulation that houses would be built to certain standards to form part of

a harmonious scheme, and would revert to the landlord at the expiration of the lease. These may have been the pioneer examples of ground or building leases which provided the basis for the development of so much of Georgian and early Victorian London—the landowner did not actually develop, but retained the ownership of the land and control of the initial building, and, eventually, enjoyed the reversion of the property his lessees had built. Later, the normal length of ground lease was ninety-nine years. Nothing survives outwardly of the original houses in Bloomsbury Square; the subsequent development of Bloomsbury is described later.

St James's Square was developed in much the same manner, but its clients were at the top of the social scale. Its situation near St James's Palace, which became the chief royal palace for a time after two serious fires at Whitehall Palace—foreign ambassadors are still called to the Court of St James—ensured the square's social standing. The surrounding area became the centre of gentlemanly London, which it remains in some measure today with its clubs, many of which developed out of coffee houses when these were still, at different social levels, customary places of meeting. Like Bloomsbury Square, St James's Square was not built uniformly; the houses were erected, and in most cases later rebuilt, piecemeal under individual building leases—so that there was general conformity in style and scale rather than uniformity of design. No original houses survive outwardly in the square, but several of eighteenth-century date remain.

North of Piccadilly—which was originally a main route west out of London—

75. **King's Bench Walk, Inner Temple, London**. The Great Fire reached as far as the Temple (**XVIII**). These replacement buildings attributed to Wren, 1678, give some idea of the style of domestic rebuilding in the City after the Fire, although, as lawyers' chambers (page 128), they are not quite typical. Note the carved brick doorway (page 191). The sash windows are probably an early modification—they become general after *c* 1700.

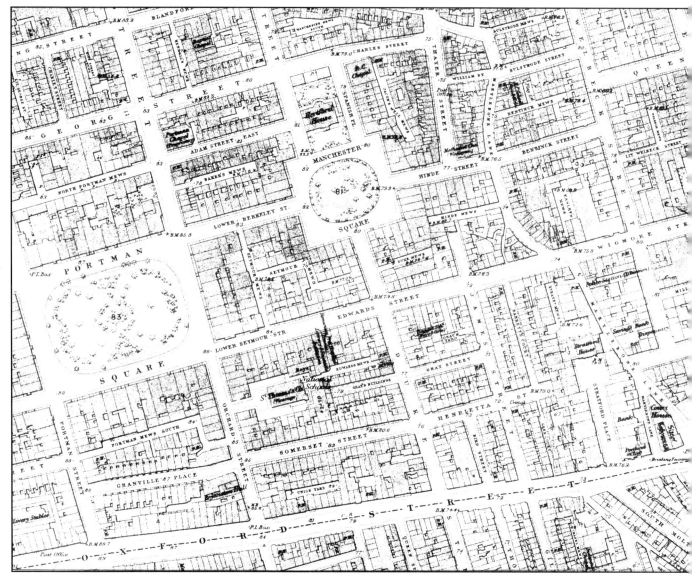

fashionable building took place, at first fairly sporadically, then more regularly, after 1700. Hanover Square was started in 1717, Berkeley Square in the 1720s, and Grosvenor Square at about the same time. The last was the centrepiece of the first part of the Grosvenor Estate to be developed—on land which the Grosvenor family, landed gentry from near Chester, obtained through marriage with an heiress in the seventeenth century. North of Oxford Street (which follows the line of the Roman road to Silchester and Bath), development started around Cavendish Square about 1720. The pattern continued through the eighteenth century, each new well-to-do neighbourhood being centred on a square, off which streets led, lined by houses a little less fashionable than those facing the square itself.

The London Georgian town house, whether upper class or bourgeois, was

136

unusual in the European context. In Paris, despite the early example of the Place Royale, the possession of an entire town house by one family became exceptional. Even the rich in Paris came to accept apartments on one floor only of a multi-storey building—the first floor was normally the most desirable. The same came to be the pattern in most major Continental cities, apart from Italy, where the tradition of the urban *palazzo* survived. There were a few equivalents of such *palazzi* in London; among them were Devonshire House in Piccadilly (demolished); nearby Burlington House, converted in Victorian times to the present Royal Academy; Spencer House, which survives, facing Green Park (*c.* 1760); Marlborough House, originally by Wren, now a royal residence; and Buckingham House, built for a Duke of Buckingham and rebuilt by Nash for George IV as Buckingham Palace. Such aristocratic town houses were exceptional and were not the main residences of the families—the Devonshires lived at Chatsworth, the Spencers in Northamptonshire, and the Marlboroughs at Blenheim Palace. More usually, landed families kept an outwardly more modest town house in a square or street of the West End, which they occupied periodically. The typical upper-class town house had main rooms on the first floor, following the Italian tradition of the *piano nobile*, kitchen in the basement, and servants' sleeping quarters in the top floor or attic. This provided the model for smaller town houses down the social scale.

The typical exterior of the London town house of the late seventeenth and eighteenth centuries changed gradually, partly through legislation. Sash windows, invented in Holland, became universal in England after about 1700; earlier mullioned and casement windows were replaced by them. In 1706 and 1708 were passed two Building Acts, applying only to the built-up area of London, which made wooden cornices and eaves illegal, and controlled external woodwork elsewhere. Henceforth, the lower ends of house roofs had to be set behind brick or stone parapets, giving Georgian façades in London their characteristic horizontal rooflines, with little of the actual roofs visible from the streets—an effect entirely different from that of older houses, where more of the sweeping angles of the roofs are visible. Windows had to be set back four inches from the wall surfaces—hitherto they had usually been flush with the walls. Wooden bow-windows, which later became fashionable elsewhere, were prohibited in London through these Acts. The next legislation came with the Building Act of 1774, which required that the wooden frame of each window should actually be set back behind the brickwork of the opening, and prohibited wooden porches or projecting doorcases, ensuring that very little woodwork was exposed externally. All these restrictions, of course, were intended to reduce the effects of fire.

The houses of the mid and late seventeenth century were typically of dark red brick. In the first half of the eighteenth century the normal practice was to combine grey-brown brick with red brick on façades, the red being used for dressings, including cornices and window or door frames. Especially notable were the bright red, thin and usually tapering 'rubbed bricks', used on the structurally sensitive tops of window and door openings, which were either slightly arched, a fashion which went out after the early eighteenth century, or flat; in each case the bricks were formed to exactly the right size through cutting or rubbing. After about 1725, there was a tendency towards greater simplicity in house façades; red brick became less acceptable, and by the end of the century most London house fronts were entirely of the rather drab buff-brown 'London stock' brick.

Map XIX *Opposite* **Part of Georgian London**. Portman Square, laid out *c* 1761, retains its typical informal garden (page 146). Manchester Square was laid out from 1776 in front of Manchester House, later Hertford House (now containing the Wallace Collection), which was the town house of the Duke of Manchester. His country seat was Kimbolton Castle, Huntingdonshire (**18**), and he took his title from nearby Godmanchester.

Note the wavering Marylebone Lane, following the line of an old country track which led to the village of Marylebone further north. The map dates from the mid-nineteenth century.

The middle of the century was the period of pattern-books providing models for house designs, which circulated among builders, ensuring the remarkably consistent good proportions characteristic of the time. Wooden doorcases of this period—until they were prohibited in London under the Act of 1774—were often modelled on the specimens illustrated in pattern books. Typically, a door frame would consist of wooden columns attached to the wall, supporting a pediment over the door, with perhaps a decorative fanlight. Basements were usually one-third to one-half above street level, so that stepways were necessary up to the front door at elevated ground level—giving a distinction and dignity to the entrance to each house.

One of the best localities in London in which to appreciate early Georgian town houses of fairly moderate scale is Westminster. In Queen Anne's Gate are houses of just before the 1706–8 Acts, of three storeys, with wooden eaves, window frames flush with the walls, keystones over the windows—which later became unfashionable—and densely decorated canopy porches typical of the period (76). Barton and Cowley Streets, behind the Abbey, were developed in the 1720s and later; the houses, like those in Queen Anne's Gate, are of brown brick with red dressings, but they have parapets, not eaves, in accordance with the 1706–8 Acts. But they also have flush window frames, clearly against the provisions of those Acts, suggesting that in this respect the Acts were not at first always strictly enforced. Beyond, in Lord North Street, are simpler houses of the same period (77). This street makes an unforgettable picture because it ends in the stupendously eccentric Baroque church of St John, Smith Square, by Thomas Archer (1714–28), now a

76. Queen Anne's Gate, Westminster was started just before the Building Acts of 1706–8, which would have prohibited the wooden cornices, the densely carved door canopies and the wooden window frames flush with the walls. Sashes were then an innovation. Also characteristic of the early 18th century are the keystones, and string courses at each floor level.

concert hall, with four corner turrets—providing an extreme contrast between fairly modest domestic building in brick, and grand public architecture in Portland stone.

The powerful and individualistic Baroque style of St John's was paralleled in the churches of Nicholas Hawksmoor (80) and, more moderately, those of James Gibbs (78, 79). Then architectural fashion reverted to the classicism favoured by Inigo Jones. The great monument of Palladianism in London is Somerset House, built to the design of Sir William Chambers from 1776 as Government offices, on a site that had been occupied by one of the many Strand palaces, that of the sixteenth-century Protector Somerset. It has quite a modest, dignified façade to the Strand, and a magnificent, but restrained, frontage to the Thames, on two tiers—when built it faced the river more directly; now the Embankment lies between. Somerset House is an interesting counterpart to the earlier Horse Guards in Whitehall, a posthumous work of William Kent (1750–60) and a less sure piece

77. Lord North Street, Westminster dates from *c* 1720—even though not every house conforms with the Building Acts of 1706–8 (page 137). The fairly modest houses contrast with the tremendous St John, Smith Square, by Thomas Archer, 1714–28 now a concert hall.

78. *Above* **St Clement Danes**, just outside the City boundary at **Temple Bar** (page 124); rebuilt by Wren 1682; steeple completed by James Gibbs, 1719. Behind, left, the complex composition of the Gothic Law Courts, by G. E. Street, 1874–82.

79. *Right* **St Mary-le-Strand**, by James Gibbs, 1714–7; its steeple counterpoints St Clement Danes further along the Strand. Its islanded situation results from street widening, *c* 1900.

141

of classical design, but remarkable in being the first purpose-built Government building to be erected in Whitehall, where the rambling Tudor palace had been largely destroyed by fires in 1691 and 1697, fortunately sparing Inigo Jones' Banqueting House.

The heyday of Bath

Bath in its heyday was a metropolitan resort. Water with special chemical qualities had been drunk, and bathed in, both in Roman times and from the later part of the Middle Ages. There were small stone public baths fed by some of the springs, open to the sky, in the seventeenth century, which were on occasions visited by notable people, including royalty.

But the most fashionable place of resort in the seventeenth century was Tunbridge Wells. Here springs with strong mineral content were discovered in a deeply rural setting in 1606 and 1608. Fashionable people were attracted, including the Queen, Henrietta Maria, who came in 1630. At first they stayed in neighbouring country houses, or lodged in nearby villages—the sheer rusticity of the area appealed to the sophisticated courtiers of the period. Something like a village grew around the main spring after the Restoration; a small church, characteristically dedicated to Charles I as a martyred king, was built in 1676 (its exquisite plaster ceilings are completely unexpected behind the plain exterior). A colonnade brought a touch of formality in 1687, initiating the Pantiles, a delightful amalgam of half-rustic, half-sophisticated buildings of the seventeenth century onwards.

In total contrast, Bath became, in the eighteenth century, the finest city in England, and one of the finest of its period in Europe. Previously it was a small, but for its size unusually dense, city, hemming in the site of its dissolved Abbey of which the great church survived; it had a share of the West of England cloth trade. Fashionable people visited the city in increasing numbers after about 1690, and came to expect more than just facilities for bathing or drinking the waters. Amusements and distractions were limited until 'Beau' Nash obtained the post of Master of Ceremonies in 1704, and reorganized the social life according to rigid conventions and strict timetables. Another influential figure was Ralph Allen, an entrepreneur who promoted, to his considerable profit, cross-country postal services throughout Britain, at a time when official posts ran only on routes radiating from London. He bought local quarries, and promoted the use of Bath stone. He built for himself Prior Park, a Palladian mansion overlooking the city in whose development he was greatly involved. John Wood was a native of the city who, after working in Yorkshire and the West End of London, returned to Bath in 1727 and became architect and, in many cases, promoter, of most of the best buildings in the city from then till his death in 1754, when his work was continued by his son, also John. Both Wood and Allen had extraordinary ideas of restoring Bath's lost Roman glory, by means of latter-day versions of some of the features of Imperial Rome itself, including the Forum and Colosseum, which they knew only from often inaccurate representations. Had they been more educated, sophisticated men, their initially strange ideas might not have been realized in the magnificent, not very Roman, form which they eventually took.

Wood's first large-scale venture was Queen Square, started in 1729, modelled on the West End squares but in Bath stone, and very different in execution from the 'Forum' of his initial dreams. In one respect it was specially significant. Hitherto, nearly all London squares after Covent Garden had been built up piecemeal, house by house, to produce a pattern of general conformity but individual variety in house fronts. Only in Grosvenor Square, where Wood had worked, had there been any attempt, after Covent Garden, to design one side of a London square in a uniform style—and not very successfully. In Bath, the whole of one side of Queen Square was treated on a monumental scale, as if it were a single palace, with the central part given prominence under a broad pediment. The only indication that the palatial building is really a row of houses is that there is a door on the ground floor, rather than a window, every three bays. Not until forty years later was anything comparable built in a London square.

Queen Square is at the foot of a long, fairly steep slope. Gay Street, climbing northwards, was built with three-storey stone-fronted houses—Bath versions of London town houses—stepped regularly up the incline. It leads into The Circus, which was started by the elder Wood in 1754, the year he died. It was the realization of his extraordinary idea of an English version of the Colosseum turned outside-in. It was the first perfectly circular space in the history of British town-planning, and it has the simple but supremely effective characteristic of being divided into three segments. Later Circuses in Britain were usually at crossroads, which meant that they were divided into four segments—so that one looked along either of the intersecting axes without necessarily appreciating, unless there were a major feature at the intersection, the circular form. In Bath only three streets converge at The Circus, so that as you approach along any one of them the view is closed by the centre of the opposite segment, and the eye appreciates in full the form and extent of the space. The segmental blocks consist entirely of uniform houses, the separate identities of which are indicated only by their doors at intervals. The trees which now grow in The Circus were not planted until much later; originally the circular space was open and paved, with no contrasting landscape.

One of the streets leading off the Crescent passes the Assembly Rooms, the main centre of Bath social life from its opening in 1771 (it has been reconstructed after bomb damage). Another, Brock Street, a thoroughfare of 'standard' Bath town houses, opens suddenly and magnificently on to the finest classical urban composition in Britain, the Royal Crescent, designed by the younger John Wood and started in 1767. This too was something unprecedented, a series of houses on a curve—which was not a simple segment of a circle, but a semi-ellipse. We do not know whether the elder Wood had such a climax in mind for his Bath development; certainly the unrivalled sequence Queen Square—The Circus—Royal Crescent, with the connecting streets, took shape, section by section, over forty years. It was all totally urban, with spaces completely enclosed by buildings, until one reached the Crescent which, on its hillside site, faces over a landscape which was more open and idyllic in the eighteenth century than it is today. The relationship of the Royal Crescent to this informal setting is comparable to that of an eighteenth-century country house to surrounding landscape planted in the manner of 'Capability' Brown.

The idea of the crescent, or curved range of houses, soon became fashionable. Dozens of crescents were built over the next eighty years, in resorts and residential areas, with curvatures ranging from slight to bold. Bath itself has one of the most original and effective later examples, Lansdown Crescent, further up the hill from the Royal Crescent, started in 1789 (**82**). It has a sinuous form, which is related to, though it exaggerates, the folds of the ground on which it is built; like the Royal Crescent, it faces over informal descending landscape. The architect was John Palmer. The final major development in Bath, that around Great Pulteney Street (**81**) from 1788 onwards, is described later.

Bath had few serious rivals till the later eighteenth century. One magnificent crescent was built at Buxton by the Duke of Devonshire in 1780, to the design of John Carr of York, as part of the promotion of this remote moorland town as a resort, but little more significant development followed there for several decades. Cheltenham had begun to develop by that time, but its story is essentially one of the Regency period.

Fashionable London from 1770
The Earl of Southampton's estate at Bloomsbury (page 134) passed through marriage to the Dukes of Bedford, already owners of Covent Garden, in the later seventeenth century. Much of it remained undeveloped for several decades. In 1776 the Duke began Bedford Square, remarkable not only as the best-preserved major Georgian square in central London, but also as the first in the capital, apart from Covent Garden, where whole sides were designed uniformly as architectural compositions, mainly in buff-brown brick, but with centrepieces brought out in stucco—an early use of this form of hard plaster intended to imitate stone (**83**). The effect is less palatial than in John Wood's earlier Queen Square in Bath, and the individuality of the separate houses at Bedford Square is brought out by the emphatic doorways. These are set back behind arches—as required in the 1774 Building act just passed—but the arches are emphasized by mock rusticated stonework which in fact is executed in Coade Stone, one of the earliest examples of this remarkable, hard-wearing product which was manufactured in Lambeth by Mrs. Eleanor Coade—whose seaside house at Lyme Regis has a façade treated wholly in her product.

The Adam brothers, particularly Robert, dominated fashionable London building in the 1770s. Their house exteriors were in restrained, even austere, Palladian styles, but their interiors at their best were brilliant with delicate plasterwork of classical Roman inspiration. Some of their finest surviving interiors are in three

81. Pulteney Bridge and Great Pulteney Street, Bath. Bath is specially noted for its Circus and Crescents (**82**), but this vista is straight and almost Parisian in character. In the foreground the shops on Robert Adam's Pulteney Bridge, 1770, across the hidden Avon. Great Pulteney Street was started in 1788 (page 156); the view is closed by the Holburne of Menstrie Museum, built as a hotel in 1796.

country houses on the outskirts of London—Kenwood, Syon House and Osterley. Their extensive developments in London have on the whole suffered badly. Little remains of their speculative scheme called the Adelphi, which included a terrace of houses on a podium overlooking the river, south of the Strand; the Royal Society of Arts building in John Adam Street is a survivor of this scheme. Two sides of Fitzroy Square, built in 1790 and restored after bombing, are externally theirs— faced in stucco, which was coming into general use at that time. One of the best preserved Adam town houses is the old Courtauld Institute in Portman Square, a survivor in a square otherwise largely wrecked by appalling post-war redevelopment, apart from the central garden. Not far away, Portland Place was laid out from 1776 by the Adams. Its width is due to the owner of Foley House at its southern end, where the former Langham Hotel stands, wanting to retain his view northwards to the Hampstead hills. A few Adam houses survive in Portland Place,

82. Lansdown Cresent, Bath. The nearby Circus (c 1755) and Royal Crescent (c 1770) started the fashion for curved groups of houses. Lansdown Crescent (1789–92) developed the idea, with its sinuous frontage taking up, and exaggerating, the form of the hillside on which it is built. Curvature in town planning remained a particularly British characteristic. Note the lantern arches; such ironwork became plentiful after the invention of Henry Cort's refining process in 1784 (page 172).

overwhelmed by the scale of later development. The streets to the west were built in the following decades, not by the Adams. Harley Street in particular is a typical late Georgian upper-middle-class street with its almost anonymous gentlemanly façades, their ground floors stuccoed in imitation of stone; almost the only decorative features are small iron balconies at first floor level.

Many charitable institutions were founded or expanded in London in the eighteenth century. The ancient St Bartholomew's Hospital was rebuilt from 1730 onwards to the design of James Gibbs—architect of two of London's most familiar churches, St Martin-in-the-Fields and St Mary-le-Strand (page 79). Guy's Hospital in Southwark was founded in 1722. Both St Bartholomew's and Guy's retain many of their Georgian buildings. The Foundling Hospital, established in 1742 by Thomas Coram, a seafaring merchant, was a home and school for orphans, which built up a great musical tradition. Its now demolished buildings, by Theodore Jacobsen, who was also concerned with the very large Royal Naval Hospital at Gosport in Hampshire, stood on the edge of Bloomsbury. The Foundling Hospital started to develop the adjoining fields in the 1790s, with Brunswick Square and the still fine Mecklenburgh Square.

The Bedford Estate resumed development of Bloomsbury in 1800 when Bedford House, the original Southampton House, was pulled down, and a new street, Bedford Place, laid out on its site, leading to a large new square, Russell Square, with further streets and squares beyond. The highly successful contractor who built much of this new quarter, as well as parts of the Foundling Hospital Estate, was James Burton, father of the better-known Decimus Burton. The surviving houses in Bloomsbury of the date, especially in Bedford Place, illustrate the severe external simplicity of fashionable town housing at the end of the century. As in Harley Street, the ground floors are stuccoed; the upper floors, usually two plus an attic, are in brown brick; simple iron balconies are the main decorative features. Later parts of Bloomsbury, built by Thomas Cubitt, had more embellishment on the façades, as the surviving west side of Tavistock Square, dating from about 1824, shows. The total effect of Bloomsbury before London University, in particular, fundamentally changed its character was one of restrained dignity, with an alternation between plain uniform streets and lushly landscaped squares.

Early London residential squares were simply landscaped, often with avenues round the edges of the central space, and symmetrical paths leading to a focal monument or fountain. Some time after the mid eighteenth century the tradition developed of dense but informal planting in the central spaces of squares—to form gardens accessible only to the householders of the squares and, sometimes, of immediately adjoining streets. This was related to the fashion for deliberately informal landscape, associated with 'Capability' Brown and, later, Humphry Repton, who created hundreds of parks around country houses, the often classical architecture of the houses contrasting with the designed informality of the landscape. The contrasts were similar in London squares; the informality of the square gardens set off the classical regularity of the enclosing houses. This is abundantly seen in Bedford Square, where the circular iron-railed garden, with its tall plane trees and thick underplanting, may date from the formation of the square. Portman Square similarly retains its central garden, but not its architectural unity (**XIX**, page 136), as does Russell Square, where the garden, originally designed by Repton has, as elsewhere, become a public space. Older squares, originally open and for-

mal, were newly landscaped, like St James's Square and Berkeley Square—where there are magnificent plane trees. The 'London plane', almost alone among forest trees, thrived in the smoky atmosphere which was characteristic of the capital until very recent times. In Bath, Queen Square, originally open, was lushly landscaped in late Georgian times; even The Circus was planted with trees.

The Prince Regent's London

The grandest town-planning scheme ever to be carried out in London until the present century was that undertaken by the Prince Regent, later George IV, and his architect John Nash. The Prince occupied Carlton House, overlooking St James's Park. At the very time he became Prince Regent in 1811, an old royal estate at Marylebone, which had been let on farming leases, reverted to the Crown. The Regent had early ideas of turning this area into a new royal pleasure ground, in conjunction with fashionable residential building. Several plans were prepared, culminating in one by John Nash in 1812. The area, then on the north-western outskirts of London, was difficult to reach from the heart of the West End, especially from Carlton House. An Act of 1813 gave the Crown power to form a new street—Regent Street—to link Carlton House with the intended pleasure ground, henceforth called Regent's Park. The Crown owned some property on a possible route, but much had to be purchased, and the line selected for Regent Street was influenced by practical considerations. The first length of street, including Waterloo Place and Lower Regent Street, crossed Pall Mall to form an axial vista from the site of Carlton House (occupied now by the Duke of York's Column,

83. **Bedford Square, Bloomsbury**, *c* 1775, the best preserved central London Georgian square, of the specifically British type where the formal architecture contrasts with the informal landscape of the central garden.

147

commemorating the Regent's brother who, in song, marched ten thousand men up and down) to what is now Piccadilly Circus. A ruthless, absolute ruler, as in France during the Monarchy or Empire, would then have extended the street straight to its intended destination, but this was not practicable in Regency Britain. Instead, Nash swung the new street west then north, so avoiding substantial property in Soho, and taking the line of a relatively poor old street, Swallow Street, which bordered affluent Mayfair—to which Regent Street provided a new, definite, eastern boundary. This explains the changes in direction of Regent Street, which Nash formalized into the sharp curve of the Quadrant.

Of Nash's Regent Street nothing is left but the alignment. It was all faced in stucco, by then a fashionable material, painted as if to resemble stone. The original Quadrant was completely plain, relying on its shape and proportions for effect, except for a very handsome colonnade which covered the pavement and sheltered the shops. The colonnade was removed early, and the Quadrant as it survived into the early twentieth century was simple but noble. Its present elaborate replacement, in Portland stone, has a scale much larger than Nash's.

North of the Quadrant, the original buildings of Regent Street were built separately and piecemeal, to good overall effect. Past Oxford Circus which, unlike Piccadilly Circus, retains its original circular form, there was a major alignment problem. It was decided to make use of the Adams' Portland Place, because of its width (page 145), as part of the *route royale*, but a direct alignment to its southern end would have meant buying expensive properties. So Regent Street had to make a double bend to link with Portland Place. Nash responded to the architectural challenge by siting a new church, All Souls, on the outside of the first bend, aligned at an angle. Its round portico, encircling the base of the steeple, acted as a pivot, visually speaking; it drew the eye round the corner in preparation for the second turn into the (now severely compromised) Augustan splendour of Portland Place. This was a master-stroke of pragmatic town-planning.

Nash's grandiose plan for Regent's Park was modified in execution, but what took form is magnificent enough. Portland Place opens into Park Crescent, a double quadrant of stuccoed houses (virtually all rebuilt after bombing), the ends of which are continued straight, across Marylebone Road, to form two sides of Park Square,

84. Chester Terrace, Regent's Park, one of the terraces which make the dramatic backcloth to Nash's park; finished in stucco—a hard plaster intended to imitate stone. However it needs to be frequently repainted, so that the effect is different from that of weathered stone.

which at its north end merges with Regent's Park itself.

Nash had for several years been in partnership with Humphry Repton, the great landscape designer in the Picturesque tradition—the basis of which was the creation artificially of irregular, apparently natural scenes such as might have been shown in a landscape picture of the time, hence the term. This could be achieved through studied planting, moulding of slopes and declivities, and often, where practicable, the formation of water expanses with intricate shorelines. Although the partnership was broken, Nash remained a superb landscapist very much in the Repton manner, and this is seen in Regent's Park today—particularly in the masterly effect of the branching islanded lake with its winding wooded shores, and the contrasts between wooded areas and sweeping grassy expanses. The lake was formed from two converging streams. But Regent's Park is not simply a landscape creation of its own right; it is also the foreground to the fabulous terraces of what were originally houses which Nash, and others, designed round the peri-

85. Cumberland Terrace, Regent's Park, 1826, the grandest of the terraces surrounding the park like huge pieces of theatrical scenery.

meter (**84, 85**). The most grandiose of these is Cumberland Terrace, with its dramatic pastiches of classical motifs in stucco. 'Dramatic' is the right term, for this and the other terraces look like stage sets seen from the park. (The fate of Nash's Regent's Park terraces has been curiously different from that of his Regent Street; they have been mainly rebuilt, either behind the original façades, or in total external replica, following war damage and neglect.) This is the ultimate development in the relationship of grand architecture with informal landscape.

Nash had another bold idea, very significant in the history of town-planning, in his designs for Regent's Park. He intended to place a ring of villas in the centre of the park. Each was to have its own, well-grown plot, so located that other villas would not be seen from it, and the occupant could deceive himself, and his guests, that all around was his demesne. Although not entirely without precedent, these villas can be called the precursors of detached suburbia. Only a few were ever built, including The Holme, latterly Bedford College, which looks—deliberately—rustic and idyllic when seen among trees from across the lake. Even more suggestive of developments that were to come are the two Park Villages on the edge of Regent's Park (**144**).

When the Regent became King in 1820, he persuaded Parliament to allow the rebuilding of Buckingham House as his new palace. Carlton House was demolished, and over part of its site Nash built Carlton House Terrace, overlooking St James's Park. The transformation of the latter was one of Nash's last and greatest works. St James's Park was originally marshy fields, which were drained and formally landscaped, rather ineptly, in the seventeenth century, with two avenues on the lines of The Mall and Birdcage Walk, and a straight 'canal' in between, fed by a natural stream. Nash transformed it into one of the most successful urban picturesque landscapes in the world (**86**). The canal was enlarged into a winding, branching, islanded lake with, eventually, thick planting along its banks. The rest of the park was turned into an alternation of glades and thickets, slightly undulating, threaded by shady paths. It is the perfect realization of concentrated, contrived landscape in the heart of a metropolitan city, and the view from the bridge along the lake, thanks partly to the skylines of later, Victorian buildings which were consciously designed with this view in mind, is one of the most effective of its kind.

Nash's influence extended further. The alignment, at least, of Pall Mall East, and its continuation to the Strand, was his, as was the outline of Trafalgar Square. Unfortunately, the buildings around the latter were not designed by him, and William Wilkins' National Gallery proved architecturally inadequate for the site. The nearly contemporary British Museum is better as a building, but it has no particular setting—and Sir Robert Smirke's Greek Revival design cannot compare with the work in the same style by the unknown (in London) Thomas Harrison at Chester (**117**). The greatest architectural genius of the age was Sir John Soane, but his Bank of England, started in 1788, was wrecked through enlargement between the wars; his most effective memorial is his extraordinary house and collection, now Sir John Soane's Museum, in Lincoln's Inn Fields.

Regency resorts
The Prince Regent's legacy is not only in London. Brighton is his progeny. Sea bathing was practised for pleasure in a few places in the early eighteenth century,

notably Scarborough, an ancient port which also had a medicinal spring. The first town to become fashionable wholly as a seaside resort was Weymouth. This too was an ancient port, where trade was languishing. In the early 1760s Ralph Allen of Bath promoted some building there, and suggested that visitors to Bath might travel on to Weymouth, by the newly opened turnpike road, to enjoy bathing and also to take sea water—it was held that drinking sea water was itself effective in relieving some complaints. But it was the patronage of royalty that made Weymouth—and sea bathing—fashionable. The Duke of Gloucester came there from 1780 onwards, followed, in 1789, by George III himself, who first dipped into the sea to the strains of 'God Save Great George Our King', as the first line of the national anthem then ran. Thereafter not only Weymouth, but bathing generally, became unquestionably fashionable. Bathing, from then right through the Victorian period, was performed decorously from 'bathing machines', really wheeled huts drawn as far as possible into the sea by horses, for the occupants to take the plunge. At Weymouth a succession of terraces was built along the gently curving bay overlooking the beach, to the north of the old harbour town (**XVI**, p. 116). They consist mainly of brick versions of the typical Bath town house—perhaps strangely in a place which adjoins the quarries where the finest stone in England is extracted, at Portland. But Portland stone was expensive, even locally, and there were nearer deposits of clay suitable for brickmaking.

Brighton had been a fishing town of some importance; it was the nearest on the south coast to London, and fish from there could be carried overland to Billingsgate in time for it to be still saleable. It had no harbour; the fishing boats were beached. But they could be more than offshore vessels—it was a Brighton fisherman who brought the future Charles II safely across to France after the Battle of Worcester, not knowing that he was ensuring the future prosperity of his town by saving the Royal line.

86. St James's Park, redesigned by Nash from 1828, is one of the finest pieces of contrived landscape in any large city. But the buildings in the background—the Foreign Office with its Italianate tower and Whitehall Court with its fantastic domes and turrets—came later.

The fishing town was in decline when visitors began to bathe there in the mid eighteenth century. A local doctor, Dr Russell, published discourses on the medical value of sea water in the 1750s. Royalty came to Brighton before Weymouth—the Duke of Gloucester in 1765, and the Duke of Cumberland from 1771. But more important than these brothers of the King was the heir to the throne. The Prince of Wales, as he then was, first came in 1783. Two years later he married, legally but secretly, Maria Fitzherbert, and in 1786 he built the first, simple, Pavilion to the design of Henry Holland, architect of Carlton House. Several years later he employed Nash to transform it into the fantastic oriental palace it is today. Fashionable and, perhaps more importantly, would-be fashionable visitors came to Brighton in increasing numbers as the Prince of Wales became successively the Prince Regent and George IV.

Old Brighton was a town of alleys—the present Lanes—with traditions of building in local pebbles, flints, and also bricks and tiles, often baked to a glossy black or grey through salt water being added in the process. These traditions it partly shared with neighbouring Lewes. Most of the early resort houses were built, like

87. Kemp Town, Brighton.
The grandest developments in Brighton date from the 1820s when the former Prince Regent was King. Lewes Crescent is part of a scheme by Amon Wilds, father and son (**26**), and Charles Busby. Despite alterations, some of the original canopied balconies survive over the porches.

88. 26 Old Steine, Brighton, by Amon Wilds and Charles Busby (**87**); the 'ammonite' capitals, based on spiral shell fossils, are their hallmarks. The delicate iron balcony is characteristic of 'Regency' resorts; the convex façade is a Brighton speciality.

the Pavilion itself, not facing the sea but bordering the Steine, a long irregular open space which followed the course of a dried-up stream. Some of the earliest fashionable houses were faced in the traditional local materials—pebbles with brick dressings, or 'mathematical' tiles made to look like bricks (112)—but stucco quickly became the normal facing material for houses in the town (88). From the start there was a liking for bow windows, either rounded or diagonal-sided, usually on all floors in continuous vertical succession (89), and sometimes embellished with iron balconies. Extension of the town laterally, facing the sea, began about 1800 when the gently curved, shiny black-tiled Royal Crescent was built with its diagonal-sided bow windows—much more modest than its namesake in Bath. Over the next decades, street after street of mainly bow-windowed houses were built at right-angles to the shore, interspersed by a few small grassed squares open to the sea.

The crescendo was reached in the 1820s when George was King. Two builders, Amon Wilds father and son, originally from Lewes (26), partnered with Charles Busby, an architect who had practised in America, to design two of the most spectacular development schemes of the period outside London. One was Kemp Town, on the eastern extremity of Brighton, promoted by a local magnate T. R. Kemp, consisting of two quadrants of houses flanking the entrance to a three-sided 'square', in plan like the top of a bottle, set on a clifftop (87). The houses are of the London 'Regency' type, mostly stuccoed, with balconies. The other scheme, Brunswick Town, was on the town's western edge—actually in the old parish of Hove which, as a borough, retains its administrative independence to this day. Here, the houses facing Brunswick Square, an elongated space open to the sea at one end, are boldly folded out in broad, shallow, columned bows rising through three storeys—a pattern continued in some of the adjoining streets. Brighton was

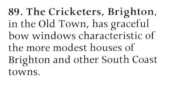

89. The Cricketers, Brighton, in the Old Town, has graceful bow windows characteristic of the more modest houses of Brighton and other South Coast towns.

already big and fashionable when the railway came in 1841, after which it became bigger and more popular, but still stayed fashionable, even after disapproving Queen Victoria, the antithesis in almost every way to George IV, sold the Pavilion to the Town Council in 1849.

Many would-be Brightons were hopefully developed in this period, especially along the southern coasts. Some eventually succeeded—like Worthing, which has some pleasant bowed terraces and a spectacular sinuous 'Crescent', or Ramsgate, which retains several impressive buff-brick terraces of the 1820s and 1830s, with a profusion of ironwork. Others never got much beyond a single Crescent, like Alverstoke, close to the monumental Royal Naval Hospital (page 146) at Gosport, or Hayling Island, where the Crescent, started in 1825 by the Bloomsbury-based builder Robert Abraham, was never properly finished.

Very different from Brighton were the seaside cottage resorts of the South-West, particularly Sidmouth. Here a coastal market town—there was hardly any fishing trade and no harbour—expanded after 1800, partly with Regency brick and stucco terraces, but mainly with a delightful assortment of *cottages ornés*, or rustic villas designed like over-large cottages, each in a luxuriant garden (**90**). Many are thatched; some are playfully 'Gothic'; a secluded group in a cul-de-sac is called the Elysian Fields.

Despite the huge development of seaside resorts, inland spas continued to be fashionable. Cheltenham became a leading resort when Bath was, relatively, declining. It had been a small market town under the slopes of the Cotswolds. Springs with chemical properties were found and exploited in a small way in the mid eighteenth century. Major developments began about 1810, with the building of terraces, crescents and individual villas, faced in Cotswold stone or stucco, set amid the lushly planted landscapes of public spaces and private gardens—an amal-

90. Sidmouth, Devon, a retirement resort of the early 19th century, has romantic *cottages ornés*, and villas with broad verandahs, of which this is a fairly late example, set in lush and often exotic greenery.

gam of grandeur and deliberate informality more subtle than that of Nash's Regent's Park. The buildings associated with the two main springs are, appropriately, among the most prominent—the domed Montpellier Spa with Ionic columns, and caryatids between the adjoining shops, and the grander Pittville Spa with an Ionic frontispiece. A resort such as Cheltenham was not only a place of hoped-for cures and social gaiety, but also a haven of retirement for people from industry, commerce, the armed forces and, increasingly, for those who had made a career in India or other parts of the developing British Empire where service, whether civilian or military, usually ended fairly early in life.

Clifton has a grander site than Cheltenham. It was partly, but not wholly, an appendage to Bristol. This merchant city had its first formal square, Queen Square, in the early eighteenth century; its Georgian terraces were at first mostly of brick, but increasingly of Bath stone as that material became more easily available. A mud-girt medicinal spring by the tidal River Avon at the entrance to the dramatic Clifton Gorge became the centre of a half-rustic spa called Hotwells; its houses climbed the steep slope to the old hilltop village of Clifton where a few merchants' mansions already existed. In the 1790s grand developments started, including a long shallow crescent along the rim of a deep gully (Royal York Crescent), and a shorter sharper one backing on to the edge of a precipice. Other terraces, and villas, spread along the edges of the half-wild Clifton Down which bordered the Gorge. An urban centre developed round the classical Assembly Rooms of 1806–11 in The Mall. This was designed by a local builder-architect Francis Greenway, who was later transported to Australia for fraud, and who became the 'father of Australian architecture'; there are buildings by him still in Sydney. The grandest Clifton buildings are early Victorian, but the visual centrepiece is Brunel's fantastic Suspension Bridge across the Gorge, finished in the 1860s. Suburb, or resort in its own right, Clifton has the most spectacular combination in England, after Durham, of grand-scale architecture and dramatic land-form.

The last and one of the grandest stages of Georgian development in Bath was centred on Great Pulteney Street, which lies across the River Avon from the main part of the city, and is reached by Robert Adam's delightful Pulteney Bridge, flanked by little shops, which was built in 1770 (81). Great Pulteney Street, started in 1788 was designed by Thomas Baldwin, architect also of the Guildhall and the Pump Room in Bath. With its wide, straight alignment, it possesses much of the grandeur of a Paris boulevard and has few counterparts in England, although it resembles some of the streets in the New Town of Edinburgh. The view is closed by the classical Holburne of Menstrie Museum, originally built in 1796 as a hotel and assembly rooms. Behind this building, in typical 'Regency' contrast, are the romantically landscaped Sydney Gardens, through which pass the Kennet and Avon Canal, and also—deliberately exploited as a visual feature—Brunel's railway to Bristol of 1840–1 set in a shallow cutting. By then Bath's heyday had passed; the most fashionable spas were Cheltenham; Leamington, which grew rapidly from a village after 1800; Harrogate, known as a rural 'spaw' in 1598 (the first known use of the term in England), but not recognizable as a town till the early nineteenth century; and, once again, Tunbridge Wells. At the last-named, Decimus Burton designed the delightful Calverley Park from 1829, with a crescent, in the attractive local sandstone, and many villas set in lush gardens—a charming piece of 'Regency' urban landscape.

The threshold of Victorian London

With Decimus Burton we return to London. His is the Athenaeum of 1828–30 in the heart of Nash's West End, facing the former United Services Club, designed by Nash, but altered by Burton, on part of the site of Carlton House. They mark the beginning of nineteenth-century Pall Mall 'clubland', grander in scale than the older 'clubland' of St James's. Next to the Athenaeum are the Travellers' Club (1831) and the Reform Club (1837–41), both by Sir Charles Barry, in the newly fashionable 'Italianate' style, taking his inspiration from Renaissance Italy, rather than, as Nash and Burton did, from ancient Greece and Rome. Barry is known, above all, for his new Palace of Westminster, built after the old Palace was destroyed by fire in 1834; its Elizabethan style was required—one of two alternative styles, the other being Gothic—as a condition of the competition that Barry won. In some ways it is a Classical building in its external design, though not in its style, but the asymmetrical positioning of the two towers and other skyline features, especially as seen from the river, is as much a masterpiece of 'Picturesque' composition in architecture as Nash's St James's Park is in landscape. Unfortunately, Westminster Hall, which used to be more dominant in the old, rambling, basically medieval, complex of Palace buildings, among which it almost alone was saved from the fire, is now externally overshadowed by Barry's buildings.

The last major development of high architectural quality in the Georgian tradition in London was Belgravia. This was on land owned by the Grosvenor Estate which employed Thomas Cubitt, who had built the northern parts of Bloomsbury, and whose firm became the most successful of early Victorian building contractors, organizing all stages of construction. Eaton Square, developed partly by Cubitt between about 1825 and 1850, is an exceedingly long 'square', with ranges of terraces, some stuccoed, some in buff brick with stucco Classical features, facing over private-communal landscaped gardens in the Georgian tradition. A main road runs axially through the garden area—an appropriate exit from the West End, with its fitful grandeur and lush landscapes of the Renaissance to Regency era.

14
The Age of Industrial Change

What was the Industrial Revolution? Mainly it was the result of huge advances in the techniques of manufacture, particularly of textiles and metal products, which led to tremendous changes in society and in the setting of people's lives. It was a 'revolution' only in the widest context of human history, since it took place over several generations. It reached a crescendo at the end of the eighteenth century and continued into the nineteenth. This chapter deals with industrial changes and their effects on towns from the seventeenth to the early nineteenth centuries.

Textiles

Already by Tudor times, much of the wool industry was organized on a fairly large scale by entrepreneurs with considerable capital resources, who might employ dozens of workers at the different stages of production. But their machinery was rudimentary and hand-operated, and—this is specially important—they nearly all worked within, or close to, their own homes. Only fulling—beating the woven cloth—was mechanized by the simple use of water-powered hammers (see Chapter Ten).

There were some significant early developments in hand-operated machinery. One of the first was the stocking-frame, invented in 1589 by William Lee of Nottinghamshire, which produced knitted stockings, at first from worsted yarn, later also from silk. Many of these were set up in London, particularly around Shoreditch, but during the eighteenth century the industry developed mainly in the Midlands.

Refugees have repeatedly stimulated the development of British industry. Flemings introduced the 'New Draperies' in the 1570s. A hundred years later, thousands of Huguenots fled to England, bringing various skills, including those of silk weaving. Huguenot silk weavers settled in Shoreditch and Spitalfields, using fairly sophisticated hand-operated machinery; they produced fabrics of high quality such as had previously been imported. Others settled in Coventry, where a silk ribbon industry developed. At both Spitalfields and Coventry, eighteenth-century houses survive with wide-windowed top floors where the looms were installed.

The silk yarn used in the weaving-looms and knitting-frames was produced from the raw silk—imported from the Mediterranean and the East—by a process called 'throwing'. This was equivalent to spinning yarn from raw wool, but more complicated, and it was done for a time with hand-operated machinery. Increased demand for silk yarn provided the stimulus for the first main stage of the Industrial Revolution as it applied to textiles.

In 1719 Thomas Lombe opened in Derby a factory for silk throwing, using water power from the River Derwent to drive the machinery. This was the first time in Britain that textile machinery, other than fulling hammers, was driven by non-human power. (In fact such machinery was already in operation in north-west Italy, which Lombe used as a model.) And Lombe's was possibly the first building which we should recognize as a 'factory'—where large numbers of people worked together, necessarily subject to operational discipline and precise timekeeping. Traditional hand-machine operators, by contrast, worked in their own home or workshop, to their own timetable and at their own pace.

Lombe had a patent for his machinery, but, after it expired in the 1740s, other silk yarn factories were built. This happened especially in Derbyshire; in Cheshire, for instance at Congleton and Macclesfield; and in Dorset as at Sherborne and at Gillingham, where the former factory of 1769 survived until a recent fire, though without its machinery, as the oldest extant building of its kind. It should be emphasized that these early factories were for producing yarn, which would be used by the silk weavers and framework-knitters of London, the Midlands and elsewhere. Silk weaving, as distinct from throwing, remained a hand-operated, though highly skilled, craft for many years.

Silk manufacture was never more than a limited luxury trade in Britain. Cotton manufacture, on the other hand, became the most important single industry in the country. Like raw silk, raw cotton was imported, at first from the Middle and Far East. The early imports came into London, but by 1600 certain merchants in Manchester, then a very small town, obtained regular supplies of cotton through London. (It was only later, when cotton-growing developed across the Atlantic, that Liverpool became the port of entry.) The Manchester merchants distributed the raw cotton locally for spinning, after which it was woven, together with linen or worsted, into fabrics known as fustians, for which Lancashire became increasingly noted until the later eighteenth century. There has been no entirely satisfactory explanation why Manchester, which had been a very small wool weaving centre should in the first place have become a centre for cotton processing; the damp climate, suitable for the industry, may have been a partial reason.

Pure cotton fabrics, called calicoes, often dyed or printed in brilliant colours, were imported from India before 1700. Around that time Huguenot refugees, who had settled in Wandsworth and other places round London, set up workshops for printing fabrics—a skilled operation requiring various dyestuffs. Legislation (the Calico Act of 1720) forbade for a time the import from India of cotton fabrics that had already been dyed or printed, but permitted the import of uncoloured fabrics, which continued—so stimulating the newly-established English fabric-printing industry, which developed further round London, in places where there were good water supplies, and, a little later, in Lancashire.

A series of developments in hand-operated machinery stimulated the growth of the fustian industry in Lancashire, beginning with John Kay's flying shuttle (for weaving), introduced in 1733, followed by James Hargreaves' spinning jenny in 1764. The latter aroused hostility from cotton spinners using the older tools, fearful of losing their jobs. Hargreaves' cottage in the Lancashire village of Oswaldtwistle was attacked, and the machinery destroyed; he moved to Nottingham.

The real begetter of the Industrial Revolution in cotton production was Richard Arkwright, who developed the water frame, or spinning machine driven by water power. He first experimented in Preston but, again, hostility drove him from Lancashire, and he settled in a small village called Cromford, beside the River Derwent

91. Masson Mill, Cromford, Derbyshire. Richard Arkwright built the first water-powered cotton mill nearby in 1771; Masson Mill with its Venetian windows dates from 1783, with large Victorian extensions.

north of Derby. Here he built the first cotton spinning factory in 1771 (part survives), followed by another in 1777, and a larger one, Masson Mill, in 1783—the fine façade of the last remains as the centrepiece of a bigger, still operating, factory (**91**). It is said that Arkwright deliberately chose a remote spot without existing textile workers, who might have been hostile—the workforce for his mills moved in from surrounding agricultural and lead-working areas. To house them, Arkwright built a street of houses, North Street, in 1776—the oldest extant workers' 'model' housing in the country. They are of three storeys, the lower two domestic, the top storey, with wide mullioned windows, intended for stocking handlooms using the yarn from the factories.

From the later 1770s spinning mills with water-driven machinery—at first on the Arkwright model, later in improved forms developed by Samuel Crompton—were built in increasing numbers. Some were in the Midlands, as at Belper, Derbyshire, where the Strutt family built up a complex industrial enterprise, but the main area of cotton expansion was Lancashire. By this time, raw cotton production had developed hugely, both in the West Indies, and in the southern North American colonies, and was imported through Liverpool. The flow was interrupted by the American War of Independence, but resumed and went on increasing. Cotton yarn produced by water-driven machinery was more reliable than hand-spun yarn, and could readily be used for pure cotton fabrics, instead of being woven with worsted or linen to produce fustians. So the large-scale import of calicoes from India ceased, and Lancashire and adjoining counties produced ever-increasing quantities of pure cotton goods.

The new water-driven spinning mills were built astride fast-flowing streams, particularly those of the Pennines. Some were in or near established small towns

like Bury or Rochdale, which already had hand-spinners, but many were set up on completely rural sites, round which villages and towns developed, such as Todmorden (92).

In the 1780s there was another revolutionary development in textile manufacture. James Watt, in conjunction with the industrialist Matthew Boulton of Birmingham, perfected the steam engine, which was applied to spinning machinery. The first steam-driven cotton mill was built near Nottingham in 1786; the first in Lancashire at Warrington a year later. It was no longer necessary to build a factory on a powerful stream, though a water supply was still needed, for processing and raising the steam. The best sites for early steam mills were usually by canals—fast expanding at the time—which provided transport for fuel, raw materials and finished goods as well as water supply.

These early developments at first affected cotton spinning only. Cotton continued to be woven on hand-operated machinery for some time, but weaving necessarily expanded in proportion to the production of spun yarn. So, paradoxically, the end of the eighteenth century and the beginning of the nineteenth was the heyday of the handloom weaver, and this must have led to curious domestic arrangements. Traditionally, women spun and men wove (page 108); the tradition was continued in the spinning mills, which always employed a high proportion of females—and children too before the Victorian Factory Acts. During the transition period, men would have remained in or near home, operating the looms in lofts or small workshops, while women worked in large numbers in factories. But from about 1800 it became common for weaving sheds to be built alongside the spinning mills, where weavers worked in factory conditions, though using handlooms. It was not till after about 1820 that steam-driven weaving machinery

92. **Todmorden**, on the Yorkshire–Lancashire border, grew from a hand-weaving village into a town as first water-powered, then steam-powered, textile mills were built beside the streams, canal, and, later, railway. The leading mill-owners were the Fieldens, influential promoters of factory reform. They employed John Gibson (**130**) to design the Town Hall, 1870, whose Classical form contrasts serenely with the dour terrace houses and rugged Pennine setting.

161

became general in the cotton industry.

Manchester was a small town which grew a little in the seventeenth century under the impetus of its developing textile trade, and a great deal in the eighteenth. At the 1801 census it was, with contiguous Salford, the largest town in England after London. What distinguished it, other than its size, from adjoining textile towns was the concentration of merchants who dealt with finished fabrics from all over Lancashire—their main meeting place was the Royal Exchange opened in 1729—and the development of specialized commercial, servicing and cultural facilities which served the whole region. It had a big 'patrician' class as well as a huge proletariat, and more middle gradations of society than smaller industrial towns; it became volatile politically, as the events leading up to the 'Peterloo' massacre, and, later, the Corn Law and Free Trade agitation testified. Not a great deal survives of pre-Victorian Manchester, apart from the medieval core with the present Cathedral and Chetham's Hospital (page 87). There are some Georgian town houses, now offices, in King Street and elsewhere, some merchants' villas on what were the half-rural outskirts, and two fine Classical monuments of middle-class urban culture—the Portico Library of 1806 by the great Thomas Harrison (page 197), and the former Manchester Institution and Athenaeum of the 1830s, now the Art Gallery, by Barry.

The other main cotton manufacturing centres which developed from the 1770s were mostly old-established, though hitherto small, market towns on the edge of the Pennines, like Bolton, Bury, Blackburn and Stockport, or right in the Pennines like Burnley (128) and Rochdale. They grew so much in Victorian times that they retain little of their earlier character—apart from Stockport with its extraordinary market place, medieval in form, which is infilled with a Victorian market hall, and is approached by steep alleys. Oldham, on the other hand, was almost entirely a creation of the early cotton boom period, and so were most of the smaller towns and large villages which grew beside the mills between the principal cotton towns. But Preston, north-west of the main cotton area, was a substantial ancient town ('Proud Preston'), which also became dominated by the textile industry. Accrington, entirely a new creation as a town, was a centre of the cotton printing industry, in which the Peel family, of Victorian political fame, were prominent.

The woollen industry, unlike that of cotton, was an ancient trade which adapted and expanded during the Industrial Revolution. Before, the chief wool processing areas were in the West of England and East Anglia, with another, originally less important, in Yorkshire (see Chapter Ten). The industry in East Anglia, with the important exception of Norwich, declined steadily after the Civil War, and was largely extinct outside Norwich by 1800. The West of England textile industry, however, remained important into the nineteenth century. That of Yorkshire expanded, at first steadily, then dynamically, until it became the chief wool manufacturing region in Britain.

In Yorkshire the old pattern of cloth production persisted into the late eighteenth century. Many of the clothworkers lived in cottages, often associated with smallholdings, scattered over the hilly country of the West Riding. Different members of the families prepared the wool—which was often obtained from itinerant pedlars—carded it, spun it and wove it, usually into small, coarse fabrics called kerseys. These were taken weekly to the cloth or 'piece' markets, of which the oldest-established were in Leeds, Wakefield and Halifax (page 110). Most of the early Yorkshire clothworkers were commercially independent, unlike those of other regions where there were more large-scale clothiers, but, as the industry developed in Yorkshire, more and more of it came under the control of larger entrepreneurs.

Leeds became a market town in 1207, when the present main street, Briggate, was laid out leading north from the bridge over the River Aire, west of the original village whose form is still suggested by the twisty streets around the parish church of St Peter. The town expanded significantly, under the impetus of the developing cloth industry, in the seventeenth century and grew fast in the eighteenth; it retains fine Georgian town houses round Park Square (132). The new church of St John, built in 1634, a late example in the Gothic style, and that of Holy Trinity, built in 1727 with a classical steeple, later heightened like that of a London church of the period, testify the town's continuing growth. A Cloth Hall was first built in 1711 and replaced in 1775 (a fragment remains), where undyed cloth from the surrounding area was sold. Another Cloth Hall, for dyed cloth, was built in 1756 but does not survive. Neither of the Leeds Cloth Halls was as magnificent as the surviving Piece Hall in Halifax (93). Halifax began as a remote moorland-edge market town which was already rich enough, through weaving, in the fifteenth century for a grand parish church to be built. Its Georgian prosperity is shown by the surviving cloth merchants' houses in what were the fringes of the town,

93. The Piece Hall, Halifax, Yorkshire, 1779, is the most impressive monument of the pre-Industrial Revolution cloth trade in England. Hand-weavers sold their pieces of cloth in small shops behind the galleries or on the space in the middle. Rapid changes in technology and distribution soon made the Piece Hall redundant; now it is a showpiece, put to varied uses.

some with associated wool stores. The Piece Hall (i.e. cloth hall), opened in 1779, is a huge rectangular composition of two- and three-storey blocks round a central open space (93). Each floor is divided into small rooms, or shops, set behind colonnades, the whole having an Italian Renaissance character. The market was held on Saturdays. The richer clothiers rented shops; the smaller, independent, producers paid to display their 'pieces' on the central space. This is by far the most impressive monument of the pre-Industrial Revolution cloth trade in Britain, apart from the churches and clothiers' mansions built from its wealth.

There were other Cloth or Piece Halls in Wakefield, which lost its earlier preeminence as a cloth-marketing centre; in Huddersfield, which grew from small beginnings in the late eighteenth and early nineteenth centuries; in Bradford, which, although an ancient village and large parish with a long tradition of weaving (64), did not become an important marketing centre till the time when its Cloth Hall was built in 1773; and in Colne in Lancashire. None of these four survives. The Cloth Halls became obsolete as the trade became more dominated by larger entrepreneurs, who might employ or commission clothworkers, or buy their products direct. These merchants might 'finish' the cloths, including fulling (page 108), dyeing, and shearing, or dressing the fabric. Many of the finished products were sent along the rapidly improving navigation system based on the Rivers Aire and Calder down to the port of Hull, for overseas export or coastal transit, or went overland to London or elsewhere.

The mechanical improvements pioneered in the cotton industry were adopted more slowly in the wool industry. The spinning jenny and flying shuttle were used in the manufacture of the heavier woollens from the 1770s, but it was not until about 1820 that power-driven machinery was introduced for spinning woollen yarn. Power-driven woollen weaving came even later. However, one important process, that of carding the wool before spinning, was successfully mechanized by about 1790. From that date, carding mills were built beside streams and rivers, often alongside older fulling mills. Sometimes accommodation for hand-operated jennies was provided beside the carding mills, so that many spinners who were, as usual, largely women, worked under factory conditions while still operating hand machinery. Woollen weaving continued, on a large scale, as a cottage industry for longer—much of it was done in upland villages like Heptonstall (94, 95) or Haworth, which still have stone-built cottages with wide windows to provide light for looms. (Haworth, when the Brontë sisters lived there, was truly on the edge of industrial England; steam-powered spinning mills were advancing in the valley below; weavers worked in the hillside village; westward were wild moors.) However, handlooms were increasingly brought into weaving sheds beside the mill buildings, as in the cotton industry, so that more and more of the woollen industry became concentrated in factory complexes. The first truly comprehensive woollen factory in Yorkshire, where all the manufacturing processes were carried on, was at Bean Ing in Leeds, built by Benjamin Gott in 1792; it was also the first factory in Yorkshire where steam power was used to drive machinery.

All that has so far been written about Yorkshire textiles concerns the production of the heavier woollen, as distinct from the lighter worsted, fabrics (page 110). Worsted production in Yorkshire began about 1700, and steadily increased after the middle of the century. Water-driven machinery was adapted for spinning worsted yarn in the 1790s, after which numerous worsted mills were built in the

94. *Left* **Heptonstall, Yorkshire**, high on the Pennines, remained a hand-weaving village while water- and steam-powered mills developed in the valleys below. These 19th century cottages in local stone are very traditional for the date; the wide windows provided light for looms inside.

95. *Below left* **Methodist Chapel, Heptonstall**, late 18th century, typical in its austere elegance of early Nonconformist chapels (**14, 109**); the octagonal plan, with galleries and central pulpit, is convenient for preaching. Note, in the background, mill chimneys in a nearby valley.

deep valleys around Huddersfield and Bradford. As with other types of fabric, the weaving of worsted remained hand-operated for longer than spinning, with handlooms gradually being brought into weaving sheds.

The Huddersfield area came to specialize in fine fabrics—both worsted and, to a lesser degree, woollen. Huddersfield, like Bradford and Halifax, competed successfully with Norwich, the traditional centre of the worsted industry. The Norwich manufacturers were slow to adapt to new machinery, and when they did, after 1830, it was too late. The Norwich worsted industry collapsed, and Yorkshire was henceforth the centre of the trade. Huddersfield also came to specialize in 'fancy' woollens, including twills, in which it competed successfully with Bradford-on-Avon in Wiltshire.

Labour conflicts seem, on the whole, to have been less violent in Yorkshire during the eighteenth and early nineteenth centuries than they were in Lancashire, the Midlands, or the West of England. Among the worst outbreaks of violence in Yorkshire were those of 1812, principally in the Huddersfield area, over the introduction of power-driven machinery for shearing worsteds—hitherto a very skilled job, consisting of trimming off loose ends from the finished fabrics. The rioters were called 'Luddites' (p. 170) after their counterparts of a year before in the Midlands—where, however, the disturbances had a very different cause.

The urban pattern that developed in the Yorkshire wool area was broadly similar to that in the Lancashire cotton area, but with important differences. Leeds was the chief town in the area from at least the eighteenth century, but it did not become as dominant as Manchester did in the cotton region. Bradford, hitherto very small, grew explosively from about 1790, and by 1850 was unquestionably the most important centre of wool manufacture (for both woollens and worsteds) in Britain; Leeds, by contrast, was less exclusively concerned with textiles, and had wider interests as an important regional centre. The two contiguous cities developed very different characters, even to their building materials; Leeds was largely of brick except for its public buildings; Bradford, like Halifax, was essentially a Pennine town and mainly built of local stone. Huddersfield, where a single family, the Ramsdens, owned and controlled much of the town and its surroundings, developed after 1800 in a fairly orderly way with regular streets and Classical façades, some of which survive. Its architectural climax came in the early Victorian period, with the superb Corinthian façade of the railway station of 1847.

Few people would have predicted around 1760 that the cloth industry of the West of England (page 110)—Wiltshire, eastern Somerset and Gloucestershire—would soon be eclipsed by that of Yorkshire. The traditional product of the West was fine broadcloth, a high but fluctuating proportion of which was exported by London merchants. Gloucestershire became famous for its scarlet cloths, Wiltshire in the seventeenth century for its 'Spanish medleys', using imported Spanish wool, dyed before weaving. The region, unlike Yorkshire, was dominated since Tudor times by large-scale clothiers who might employ hundreds working at the various stages of production in their homes. One clothier family was that of the Yerburys of Bradford-on-Avon, who developed a trade in 'fancy' or twilled cloths, and built a fine country house on the edge of the town, Belcombe Court, for which they employed John Wood of Bath, in 1734. Eleven years later, Paul Methuen, from another Bradford cloth dynasty, bought nearby Corsham Court. Unlike the Yerburys, the Methuens severed their connections with manufacture and became

96. *Left* **Weavers' Houses, Bradford-on-Avon, Wiltshire,** set on the hillside seen in **98**. They date from the 17th century—the town was a major weaving centre from the 15th to the 19th (pages 110, 169).

97. *Below left* **High Tory, Bradford-on-Avon**. The houses, further up the hill from **96**, were built for prosperous 18th century clothiers, who probably employed weavers and spinners elsewhere.

98. Bradford-on-Avon from the river. The mill, with Gothic arches, dates from 1857, during the last phase of the town's prosperity as a weaving centre; it is now offices. Gabled houses of the 17th century and classical terraces of the 18th (**96, 97**) are built in tiers up the hillside.

county gentry—following a course common among successful trading families since the Middle Ages. Many lesser but still substantial clothiers flourished in the western textile towns, as their surviving stone-built town houses in Trowbridge (**99**), Bradford-on-Avon and Frome testify, and all these towns retain large numbers of clothworkers' houses and cottages from the early seventeenth century onwards (**96, 97, 98**).

In Gloucestershire, the textile industry was centred on Stroud, and developed along the deep Cotswold valleys where fulling-mills were built beside fast streams. Even in the seventeenth century there were concentrated centres of production, where dyeing and finishing were carried on beside the fulling-mills, and raw wool was stored before being distributed by the clothiers to the domestic workers. Nailsworth, Dursley and Painswick (**113**) were other Cotswold towns concerned with weaving.

The West of England, on the whole, adopted mechanical improvements slightly more slowly than Yorkshire. The Western workforce seems to have been more volatile. There were frequent strikes against reductions in wages during the slump periods, and spirited opposition to the introduction of machinery on some occasions. When a clothier called Phelps tried, in 1791, to install water-driven carding machinery into his mill at Bradford-on-Avon, a mob threw the machinery into the river and smashed the windows of his house—Westbury House, which still stands, by the bridge. So Phelps set up in Malmesbury, several miles away, where the textile industry had slumped and there were plenty of unemployed workers who had nothing to lose. The splendid factory which he built there still survives, now in part a furniture showroom. Like the contemporary, but vanished, Bean Ing factory in Leeds it was comprehensive, including space for carding (water-powered), spinning and weaving (both hand-operated), as well as fulling and finishing. Many more cloth mills were built in the West of England textile area after 1810, and probably more early examples survive than in Yorkshire. The finest is Stanley Mill outside Stroud, dating from 1812–3. Coal for steam power came from the small Somerset coalfield, or from Wales up the Severn and Stroud-water Canal.

The prosperity of the Western cloth industry was particularly erratic in the first half of the nineteenth century. It suffered from increasing competition for the finer types of cloth in which it specialized, and failed to adjust to changes in demand or taste as readily as Yorkshire. There was a terrible slump in the region in the 1840s, when every cloth factory in Bradford-on-Avon was closed, following competition from Yorkshire; neighbouring Trowbridge proved to be more resilient, and, like Stroud, saw a limited revival in the cloth industry in the mid nineteenth century. Even Bradford-on-Avon had a small resurgence; the town's most prominent building today is a Gothic cloth factory built beside the river in 1857, now offices, which looks splendid against the backcloth of a steep hillside piled with terraces of earlier stone-built workers' cottages, interspersed with classical

99. **The Parade, Trowbridge, Wiltshire**, where the wealthy clothiers of the town lived in the 18th century. Note the rich details—columns, cornices, stringcourses, quoins, window frames—which are characteristic of early Georgian architecture. The houses are in near-local Bath stone.

clothiers' mansions (98). But this was just one cloth factory, compared with the dozens which dominated Bradford in Yorkshire, originally much smaller than its Wiltshire namesake, but by Victorian times over thirty times as big. The contrast between the two Bradfords, which both, at different times, gained great wealth from the processing of wool, is poignant.

There was another cloth-making region in Devon and western Somerset, which specialized in serges or light draperies. Tiverton was an important centre. On the whole, cloth making in this region declined after its seventeenth-century heyday, but was partly replaced by silk manufacture, and lace-making.

Lace-making was a highly skilled cottage industry which flourished in the seventeenth and eighteenth centuries in certain areas, notably Devon and Dorset, and also Northamptonshire and northern Buckinghamshire. It developed in Nottingham in association with the already established hosiery knitting industry; stocking-frames were adapted to lace-making, and in the 1770s there were great improvements in hand-operated lace machines. A further development was the bobbin-net machine, invented by John Heathcoat of Leicestershire. When he tried to instal some in a new factory at Loughborough in 1816 it was attacked by a mob from Nottingham. He thereupon moved to Tiverton in Devon, where a closed textile factory and unemployed labour were available, although he brought some skilled workers from Loughborough. For the first time, water power was applied to lace-making machinery. The Heathcoat family provided housing and community facilities in the adjoining Tiverton suburb of Westexe, most of it of mid nineteenth century date but handsomely Classical in design (153). The new machinery was soon accepted in the Midlands, and Nottingham developed into the chief lace-making centre of Britain.

Nottingham, Leicester and, to a lesser extent, Derby were centres of stocking knitting—on the hand-operated frames invented in 1589 (page 158). In the later seventeenth and eighteenth centuries, as the industry declined in London, Leicester came to specialize in stockings knitted from worsted yarn; Nottingham in stockings from cotton yarn; and Derby from silk yarn, which provided an incentive for the early silk mill there. The industry was largely controlled by merchants in these towns, who employed hundreds of knitters working at home, often on frames which they hired from the merchants. The workers lived not only in the main towns, but also in dozens of villages and small towns around, where cottages with wide-windowed rooms or lofts for the frames can still be seen. It was some of these framework-knitters who revolted in the original Luddite riots of 1811, which were directed not against new machinery, for none was then being introduced in their industry, but against low wages and long hours, especially when compared with those of the local lace-makers, or the operatives of the new spinning mills. However the name 'Luddite' (from the framework-knitters' leader, Ned Ludd) was soon applied to workers who did revolt against new machinery, as at Huddersfield in 1812 and at Loughborough in 1816, already described. Stocking knitting was finally mechanized, with steam power, in the 1840s.

Metal processing and mineral extraction

In metal manufacture, we associate the Industrial Revolution particularly with the use of coal, or coke, in the processing of iron. The two most important dates are 1709—when Abraham Darby successfully smelted iron with coke—and 1784, when Henry Cort first used coal for the equally important refining process. It was after the second invention that the iron industry really expanded. These two dates correspond remarkably with those of the first water-driven textile mills, and the introduction of steam power in textile manufacture.

Coal became important as an industrial fuel in the late sixteenth and seventeenth centuries, in the production of glass, salt, soap, dyes, sugar, and, in the form of coke, malt, as well as in some stages of metal processing (see Chapter Ten). The most important early sources of coal were Tyneside and Wearside, from which large quantities were shipped to London and elsewhere, mainly for domestic use, but there were also early coal workings in Cumberland, Staffordshire, the Bristol area, the Forest of Dean and South Wales.

Some very important early technological developments took place in South Wales. Works for the production of wire, using water power, local iron ore, charcoal and possibly a little coal were set up by the Government in 1567 at Tintern, close to the recently abandoned abbey. More significantly, at Neath in the 1580s, close to the remains of another abbey, copper was successfully smelted using coke—well over a century before this was done with iron. The copper ore came from Cornwall, where there was little timber and no coal—hence its transportation to Wales where there was plenty of both sorts of fuel (page 112). Copper was used in alloy with zinc—dug from the Mendip Hills in Somerset—to make brass.

Copper and brass production languished in the mid seventeenth century, but revived in the 1690s, when two works were opened in the coalfield east of Bristol, and another at Redbrook on the River Wye above Tintern. In 1699 Abraham Darby, a Quaker who had worked in the malting industry, in which coke was used, came from Birmingham to Bristol. In 1702 he set up a brass foundry just outside the city where he produced 'hollow ware' pots and other utensils; skilled Dutch workers were among the employees. A few years later, Darby moved to Coalbrookdale in Shropshire where he modernized an old furnace and conducted his epoch-making experiment in the use of coke for smelting iron. However, at first, the smelted iron was suitable only for casting objects such as pots and pans, which Darby continued to produce, more cheaply in iron than he had done in brass. His son Abraham improved the smelting techniques to produce metal suitable for wrought iron about 1750. The family's final triumph, that of the third Abraham Darby, was the building of the amazing Iron Bridge across the River Severn in 1778–81.

Despite all the industry on the small Shropshire coalfield, including tile, pottery and (at Coalport) porcelain making as well as iron works, no substantial town developed there. Older small villages like Madeley grew into larger villages; the small market town of Wellington increased a little in status; and Ironbridge never became more than a straggle of buildings on the slopes of the Severn Gorge.

It was not Shropshire which developed into the main iron-processing region of the Midlands, but what we know as the Black Country. There were furnaces and forges in the area in the sixteenth century, using local iron ore. Birmingham (page 112), still a small town, was already noted for nails and cutting tools. Water-driven grinding mills were set up on streams nearby; the name of one, Pebble Mill, is still commemorated. The town supplied the Roundheads with swords.

Coal was used in the late 16th and 17th centuries for re-shaping refined iron into bars and sheets, and in blacksmiths' work. One very important innovation was that of the slitting mill. The first in England was set up at Dartford, Kent, in 1588; many were built in the Stourbridge area, on the edge of the Black Country, after 1620. These mills, driven by water power, slit iron sheets, which had been formed by beating or rolling, into rods, which were shaped, with further heating and processing, into wire or nails. Nailing became a cottage industry in the Black Country, carried out in small one-man forges, often on cottage plots which began as 'squatters' encroachments on the once extensive heaths of the area. Brierley Hill, Gornal, Lye and other towns and districts round Dudley and Stourbridge originated in this way. The nailors, however, were seldom independent; their output was usually controlled by 'nailmasters' who supplied the rods, and marketed the nails—generally in Birmingham.

The first large-scale furnace in the Black Country, using coke according to the methods pioneered at Coalbrookdale, was opened at Bilston by John ('Iron Mad') Wilkinson, who came from Shropshire, in about 1758. The enterprise was extended to include a forge as well, using a steam engine to circulate water for power as early as 1775, and a more advanced engine, from Boulton and Watt, to drive a forge hammer in 1782.

In 1784, Henry Cort, a private contractor to the Royal Navy, invented the 'puddling' method of refining iron with coal in his small forge at Titchfield, not far from Portsmouth. Cort was unlucky; he was cheated by a partner, and treated meanly by the Admiralty; he gained little or nothing personally from his invention. But it was epoch-making. Hitherto iron, even if smelted with coke, still had to go through a complicated series of processes, using charcoal, before it was properly refined, with impurities eliminated. Only iron refined in this way could be processed as wrought iron before Cort's invention. Cort's process not only used coal (not coke) instead of charcoal, but was much simpler than the old method. It enabled wrought iron to be produced in vastly increased quantities, and made possible the huge subsequent developments in the use of iron in construction, machinery and engineering work. Many such developments took place in the Black Country in the late eighteenth and early nineteenth centuries.

Meanwhile Birmingham developed its own distinctive activities, and grew steadily from a small town into the largest city in the Midlands. In the later seventeenth century its range of products extended to toys, trinkets, buckles, buttons and other similar objects to which the term 'Brummagem'—an old popular variant of the name Birmingham—came to be applied. At first these were of iron, but brass was widely used in the eighteenth century. This was brought initially from Bristol. Then, after canal connections were opened, it came from Warrington and other places in the North-West where brassworks developed, using copper from Anglesey. Another local industry, the production of jewellery, which developed from about 1690, was stimulated by colonial expansion. With other 'Brummagem' products, it was taken by the slave-traders from Bristol and Liverpool, and bartered in Africa for cargoes of human beings who were dispatched across the Atlantic (page 178).

These goods were made in small backyard workshops, or in converted rooms in houses. Even new houses were taken and partly converted in this way. By the mid eighteenth century, larger workshops or small factories employing up to about forty people became common. But the most significant development in Birmingham's early industrial history was the establishment and astonishing growth of Matthew Boulton's, later Boulton and Watt's, factory at Handsworth on the town's outskirts, opened in 1761. At first it produced typical Birmingham goods like trinkets and toys, some silver-plated, to a higher standard than was sometimes customary, so raising the reputation of 'Brummagem'. An early steam engine was installed for the circulation of power, and by 1770 about 700 people were employed—making it one of the largest, if not the largest, private centre of employment in the country at the time. The royal dockyards were larger as discussed at the end of this chapter. James Watt, already famous for his successful experiments with steam power, went into partnership with Matthew Boulton, and under an Act of 1777 the firm had virtually a monopoly for producing steam engines for twenty-five years. British industry owed much to this firm's products during the period of monopoly.

Birmingham developed not only as an industrial town, but also as a regional centre for merchanting, finance and services, much as Manchester did in the cotton region. Lloyd's and Taylor's (now Lloyd's) Bank was established there in 1765, and the Midland Bank also has roots in Birmingham. An early eighteenth-century middle-class residential area developed north-west of the original town, including a Square, but this has all vanished, apart from the Baroque church of St Philip (1709–15) by Thomas Archer, now the small but handsome Cathedral. Birmingham became an intellectual centre; the famous Lunar Society, founded in 1766, had as members the industrialists Matthew Boulton and Josiah Wedgwood, whose firm in Staffordshire was already famous for its china; Erasmus Darwin, father of the more famous Charles; and Joseph Priestley, scientist, philosopher and Unitarian preacher. Although based on Birmingham, its meetings were sometimes held in Lichfield, where Darwin lived. The Society ended after a mob viciously attacked Priestley's home and laboratory, and also his chapel.

Birmingham was not the only centre in the region. Walsall and Wolverhampton were ancient market towns which developed distinctive trades—lock-making in Wolverhampton and surrounding villages, notably Willenhall, and saddlery at Walsall. Dudley was an ancient hill-town beside a medieval castle—the seat of the Earls of Dudley, who moved to nearby Himley Hall after a fire in the Castle in 1750. The Dudley family were active early in exploiting their extensive lands; 'Dud' Dudley, bastard son of one of the Earls, almost succeeded in using coke for smelting iron in the seventeenth century. Stourbridge became a major centre of glass-making, using coal, as well as of various branches of metal manufacture. In between the towns were various straggling villages; Wednesbury had forges and mines since Tudor times; Cradley Heath became famous for chains. The iron-works expanded, and with them the mineral workings—although the Black Country was never self-sufficient in iron ore; much of it came from the Forest of Dean.

Birmingham's early development took place despite a land-locked situation, without facilities for water transport. The very important links from Bristol and the Forest of Dean were via the River Severn as far up as the ancient river port of Bewdley, between which and Birmingham goods were transported by road. Major canal building in the region began in 1772 with the Staffordshire & Worcestershire Canal linking with the Severn at the newly-founded canal town of Stourport, just below Bewdley, which henceforth declined. Other canals were built, and by 1777 the Rivers Trent, Mersey and Severn were linked by canal, enabling

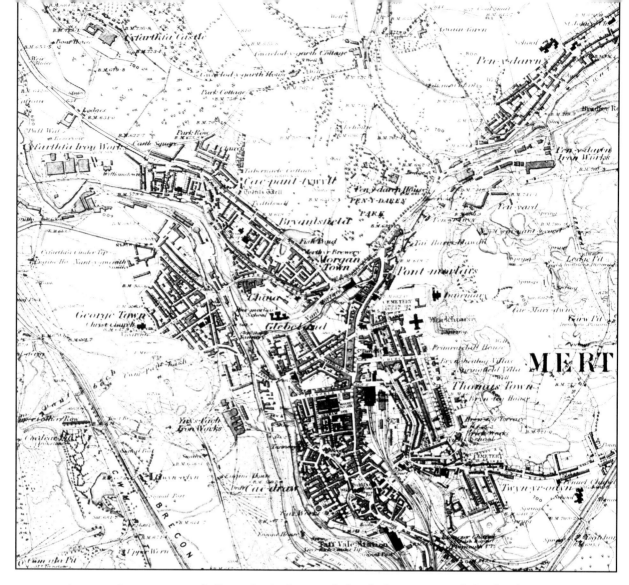

Map XX *Above* **Merthyr Tydfil** developed from a small mountain village. Cyfarthfa Ironworks, top left, started in 1766; the 19th century owners lived in mock-medieval Cyfarthfa Castle to the north. Pen-y-daren Ironworks, top right, dated from 1784; their owners built Pen-y-daren House close by. By c 1870–80, the period of this map, the haphazard groups of early workers' housing had consolidated into a close-built town, surrounded by mountain sides scarred by mines and iron workings.

goods from Birmingham, and the Black Country and the developing Potteries to be exported from Liverpool, or even Hull, as well as from Bristol.

By the end of the eighteenth century the Midland industrial area was 'black by day and red by night'. To the east, and completely separate, was the ancient city of Coventry, with its cloth industry stagnant since Tudor times, but given new life by the watchmaking and silk ribbon industries developed, under immigrant influence, around 1700. Both industries were highly skilled. While the silk weavers worked in lofts above their living rooms, the watchmakers had workshops behind their houses, initiating, or extending, the tradition of backland craft industry in Coventry which was to develop so much further at the beginning of the motor age.

In Wales, copper smelting and brass-making (page 171) developed in the eighteenth century, particularly in the valley above Swansea, which became for a time the largest town in Wales. One notable planned community in the area was Morris-

174

ton, laid out about 1793 by Sir John Morris, a copper magnate, on a grid plan with a central square, with houses graded carefully according to the wage-earning capacity of their occupants. Only the plan remains. (The dominant institutions in Morriston today are of later origin, but quintessentially South Welsh—an elaborate chapel of 1870, called the 'Cathedral of Nonconformity', and the Morriston Orpheus Choir.)

More important to South Wales for a time was the iron industry. There had been small furnaces and forges in remote places in the Taff and other valleys since the sixteenth century; Pontypool, although only a straggling village, became a centre of iron production, and also of 'japanning', or enamelling, in the seventeenth. The first Welsh iron furnace using coke was opened in 1757 at Hirwaun— then a wild spot in the mountains. Big developments began in 1759 with the opening of Dowlais ironworks, followed by others, including that of Cyfarthfa in 1766, all in the mountain parish of Merthyr Tydfil (**XX**)—named after a Celtic princess who was murdered (Merthyr means place of martyrdom), for the sake of the metal and jewels of her ring; a parable if there ever was one. These developments took place because iron ore, coal and wood for charcoal were all available. The first manager of the Dowlais works was John Guest, from Broseley near Coalbrookdale; under his grandson Josiah Guest, who eventually became proprietor, it grew into the biggest iron works in the world. Josiah's literary and aristocratic wife Lady Charlotte became a devotee of Welsh culture, and translated into English the series of Welsh traditional heroic tales which she called the Mabinogion. They lived, at first, characteristically for industrialists of that time, in what was essentially a country house adjoining the factory, with their workers at their gate. Characteristically too, following later practice in a period of change, the Guests moved away from the source of their wealth in 1846, to Canford Manor in Dorset, which they enlarged (to the design of Sir Charles Barry), into a neo-baronial domain. The firm, eventually part of Guest, Keen and Nettlefold, prospered, but its original site, no longer advantageous after it ceased to depend on local mineral resources, has long been abandoned, as have those of nearly all the other early ironworks in South Wales. At nearby Cyfarthfa, the romantic Castle, built in 1825 by the Crawshay family as their domain, has outlasted their ironworks which it overlooked, and is now the local museum.

Merthyr as a whole grew quite haphazardly, though densely, in its mountain setting; some early examples of 'model' housing have disappeared. In the next valley, above Rhymney, is the best surviving piece of early benevolent town-planning in industrial Wales, the village of Butetown (alternatively Trenewydd), built to house the workers in the adjoining ironworks—long since vanished— established in about 1802 by the Marquis of Bute. It has stone houses in severely Classical streets, recently restored. These were quite exceptional for their time; most early Welsh industrial housing was minimal by any standards.

Other iron works in the mountain valleys were established at Sirhowy, now part of Tredegar (1778), Ebbw Vale (1789), Blaenafon (1789), where part of the site is preserved as an industrial museum, and Aberdare (1800). They used the Cort refining processes from the 1780s. Towns grew from hamlets or nothing to house the workers many of whom, to judge from the surnames of their descendants, must have migrated from elsewhere in Wales. Some of these towns were linked to the Glamorgan and Monmouthshire Canals, both opened before 1800, which connected with Cardiff and Newport respectively—though both of these remained small ports until the beginning of the Victorian period.

Sheffield had a fine reputation for cutlery, edge tools and other steel instruments in the sixteenth and seventeenth centuries. 'Steel' meant, in those times, particularly hard refined iron which had gone through a series of rigorous processes to displace all impurities. No doubt the industry had originally developed because of local ore deposits, but these were not of high enough quality, and it soon came to depend on Swedish ore imported through Hull, the River Trent and the inland port of Bawtry—another remarkable example of an early industry which depended, like the cotton industry, on imported raw material. The steel implements were produced in small, individually run forges using charcoal, and sharpened on grindstones driven by water power. In the 1740s two nearly simultaneous inventions led to Sheffield's development as a major industrial town—the crucible method of steel production, using coke, invented by Joseph Huntsman, and the processing of (Old) Sheffield Plate, or silver coating over a base metal, achieved with the aid of water power. The hitherto small moorland-edge town grew very irregularly in the eighteenth century. Nearby Rotherham developed in a different way—the important iron firm of Walker's was founded in 1741.

The history of the iron industry in the North-East goes back to 1685, when Ambrose Crowley, a Quaker nail manufacturer from Stourbridge in the Black Country, set up a nail-making establishment in Sunderland, then a very small, coal-exporting town. He invited craftsmen from Liège in Belgium, then a major centre of nail-making, but it seems that the Catholics from Liège did not settle well with the local people. In 1691 Crowley moved into the country at Winlaton, south-west of Newcastle. Here, adjoining two water mills on the River Derwent, he set up furnaces and forges which produced not only nails of good quality, but also special types of iron goods such as pots, hinges, wheel hubs, hatchets, edge tools and also cannon. The iron ore was imported from Sweden—making the north-eastern location advantageous—but most of the products were sent by sea to London, where Crowley had a warehouse. It is said that Crowley developed successfully the processing of steel, using coke, before Huntsman did in Sheffield. Crowley founded two model settlements near his works, where the workpeople and their families lived according to a socialistic discipline, with welfare services

100. Needlers' Cottages, Hathersage, Derbyshire. Knitting needles were made in the area from the 16th to the 19th centuries—an industry related both to the fine cutlery trade of nearby Sheffield and to stocking knitting around Nottingham and Leicester (page 170). Note the local stone slab roofs carefully graded with the heaviest slabs above the eaves and lightest at the top.

provided—a forerunner of the better-known community established by Robert Owen at New Lanark in Scotland at the end of the eighteenth century. Unfortunately nothing survives of Crowley's establishments at Winlaton. The firm also expanded towards the Tyne west of Gateshead.

Coal extraction around Tyneside and Wearside has a long history, and a great deal was shipped to London. Coal was used increasingly in Tyneside industries from before 1600, especially in glass-making and also salt-boiling (see Chapter Ten). Most of the earliest coal pits were near the rivers or coast, but increasing demand resulted both in deeper excavations (mines rather than pits, though the term 'pit' is still commonly used in the North-East for any coal excavation), and in extraction further from the rivers or coast. The latter led to transport problems, and the earliest 'rail-ways' were simply wooden-railed tracks on which waggons ran, through horse-power or gravity, from pits to quays. Much later, around 1800, iron rails were substituted for wooden ones, and soon after George Stephenson, a Tynesider, carried out his successful experiments in steam locomotion between Killingworth Colliery and a quay on the Tyne. Successful development of steam engines led to the establishment of locomotive works in Newcastle from the 1820s—forerunners of Tyneside's great Victorian expansion in engineering.

Shipbuilding was an important North-Eastern industry through the seventeenth and eighteenth centuries; its mainstay was the building of collier ships which sailed round the often rough eastern coasts to London, and also exported coal to the Continent. The timber came almost entirely from Scandinavia and the Baltic. Sunderland in particular was a thriving wooden shipbuilding town, and so was Whitby further south. The development of steamships is described in Chapter Sixteen.

Newcastle was already one of the largest towns in England in the seventeenth century. The town spread from the riverside, up the steep slopes northward to the more level ground behind the Castle (70). Although its early seventeenth-century merchants' houses are timber-framed, the town's late seventeenth-century and early eighteenth-century expansion was in brick. But Newcastle's architectural heyday began in the late eighteenth century. This resulted not only from the town's own commercial prosperity, but also from enormous eighteenth-century agricultural improvements, and the proliferation of country estates, in Northumberland—hitherto a backward county—of which Newcastle was in effect, whatever its strict legal status, the county town. Excellent local architect-builders, including David Stephenson (no relation of the engineer George Stephenson) and William Newton, designed splendid public buildings in local stone—notably Stephenson's elliptical All Saints' Church with its London-like steeple, and Newton's Assembly Rooms with their delicate plasterwork inside. The local architectural climax came at the very end of the Georgian and the beginning of the Victorian period. Richard Grainger, already a successful speculative builder, in association with the municipal Corporation, promoted what amounted to a new city centre, mostly on vacant land on the northern fringe of the old town. Between 1835 and 1840 he formed two new main streets, of which the lesser, Grainger Street, is straight; the grander, Grey Street, climbs with a magnificent curve (101, 102). The reason for the curve was topographical, but the architects took masterful advantage of the situation, creating a superb series of Classical vistas unfolding on the curve. The projecting portico of the Theatre Royal is at a pivotal point on the inside of the curve, but the climax is the column where Grey and Grainger Streets meet, surmounted by a statue of Earl Grey, a locally based politician then nationally known for his influence in the promotion of the Reform Bill of 1832. Several architects were engaged by Grainger, especially John Dobson—who already had an extensive practice largely in Northumberland country houses—and John and Benjamin Green. Undoubtedly they were influenced by Nash's recently completed Regent Street, but Grey Street is finer than Regent Street ever was. Furthermore it is of stone, not stucco, and it is essentially intact. Other streets leading off Grey and Grainger Streets completed this Classical city centre, which today contrasts both with the ambitious recent redevelopment on one side and with the irregular, basically medieval town around the castle and the quays, dramatized now by a series of bridges.

Gateshead has always been to Newcastle as Southwark is to the City of London. Downstream, North and South Shields developed in the seventeenth century as shipbuilding and maritime towns, and were early victims of industrial pollution. Eighteenth-century visitors said that smoke from coal-burning salt-pans at South Shields put the town under a perpetual cloud.

Coal was mined in Cumberland in the seventeenth century, and iron forged at Workington in 1763. The most striking development in the area during the period was the foundation of Whitehaven. The town was laid out about 1680 by Sir John Lowther, landowner and possessor of abundant coal reserves. With its regular grid of streets, it was the first English example of Renaissance-inspired town-planning outside London. In the early eighteenth century it was the largest coal port after Newcastle and Sunderland, but the momentum of its growth was not maintained, as its mountain hinterland stimulated little general trade.

Ports

The growth of Liverpool was as much a phenomenon as that of Birmingham or Manchester. The small, corporate, medieval town hardly developed till the later seventeenth century. The original quays were by a small tidal inlet; larger ships had at first to anchor in the river itself. The first small dock dated from 1709, the next from 1734; others were built, to increasing capacity, through the eighteenth and early nineteenth centuries. The last great dock built before the steamship era, Albert Dock, of 1841–5, by Jesse Hartley, survives with its superb austere brick warehouses, supported by exposed iron columns on the ground storeys (103). They have been splendidly transformed.

There were many sources for Liverpool's wealth, but the chief was cotton. Raw cotton was first imported into Liverpool mainly from the West Indies, but later what became the Southern United States was the main source. In return, manufactured cotton goods from Lancashire were exported all over the world. After the mid eighteenth century, Liverpool overtook Bristol as Britain's principal transatlantic port, and supplanted it as the leading slave-trading base. The notorious 'triangle' consisted of the export of goods, notably cottons, together with trinkets and similar small wares largely from Birmingham (page 172), to West Africa; the shipping of humans from there to the West Indies and the American mainland; and the return to Britain with sugar, cotton, tobacco, rum, timber, and other cargoes. The slave trade was abolished after long campaigning, notably by William Wilberforce, in 1007. But of course, a great deal of the trade with North America

101. *Left* **Grey Street, Newcastle upon Tyne**, the finest Classical street in England, climbs with a magnificent curve from the old riverside area (**70**), as the centrepiece of an extension to the city centre developed 1835–40, by several local architects. The Theatre Royal with its portico, 1837, is by Benjamin Green.

102. *Below left* **Grey Street, Newcastle upon Tyne**. The street culminates at the Monument to Earl Grey (champion of parliamentary reform), 1838. The block on the left, with its tremendous domed corner (page 218), is by the local architect John Dobson.

from Liverpool and Bristol was always direct, not involving the first two stages of the ghastly 'triangle'.

The oldest buildings in Liverpool today are Georgian, and there are enough of them to give an indication of the size and, in places, splendour of the city in its early heyday. The very fine Town Hall, designed by John Wood of Bath, dates from 1754, but was altered and embellished in the 1780s and 1790s. It closes the view along Castle Street, one of the few streets of the original medieval town, which was widened in 1786, and is now lined with palatial Victorian and early twentieth-century commercial buildings whose glory has faded—a paraphrase of Liverpool's growth and decline. But the Town Hall was eclipsed in splendour by the St George's Hall, begun in 1841 and not completed till many years later—but in its Classical magnificence, Georgian rather than Victorian. It is a combined law court and public hall. Its surroundings have always been confused (though containing many fine later buildings)—since central Liverpool, unlike central Newcastle, was never planned regularly in the Classical manner. More regular, however, were the streets which were built over the higher land to the south-east of the city centre, where, for over a century, merchants, shipowners and bankers lived. Rodney Street, started in the 1780s, is largely intact, as is Abercromby Square, dating from 1815 and now part of the University area; Gambier Terrace, in a bold and hard Classical style, dates from the beginning of the Victorian era and now faces the great modern Gothic Cathedral.

Liverpool benefitted from the growth of the canal system, especially the connections with the industrial Midlands from the 1770s, and with the Pennine area a little later (128). But unlike Bristol and Newcastle, the city did not develop industrially in proportion to its status as a port, although there were numerous sugar refineries, and early glassworks. Glass-making, however, flourished in the hinterland. The Ravenhead plate glassworks was set up in 1773 amid a cluster of straggling villages which developed into the town at St Helens—served by the short Sankey Canal, formed in the 1750s to link with the Mersey at Warrington. The latter town, an ancient trading centre at a crossing of the river, became a nursery for numerous industries including brass-making, nail and wire manufacture, cotton, and, later, soap making. The last industry made use of chemicals derived from the nearby Cheshire salt deposits, which also provided raw materials for the glassworks.

Bristol is unusual among English cities in having been of first importance since early medieval times (see Chapter Eleven). As an international port, it developed steadily through the seventeenth and the first half of the eighteenth centuries. Apart from Spain, Portugal and western France, whose wines had been imported into Bristol for centuries, the port's special connections were transatlantic, particularly with the West Indies. Much Bristol and West of England capital went into the development, from about 1660 onwards, of West Indies plantations, for the production of cotton, tobacco, dyewoods and, most especially, sugar. Bristol interests, like those of other West Country ports, were also involved in the development of the American mainland colonies. Bristol was dominant in the notorious 'triangular' slave trade, already described, in the earlier eighteenth century, but later lost ground to Liverpool. Bristol's own products, including brassware, glass and soap, together with those brought down the Severn from the Midlands, were important exports to the colonies.

Bristol's waterborne connections with other parts of the British Isles were probably as important during this period as its overseas trade. It was a main port for Ireland, from which farm produce came in return for manufactured goods. It continued to have strong connections with South Wales ports, all small before the nineteenth century, such as Tenby, Carmarthen, Swansea and Newport, as well as with Chepstow and the navigable River Wye. It was, even more than before, the focus of a great deal of trade along the Severn, especially with the Midlands,

103. Albert Dock, Liverpool was built 1841–5, at the end of the age of sail and the beginning of that of steam. The warehouses, by Jesse Hartley, have stark classical simplicity; the Doric columns are of iron. 'For sheer punch there is little in the early commercial architecture of Europe to emulate the Albert Dock' (Pevsner; *South Lancashire*). It is now transformed into a museum and leisure complex.

at first via Bewdley and then through the canal port of Stourport.

Bristol declined relatively, even perhaps absolutely for a time, as a port from the late eighteenth century. This was partly because of Liverpool's new dominance in the transatlantic trade, partly because the Midlands were becoming much more orientated towards the Mersey, via the canals, and partly because of the inadequacies of Bristol itself as a port. The approach along the winding tidal Gorge was increasingly a disadvantage as ships became bigger. The main quays adjoined the River Avon and, more especially, its tributary the Frome in the heart of the city. From about 1660 they were under the control of the local Society of Merchant Venturers, who opened a small and not entirely satisfactory dock in 1775, and from time to time extended the other facilities. Drastic improvements came in 1804–9, when a new tidal channel was cut to take the main waters of the Avon through the city, and the old course of the river was turned into a non-tidal Floating Harbour (**69**). But the facilities were still not adequate, and Liverpool, London and, later, the Welsh ports provided overwhelming competition, as ships became still larger and more elaborate. But Bristol continued to flourish during this period as an industrial and commercial centre, a regional capital, and, in its suburb of Clifton, a fashionable resort (page 156).

In architecture and town-planning, Bristol illustrates clearly the change from lingering medieval to Renaissance traditions in the seventeenth century. King Street was laid out in the 1660s outside the city wall, and was built up over the next twenty years, in the medieval tradition (**104**, **105**). The street is gently sinuous; the original houses, of which several survive, have timber-framed jettied and gabled fronts. Yet, just to the south, Queen Square, started in 1699, is in the then established London tradition, with brick classical merchants' houses, of which some early examples remain, surrounding a large, genuinely square, green space. Other eighteenth-century streets and squares were built, first on the flat ground to the east where Portland Square substantially remains, dominated by St Paul's Church with its odd tall steeple, then up the steep slopes north and north-west, until, from the 1780s, they spread dramatically over the heights and hollows of Clifton, already described. But many Bristol merchants had villas or even country houses in surrounding villages like Stapleton, Frenchay and Henbury, all of which keep something of their Georgian character. Many of the merchant families were Quakers—the Quaker influence was probably instrumental in the virtual ending of Bristol participation in the slave trade before it was officially abolished. A particularly successful Quaker family were the Harfords, merchants, industrialists and bankers. They lived in a fairly modest country house, Blaise Castle at Henbury, round which they developed a romantic park. In 1811, they commissioned John Nash to design Blaise Hamlet, the famous group of retired estate workers' cottages, in romantically exaggerated 'vernacular' styles, round a miniature green. The Harfords had interests in South Wales, both in the Swansea area and in the iron industry at Ebbw Vale.

Very important to south-western England was the Newfoundland fishery, which dated back to the sixteenth century (page 115). At first ships sailed out from England in spring; the crew stayed in Newfoundland over the summer to make their catches, and returned in autumn with dried fish—often via Spain and Portugal, where there was great demand for fish. They would then return to England with wine or other imports. Many western ports participated; Dartmouth at first had the largest role, but in the eighteenth century the Newfoundland trade was centred on Poole. By this time the island was permanently settled, and Poole merchants thrived in supplying the colonists with their needs, including, notably, nets from nearby Bridport, as well as collecting and distributing the dried fish. Many a Dorset labourer, displaced by agricultural improvements or by the decline in local textile industries, is said to have found his way to Poole-based ships sailing to and from Newfoundland. Several brick eighteenth-century mansions of merchants concerned in the Newfoundland trade survive in Poole, but the tall, late eighteenth-century brick warehouses by the Quay are probably more closely associated with the coasting trade—a reminder how important coastal shipping, carrying great varieties of goods including agricultural produce, fuel, and factory products was all round Britain until the age of the railway.

Plymouth continued to flourish as a civilian port in a fairly modest way (**106**), but its later large-scale development was due more to the establishment of the dockyard at nearby Devonport.

104. *Left* **King Street, Bristol** was laid out in the mid 17th century (page 56); some early gabled, timbered houses survive. The Coopers' Hall, left, with a grand Classical facade of stone, 1746, indicates the city's long-standing fame for its imported wines (coopers are barrel-makers). The Hall has been converted as the foyer to the Georgian Theatre Royal behind.

105. *Below* **King Street, Bristol**, further east than **104**. At the end is the old course of the River Avon (**69**); the open quayside (Welsh Back) was where trows, or small vessels, landed goods from Wales. Across the river is the 15th century tower of St Thomas's Church.

106. Sutton Pool, Plymouth.
Medieval Plymouth (page 115)
developed round this inlet,
which remains a centre of
small-scale commercial trade—
the great naval dockyard at
Devonport is well to the west.
The Customs House, 1810, by
David Laing, is typical public
architecture of the time.

The naval dockyards were very special and very important in the days of sail. In the sixteenth and early seventeenth centuries the main yards were on the Thames at Deptford and Woolwich. The River Medway was first used as a permanent naval anchorage in the sixteenth century, and Chatham dockyard was established by the 1580s. It grew fairly extensively in the seventeenth century, and greatly in the eighteenth; it still retains an impressive series of Georgian buildings. A dockyard was a comprehensive industrial and servicing establishment which included not only quays or docks, but storehouses, workshops, and, usually, facilities for building ships. Naval equipment, particularly ropes, was manufactured in dockyards. Naval rope houses needed to be extremely long; that at Chatham, built in 1785, extends to over a thousand feet. But probably the most impressive buildings at Chatham date from the end of the age of sail, and the beginning of that of steam—the great Slip of 1837, with its huge timber-roofed shed, and the even bigger Ship Shop of 1847, framed in iron, a pioneer in this form of construction. It had a counterpart at Portsmouth, which was destroyed a few years ago.

For reasons of 'security' dockyards had to be walled off. Only a few senior civilian officials, as well as some naval officers, lived inside; workers lived in the adjoining towns. Ships in port, with their personnel, were often anchored in the river or harbour outside the yard, or in the case of Portsmouth in the Solent, when not being serviced or repaired.

Chatham town grew haphazardly from a village, linked from the start with the ancient city of Rochester. Devonport Dockyard, as it came later to be known, was founded in 1691, three miles from the established town of Plymouth. Devonport, originally known simply as Dock, grew into a town of its own right, reaching an architectural climax such as Chatham never attained. In 1821–4 John Foulston, a Plymouth-based architect of the Classical tradition, designed a stately town centre of which a great column, a Doric Guildhall, and an odd neo-Egyptian former library, remain, almost lost in a post-war urban desert.

At Portsmouth the Dockyard, which started in a very small way in 1485, did not really develop until the Restoration. As in other dockyards, the oldest extant buildings date from the eighteenth century, and are of local red brick—in Devonport their counterparts are of stone and granite. They include Classical storehouses and another long former rope house of 1770, (replacing an earlier one), which must have been among the largest industrial buildings in the country when first built. *H.M.S. Victory*, built at Chatham in 1759–65, and altered, also at Chatham, in 1803, is berthed in a stone dock of 1802, one of a group mainly of the same period. We can see here, as nowhere else, how the dockyards looked in the heyday of wooden ships, with their hulls and rigging set against austere and dignified storehouses, and solid stone-lined docksides. The Dockyard also retains some superb buildings from the early days of steam.

Portsmouth is also interesting for its defences. With Berwick-on-Tweed and, partially, Hull (**XVII**, p. 119), it was the only town in England fully fortified according to the post-medieval Continental practice. Solid stone medieval walls became obsolete with advances in the use of cannon in the sixteenth century (see Chapter Nine). The new pattern was one of broad earthen ramparts, faced in stone, with polygonal bastions, where guns were mounted to cover comprehensively every possible direction of attack, all set behind complicated ditches or moats. Sir Edward Lee designed defences of this type to replace the medieval walls of Berwick-on-Tweed in 1558; they were never quite completed but survive as far as they were built. Lee had previously designed similar defences round the town of (Old) Portsmouth, which stood on the eastern side of the entrance to the harbour, with the Dockyard well to the north. The Portsmouth defences were completely remodelled from 1663 under Sir Bernard de Gomme, according to the latest practice on the Continent at that time. These, altered and extended in the eighteenth century, were largely obliterated in the 1870s, but a section along the waterfront remains, together with some more conventional stone defences. On the Continent, with its repetitious international conflicts, almost every town of any consequence had to be protected in this way if it was to avoid the possibility of being ravaged either in actual conflict, or in the wake of an advancing army. In Britain there was no such necessity, at least after the union with Scotland, except at a place such as Portsmouth, vitally strategic and vulnerable from the sea. This was an important reason why British towns as a whole were able to spread loosely during the eighteenth and nineteenth centuries, while so many Continental ones were still constrained by their ramparts.

15
Georgian Country and County Towns

The last chapter considered the cities and towns which grew substantially through industry and trade. What of the other towns and cities in the Georgian era? There were great changes in the countryside during the period, resulting from many causes. The medieval communal open fields which remained in many parts of the country (see Chapter Three) were enclosed and replaced by farms with hedged fields. Marshy areas were drained, most notably in the Fens. There were general improvements in agricultural practices, stimulated by increasing demands for food from the growing industrial towns. Large country estates were formed and old ones improved and expanded, often with money made in industry or commerce. Many small-scale, locally-based crafts and trades prospered although others declined due to competing industries using new techniques. Transport facilities were extended—river navigation was improved; canals were built; long-distance road communications were steadily improved through privately financed turnpike trusts, resulting, at the beginning of the railway age, in a splendid network of highways suitable for fast coaches and heavy goods waggons. All this brought prosperity to the country towns.

Outside the fast-growing industrial towns, ports and resorts, there were two main categories of town, distinguished by their scale—'county' towns and smaller market towns. 'County' towns were usually, but not always, judicial and administrative centres, with public buildings of suitable scale, and high proportions of professional people and 'gentry' with private means. Smaller market towns were, as in the Middle Ages, the centres of trade in their local areas. Their number probably decreased after medieval times as local trade was concentrated into fewer centres, and many declined to the status of villages. Very few new marketing

107. Corn Mill, Wickham Market, Suffolk. Every town or village where there was water to harness had at least one mill for grinding corn. Later, such mills might be put to other industrial uses (pages 108, 112).

centres were established during the seventeenth and eighteenth centuries outside the developing industrial regions.

All prosperous market towns had flourishing crafts and industries which depended on local supplies and demands, notably corn milling (107, 108) and tanning. A few were engaged in industries of wider significance—extreme examples were textile towns like Trowbridge and Tiverton, or places with almost unique crafts like net-making at Bridport. Many towns prospered from passing trade—from turnpike roads, navigable rivers and canals, or coastal shipping. Some became appendages to great country houses, like Woodstock at the gates of Blenheim Palace, Kimbolton (18), and Woburn. Even quite small market towns sometimes had a significant number of inhabitants with private means—retired military or naval officers (118) and professional people; property owners; large-scale shareholders in industry; or relatives of landed gentry—whose houses were often indistinguishable from those of prosperous tradesmen, or practising lawyers and doctors.

108. Tide Mill, Woodbridge, Suffolk. Tide mills might provide greater, though more intermittent, grinding power than ordinary water mills. The incoming tide was harnessed in a pond, and the controlled outward flow drove the wheels. They were common on East Anglian creeks and around the Solent. Like many mills on the east side of England, this is timber-built and faced with weatherboarding—probably of softwood imported from the Baltic or Scandinavia.

Many of the more prosperous market towns were substantially rebuilt, or at least refronted, during the period. Hardwood timber-framing (page 51) generally ceased to be the basis for house-building during the seventeenth century, as timber became scarcer, due to demands from shipbuilding and industry, and the advances of agriculture. It remained plentiful for longer on the western side of England, north of Bristol, than in East Anglia. Softwood, or deal, imported from the Baltic and Scandinavia, came into common use for roofs and internal work, and was the main material in timber-framed building in some parts of the East and South-East, where this form of construction continued in some measure throughout the Georgian period (108). Otherwise, brick or stone became the main materials for house building from the mid to late seventeenth century onwards—earlier in some areas. Bricks were nearly always made locally, since most parts of lowland Britain had clay deposits suitable for brickmaking. Stone was preferred where it was easy and cheaper to obtain—varying in quality from the fine limestones of the Cotswold range and its continuations to the coarse rubble of some mountain areas, often rendered, or flints from the chalk downs (see Chapter Five, pp. 53–56).

The abandonment of timber-framing in favour of brick and stone broadly corresponded with the demise of the Gothic tradition and acceptance, almost universally, of Classical principles of architecture. The familiar 'Georgian house' originated well back in the seventeenth century, and evolved, with slow changes in stylistic fashion, right into the mid nineteenth century. The history of metropolitan-scale Georgian town-planning, where individual houses were usually parts of larger compositions—terraces, squares or crescents—has been covered in Chapter Thirteen. In country towns, by contrast, 'Georgian' houses were usually built singly or in small groups. They were often on the sites of older houses, so that they

109. *Right* **Unitarian Chapel, Framlingham, Suffolk**, 1717, a rare survival of an early Nonconformist chapel—simple, austere and soundly built. The chequer pattern of grey header bricks is an early example of this practice. See also **14, 95**.

110. *Opposite* **Windmill, Cranbrook, Kent**. Windmills were common by the 18th century; few remain recognizably intact. That at Cranbrook, like much of the town, is weather-boarded—this, like tile-hanging, was a common form of external cladding in the Weald of Kent.

111. Kirkbymoorside, on the foothills of the North Yorkshire Moors, has buildings in the sturdy vernacular Classical tradition of the North (**37, 38**). Some are in the light grey local stone, others in brick; many are roofed in red pantiles—which are, perhaps surprisingly, characteristic of this part of Yorkshire.

fitted into established streets, often with no special attempt at conformity with their neighbours. They were mostly built by local builders or craftsmen, sometimes self-styled architects, who might have worked with major architects on neighbouring country estates. They followed national trends, often belatedly, sometimes very individualistically, and, especially in the middle part of the eighteenth century, they were influenced by the widely circulating builders' pattern books (page 138). Because bricks were almost always locally produced, each area had its own distinctive colours and textures. Hampshire and the middle Thames valley produced bricks of deep red colour, often used in conjunction with others which were grey. In the Yorkshire plains the bricks were often of a lighter yellowish red. In some places, where there were varied types of clay deposits in close proximity, bricks of many different textures are seen together—a walk through the largely Georgian and early Victorian town of Newport in the Isle of Wight reveals an astonishing variety of colours in brickwork, as well as local stones, all from the island. National trends influenced the colour of bricks, especially in the East and South-East; after about 1800 buff or yellowish bricks were generally more fashionable than red bricks. Buff bricks, miscalled 'white', became specially characteristic of East Anglia in late Georgian times.

190

The tradition of carving in brick cornices, stringcourses, window frames and doorcases, using Classical motifs, developed, especially in eastern and south-eastern England, in the seventeenth century (**34, 75**), and continued, under Baroque influence, into the eighteenth. Examples are found in many country towns, like Chichester, Beverley, Farnham, Baldock, Godalming and elsewhere. Later, as national trends led to Georgian houses being generally simpler outside, interest came to be concentrated more on doorcases, with varied versions of Classical elements (**28**). Iron work was important; some grander early Georgian town houses were set back behind the street frontage where there was a display of wrought ironwork in railings and gates (**124**). Pallant House in Chichester, of about 1712, is an admirable example. Later in the period, iron balconies were sometimes the most decorative features of façades.

Tile-hanging—the cladding in tiles of houses which might be timber-framed, or of rough rubble or flint—was a flourishing tradition in much of Kent, Sussex and Surrey, especially in the eighteenth century. It was also common in certain Wiltshire towns, notably Salisbury and Marlborough. Normally the tiles would be hung to give an overlapping effect (**50**), but often they were specially shaped, and laid, so as to give the deceptive appearance of a brick wall—this is known as 'mathematical tiling'. Lewes has many examples (**112**); they sometimes curve round wall surfaces above and below bow windows, in ways which would be impossible with bricks. Slate-hanging was a related practice in the south-west (**63**).

While the Gothic tradition lingered, into the Jacobean period and in some places later, windows were characteristically wide and mullioned, framed in timber, stone or brick, the glazing being in small leaded panes. When the Renaissance tradition was firmly established, windows assumed Classical forms, with greater height than width, and were at first internally divided with mullions and transoms. Sash windows became the rule after about 1700 (**75**), and replaced earlier window forms. At the same time, panes were made in larger units, framed with the wooden glazing bars so characteristic of Georgian buildings, which are important in setting the proportions of overall designs. However, in smaller houses and cottages, windows often continued to be casements rather than sashes, set in horizontal, usually wood-framed, ranges.

Projecting windows—bows, bays or, in earlier periods, oriels—have a long history. In Jacobean times, substantial houses often had flat-fronted projections containing mullioned windows in wood, stone or brick, with right-angled or, more usually, diagonal ends. They were either on single floors, when they were called oriels (**25**), or in ranges running up through two or more floors. Such windows went out of favour with the onset of Classicism, but a few late seventeenth- or early eighteenth-century houses, built under Baroque influence, had bow windows of more classical proportions. Bay, or bow, windows steadily came into fashion from the mid eighteenth century—though not generally in London itself, where they were ruled out by the Building Acts unless solidly constructed as parts of the brick façades (page 137). They were however common in suburban towns and villages like Richmond or Hampstead, and, above all, in seaside resorts. Bow windows had practical advantages; they increased floor areas slightly, and greatly widened the range of vision from within—this was important on sea or river fronts or, more especially, on streets leading back from waterfronts. They

112. House at Lewes, Sussex, early 19th century, is faced in mathematical tiles arranged to look like brick, on a backing of flint, rubble or timber. They are glazed grey-black, like many bricks and tiles of this period in Lewes and Brighton (page 152). In the slit to the left of the house there is a glimpse of Lewes Castle. (See also **26, 28**).

also increased the interest and often the apparent scale of exteriors. The most typical bow windows were rounded—anything from semi-circles to shallow segments—but many were flat-fronted, with diagonal sides. They were sometimes on single floors, usually first floors since bows on ground floors might encroach on to public streets, but often ranged continuously upwards through several storeys. There were distinct local traditions. In Southampton for instance—a notable resort up to Victorian times— some of the late Georgian bows are almost semicircular, as on the Dolphin Hotel and in Bernard Street. Yet in Portsmouth, only a few miles away, the tradition was quite different; they were delicate and shallow, typically consisting of three sash windows, each following the curve, separated by wooden mullions under delicately carved cornices. In Ryde on the Isle of Wight, a resort which developed from the 1820s, the bow windows generally followed the bolder Southampton tradition rather than the more decorous examples in Portsmouth. No doubt other local comparisons can be made between nearby towns. In Brighton, whole façades were folded out (88); here the traditions were complementary to, rather than contrasting with, those of neighbouring Lewes. In Brighton and in other resorts like Ramsgate and Cheltenham, graceful iron balconies often curved round the bows (88).

Some towns stood on borderline sites for local materials—there might be nearby sources both of good stone and good clay for making bricks (pages 120, 121). In Devizes some of the many fine Georgian buildings are of Bath stone from a few miles away; others are of local red brick, though often with stone dressings. In nearby Westbury, there is the same variety round the market place, and the town's late Georgian cloth mills are of brick with stone-framed windows. Yet Trowbridge, Frome and Warminster, not far away in different directions, are almost wholly stone-built. Georgian Reading—of which a good deal survives, even though it has to be sought out—was at first very much a brick town, in deep

113. Painswick, Gloucestershire was a small but rich Cotswold weaving town. Pre-Classical houses, with mullioned windows, are mixed with others in vigorous vernacular Baroque styles. The splendid churchyard, in the foreground, has tombstones in the same vernacular tradition.

114. Abbeygate Street, Bury St Edmunds was a prosperous shopping street in a Georgian county town (page 207). This 18th century shop front is unusual for its playful Gothic details. (See also 42, 43).

red sometimes interspersed with grey, with a few earlier timber-framed survivors. But when the Kennet and Avon Canal opened in 1810, linking the town with Bath, Bath stone suddenly became easily obtainable, and most of the late Georgian terraces and early Victorian villas in the town are of that material. Later in Victorian times brick came very much into its own again in Reading.

A typical country town street at the end of the Georgian period would have buildings varied in date, style, scale, height, details and, often, materials, the result of a long period of piecemeal change. The unifying factor is the continuity of the street frontage, in terms of time and form (9, 50, 65). Established street patterns, usually of medieval origin, were seldom substantially modified in Stuart or Georgian times, even if all the houses were altered or rebuilt. A surprisingly large number of houses in old country towns were repeatedly altered, over long periods, and not completely rebuilt at any one time. We have seen how medieval hall houses were often subdivided in Tudor times, with new internal floors and fireplaces. New windows would be inserted as glass became cheaper, and in Georgian times sashes would replace older casements. Very often, entirely new Georgian façades, in brick or stone or, later in the period, with stucco facing, would be added to older, timber-framed buildings, the true age of which now becomes apparent only inside or at the back. Gardens or yards behind houses would often become encroached on (36).

A type of building particularly characteristic of the Georgian period was the coaching inn. Before the eighteenth century, overland travel was slow and cumbersome; people travelled on horseback or foot; goods were carried by packhorse or cart. Halts for refreshment, as well as overnight stops, had to be close together and frequent, and many towns on important routes benefitted disproportionately from what in modern times would seem to be very small amounts of traffic (see Chapter Four). With steady improvements in the quality and speed of coaches,

115. Martock, Somerset is a town-sized village, given urban character by the market house, c 1753, with traditional open ground storey, and adjoining column. Like neighbouring Yeovil, Martock is a centre of glove making (page 236); other industries included canvas manufacture.

and in the reliability of roads financed by turnpike trusts, the conditions of long-distance travel became very different. Overnight stops came to be further and further apart. In the early eighteenth century, travellers on the Great North Road out of London might spend the night in Stevenage or Baldock; later in the century it might be Biggleswade or Buckden; later still Stamford. Coaching inns for overnight stays would be built or rebuilt at different times in such places along the main roads (120). But horses had to be changed frequently, so there would also be numerous intermediate staging inns with large stables, where this could be done. The Georgian or older coaching inn is still familiar, with its broad archway leading into a courtyard. Sometimes, there is older fabric behind later façade, as at the George Hotel in Huntingdon, with its partly seventeenth-century galleried courtyard, behind a Victorian frontage.

Markets were still very important in the eighteenth century, although fairs had become far less significant commercially, surviving mainly as festive occasions. Shops became more numerous; the typical Georgian shop front, with its paned windows, often bowed (9), is still fairly familiar (and too often badly imitated). Many market or town halls of the traditional type—with open sided ground storeys and upper rooms, which were often the meeting places of town councils (see Chapter Eight) were built or rebuilt. Two late seventeenth-century examples are particularly fine. That at Abingdon (1678–82) is of Cotswold stone, by a Burford mason, Christopher Kempster, who worked with Wren (116); that at Windsor (1687–90) is also associated with Wren, who supervised its building after the death of its architect, Sir Thomas Finch; here the ground floor supports are straightforward columns, not arches, as at Abingdon. There are many, much more modest, Georgian market or town halls in the middle of market places or wide streets; examples are at Reigate, Amersham, Martock (115), Bridport (6) and Yarm (122). At High Wycombe there is both a handsome Guildhall of 1757 with open-arched ground storey, and single-storeyed market hall, also open-arched; the stalls on market days still extend under both buildings and out into the adjoining streets. On a larger scale, the Classical Town Hall of 1776, by John Carr of York, in the splendid market place at Newark was exceptional for so small a town, as was the Mansion House at Doncaster of 1748, by the equally distinguished James Paine—Doncaster was small when it was built. Less surprising, because of the importance of the city, is the Mansion House at York, built in 1727 in front of the medieval Guildhall. Only York and Doncaster, besides London, had Mansion Houses before modern times.

Usually on a grander scale than the Town Halls or Guildhalls were the Shire Halls in the county towns. Here the Judges came, normally twice a year, to preside over the Assizes—the High Court of the land held locally—and here the Justices of the Peace of the county met, usually quarterly, to hold their Quarter Sessions where less serious cases were heard, and other county business transacted. Normally each county would have a single county town where both the Assizes and Quarter Sessions would be held, but there were variations. Sussex had four traditional assize towns, (even though Lewes was the official county town), and Surrey had three, to which the Judges might come. In some counties the Quarter Sessions were held at different towns in succession. Where there was an undoubted centre, fine county buildings might be provided. At Chelmsford, the Shire Hall of 1791 is, apart from the nearby parish church, now cathedral, the finest building in

116. Abingdon Town Hall,
c 1680, an unusually handsome
example of its type, with open
arched ground floor and public
hall above. For a time it was a
county court house for
Berkshire, of which Abingdon
had some claim to be the
county town—but the town is
now in Oxfordshire.

the town (although it does not have much competition). At Stafford, the Shire
Hall of 1799 is of great dignity, dominating the small market place as if it were
an Italian *piazza*. At Montgomery, the Town Hall of 1748, enlarged in 1828 to
accommodate the Quarter Sessions and the Assizes for the county, dominates the
centre of the regularly planned but diminutive town, giving it urban scale and
dignity. Often the Castle continued, from the Middle Ages, to be the judicial centre.
At Exeter, the Assize Court of 1774 is set in the medieval castle bailey. At York,
the Castle was virtually rebuilt in stages in the eighteenth century, with three
grand buildings round a formal courtyard; John Carr's Assize Court is on one
side, while the other two blocks—now the famous Castle Museum—were prisons,
appropriately near the courts. The most magnificent of all county buildings is
Chester Castle, rebuilt, except for a small tower, between 1785 and 1822, to the
design of Thomas Harrison, who, after Sir John Soane, was the finest English Neo-
Classical architect (**117**). It is set round a big three-sided courtyard, entered

197

117. **Chester Castle** was rebuilt 1788–1828 by locally based Thomas Harrison, one of the best Neo-Classical architects (page 150). On the right is the gateway, or *propylea*; in the background the portico to the Assize Court, now Crown Court. Nearby were barracks and a prison (now demolished). This is the finest group of county judicial buildings in England. Only a small tower and chapel of the important medieval castle survive.

through an unerringly Greek *propylea*, with the Doric portico of the Assize Court as the centrepiece. Harrison also designed the Grosvenor Bridge nearby (completed after his death), which crosses the River Dee in a single, beautiful span.

Three towns of special Georgian character are Fareham, Blandford and Wisbech. Fareham, in Hampshire, was a medieval borough established by the Bishop of Winchester (page 72), as an extension to an earlier village, but it never achieved corporate borough status till modern times. The original village was round the church, vestigially Saxon; the High Street descends south, widening and slightly curving; an island block of buildings at its southern end represents an encroachment on the original market area. Fareham was one of several small medieval market towns in the area, but by the eighteenth century became dominant because of its advantageous position on a navigable creek of Portsmouth Harbour—an outlet for local produce to be sent to the nearby Dockyard. It was a noted brick-making centre—this industry reached its peak in the nineteenth century when 'Fareham Reds' were distributed widely (the Albert Hall is built of them). The town also had a large middle-class population—mostly naval officers, active or retired, or their relatives, due to the nearness of the Dockyard. The High Street retains a splendid series of Georgian town houses, particularly on the east side (**118**), with large long gardens extending back, related to medieval burgage plots. They are mainly of the local deep red brick, often in combination with grey, and there is a splendid range of doorcases. Some of the later houses are faced in buff brick—even in Fareham this colour became fashionable after about 1800. However, there was not a complete rebuilding of the street during the town's Georgian heyday. Some older two-storeyed timber-framed houses of the sixteenth or early seventeenth century survive, many of them refaced in eighteenth-century brick. Also, the street retains a number of small Georgian shop fronts in the ground floors of the humbler buildings—indicating that, typically for a country town, small tradesmen's premises were informally interspersed with fine patrician houses. It is not fanciful to say that this street would be readily recognizable by

Jane Austen, who must have driven through it when travelling from her home at Chawton, twenty miles or so to the north up the turnpike road, to Gosport, where for a time her uncle, a naval officer, was stationed. Fareham is now a growing and much modernised town; its old High Street remains in such remarkable preservation simply because, since Victorian times, the town's centre of gravity has moved westwards, away from the original main street.

Blandford Forum in Dorset was a medieval market town, almost completely destroyed by fire in 1731—a fate that afflicted many towns during the period (page 58). Blandford was already prosperous, as the focal point for an area with many estates, where a great deal of agricultural improvement was being carried out. It was quickly and handsomely rebuilt, largely under the direction of a family of local builder-architects, Thomas, John and William Bastard, who had already worked on some of the nearby country houses. The Bastards rebuilt the destroyed

118. Fareham, Hampshire. First developed by the medieval Bishops of Winchester (page 72) was prosperous in the 18th century as a market town and residence of Naval officers connected with Portsmouth. The house, right, 1766, has bold Georgian bows in Fareham Red brick which became well-known in the 19th century—it was used for the Albert Hall. Some older timber-framed houses remain.

119. Union Place, Wisbech, Cambridgeshire. This formal crescent, built on the site of the medieval castle by a London builder, c 1816, is unusual for a small country town. It contrasts with the splendid earlier Georgian houses, individually designed, facing the nearby Brinks, or river banks.

church and Town Hall handsomely in stone, and other buildings in brick—dark red with grey facings, in a country Baroque style which brings unusual grandeur to such a small town. The buildings were designed individually, so there was consistent variety rather than uniformity, as there was in the City of London after it was rebuilt after the Great Fire. The medieval town plan seems to have been retained largely intact, with long burgage plots which end by the banks of the River Stour (V, p. 40)—although an island block of buildings which had encroached on the wide main street was not rebuilt.

Wisbech benefitted from the drainage of the Fens. It was a small medieval town on a dry 'beach' beside a tidal river, which became silted. The huge Fenland drainage scheme of the seventeenth century gave it a rich agricultural hinterland, and river improvements in the eighteenth century made it a port again. The town

developed down-river with big bankside warehouses, some of which remain, and up-river with lines of substantial Georgian houses, mostly in local yellow-buff brick, following the curve of the river above its steep, grassy and essentially man-made banks. These riverside houses make no formal composition but are individually different, built piecemeal as if along a wide street, with water instead of a carriageway—the finest is Peckover House (1724), the home of a Quaker merchant and now owned by the National Trust. In interesting contrast is an area developed round the site of the castle from about 1810, with an oval of modest three-storey houses which might be on the fringes of Regency London—the developer was a builder from Bermondsey. This is a rare example of small-scale formal planning in a country town (119).

Two towns described in Chapter Six, Ashbourne, and Stony Stratford are inter-

120. The Cock and Bull, Stony Stratford, Bucks. Two coaching inns on Watling Street, one of the busiest roads in England before the railway age (pages 42, 65). Both were probably built after a fire which destroyed part of the town in 1742. The term 'cock and bull story' is claimed to have originated here.

121. **House in High Street, Stony Stratford**, built of local stone, in contrast to the brick of the nearby inns (**120**)—this is a 'borderline' town (pages 56, 193). The elaborate doorcase is typically early 18th century, but the wooden cornice would not have been permitted at that time in London because of the Building Acts (page 137).

esting for their partial Georgian rebuilding. Both are 'borderline' towns in terms of building materials. Some of Ashbourne's fine Georgian houses—many of which were occupied by local gentry—are faced in local brown sandstone, others in brick, sometimes with stone dressings. Around the market place, many of the back plots were infilled densely with outbuildings or cottages (**XII**, p.68). Much of Stoney Stratford was destroyed by fire in 1742, and two adjacent coaching inns, the Cock and the Bull, were rebuilt soon after; they are fine examples of their type (**120**). The local tradition is that the term 'cock and bull story' originated here. They are still hotels, serving the new city of Milton Keynes of which Stony Stratford is now the historic quarter. They, and other buildings nearby, are of brick, but much of the town is of fairly coarse near-local limestone (**121**).

Stockton-on-Tees and Yarm are old river ports. Yarm is in a bend of the tidal Tees, with a wide main street leading south from a medieval bridge. The dominant character is of the early Georgian period, when Yarm's prosperity as a port was greatest; the small market hall in the middle dates from 1710 (**122, 123**). But the town's form is medieval; long burgage plots extend behind the buildings on either side, those on the east originally ending by the river bank, where brick granaries were built in the late seventeenth and eighteenth centuries—for corn was exported from the fertile Tees valley, coastwise and perhaps occasionally overseas (**XXI**). Stockton is also of medieval origin; the very wide, long High Street was probably laid out by a medieval Bishop of Durham who had a palace here, now vanished. Again, there were burgage plots extending back, on one side, to the river—Stockton flourished at Yarm's expense in the later eighteenth century, as it was lower down the very winding river, and the building of a bridge at Stockton hindered traffic up to Yarm. The town has lost much of the battered Georgian character it retained until recently, due to redevelopment, but markets are still held in the wide street, and the dominant building is the country-town Town Hall of 1736, typically set in the middle of the street. Stockton—so much an agricultural transit town by tradition—became famous as the terminus of the railway built in 1825 to carry coal from the West Durham coalfield to the quays there (see Chapter Sixteen). But its important early role in the industrial economy of Britain was short-lived; a few years later the line was extended to the more convenient site of Middlesbrough where a new port and town were founded.

Among the towns of Georgian England, the cathedral cities had a particularly distinctive flavour. This sprang directly from the fact that the Church of England

122. Yarm, Cleveland, Yorkshire was a small port on the River Tees with maritime trade, prosperous till Stockton overtook it; the tall brick early Georgian houses give it a regular, urban character; the small Town Hall, with cupola, dates from 1710. (The name Cleveland traditionally applied to all north-east Yorkshire; the modern county is smaller.)

Map XXI Yarm. This late 19th century map (confined to Yorkshire, leaving out County Durham across the Tees) shows the medieval ground plan preserved in the largely Georgian town (**122**)—the broadening street, accommodating a market; the long plots, closely built on the frontages, mostly open behind; the lanes, or wynds, leading to the river on the east. Church Wynd (**123**) is the single built-up lane leading west, towards the riverside church. The railway, on a viaduct, overrides it all.

123. Church Wynd, Yarm, contrasts in scale with the urbane main street. Some of the 18th century cottages are roofed in pantiles (**111**), and the lane is still paved with stone setts.

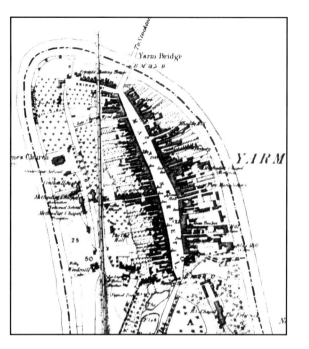

124. House in the Close, Salisbury. Some medieval houses in the Close were altered, others, like this, rebuilt, in the 18th century (**46, 47**). The facade is of Chilmark stone, like the Cathedral; the iron gates and railings are typical of the frontages to Georgian town houses which are set behind front gardens (page 191).

clergy were allowed to marry. About half of the cathedrals before the Reformation had been monastic, the rest were served by hierarchies of priests including, in each case, a Dean and Canons, all, of course, celibate (see Chapter Seven). After the Dissolution the cathedrals that had been monastic were re-organised to conform with the latter pattern (page 91), with the very important difference that the clergy were no longer necessarily celibate. This resulted in the unique domestic-clerical society of the Anglican cathedral close, which was in time caricatured by Anthony Trollope (**44, 45**). But the late seventeenth- and eighteenth-century cathedral closes were not always like 'Barchester'. Some bishops were brilliant intellectuals as well as churchmen—Bishop Seth Ward of Salisbury, a scientist, astronomer and friend of Sir Christopher Wren was a notable example—and many deans and canons were distinguished in their own right. Also, many lay people lived in or near cathedral closes after the Reformation, and contributed to their social character. Salisbury and Lichfield have splendid examples of cathedral closes as they became in Georgian and Victorian times. At Salisbury, the spacious medieval layout is preserved, decorously landscaped by James Wyatt at the end of the eighteenth century (**46**). Many of the detached medieval clergy houses remain in part, altered and adapted to seventeenth- and eighteenth-century needs; others were rebuilt. The architecture round Salisbury Close is now a delightful amalgam of all dates from the thirteenth century onwards (**47, 124**). The older work is in stone or flint, the later either in the near-local Chilmark stone—notably Mompesson House of about 1700—or in local red brick. At Lichfield, the much smaller Close (page 82) has the same atmosphere, although, owing to destruction in the Civil War no medieval buildings are outwardly evident; the prominent former Bishop's Palace of 1687, in sandstone, sets the domestic character of the Close. The gateways to the precinct have gone, but this has resulted in the Close atmosphere extending out into the adjoining part of the city proper, with decorous red brick Georgian houses, in one of which lived Erasmus Darwin (page 173).

At Winchester, Gloucester, Worcester, Durham and Peterborough, all of which were Benedictine monasteries, the living quarters of the monasteries were partly retained, and converted for administrative or clerical-domestic use. All these places have buildings visibly of medieval origin, with Georgian domestic alterations, notably sash windows; the Deaneries at Winchester and Durham are perfect examples. Such former monastic precincts have evolved into Anglican cathedral closes with the same atmosphere and general form as those, such as Salisbury and Lichfield, which were true cathedral precincts in the Middle Ages. They retain their monastic gateways; the contrasts between the modern city centres and the quiet of the Closes through the gateways are particularly impressive at Worcester and Peterborough. At Norwich, the Close, which also developed from the precinct of a monastery, is so large that it seems to be a town within a city. (**III**, p. 32)

Nearly all the Georgian town scenes described in this chapter were developed piecemeal—individual houses were built one by one, usually within already established street or spatial patterns. Outside London, the great resorts, and a few large cities like Bristol, there was little of the formal Georgian patterns of terraces, squares and crescents. Exeter was one of the few other cities to be developed on a large scale in this way. Here, Southernhay was laid out from 1805, in the form of two lines of mainly red-brick terraces facing over a long strip of landscaped garden, outside, and following the curve of, the still partly surviving city wall. Much else in the same manner was destroyed during the Second World War. From Southernhay a lane leads under a delicate iron bridge (**125**), spanning a breach in the city wall, into the totally informal Cathedral Close. Here stone-built former canons' houses of medieval origin (**45**), and Georgian buildings with red brick or stuccoed fronts face the wide grassy space which wraps round the Cathedral on three sides, and which, as in so many cathedral precincts, is wide enough in extent to set off the great building, but not so expansive as to belittle it. (Only at one end have wartime destruction, recent demolitions and unfortunate patching-up resulted in a discordant effect.) From the Close alleys lead into the busy High Street. Three types of townscape—contrived formal, spacious informal, and tight-knit, (together with an element of the formless), succeed one another in a short space.

In other major county towns Georgian town houses were set within the estab-

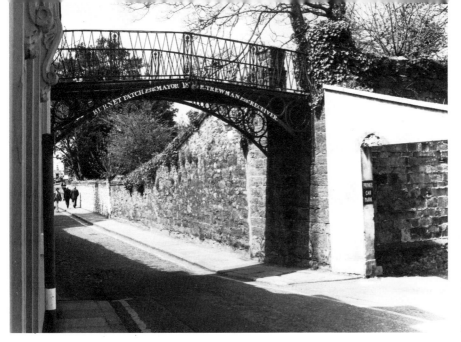

lished street patterns. At Shrewsbury a distinctive Georgian quarter developed informally to the south of the medieval centre, along a network of obviously medieval streets and lanes which had probably been loosely developed before, culminating in the great elliptical church St Chad (1790), overlooking the riverside slopes which were first landscaped in the eighteenth century. At York, the town houses of the county gentry, some of them designed by the distinguished local architect John Carr, are dispersed individually along the old streets, often adjoining older and humbler buildings, as in Castlegate, Micklegate and, outside the walls, Bootham. The Assembly Rooms, the finest of their kind in England, designed by the Yorkshire aristocratic architect Lord Burlington (1730), were the centre of the upper-class social life of the county capital. There were many other, more modest, Assembly Rooms, especially in county towns, some of them attached to inns. The most impressive surviving examples, after those at York and Bath, are at Newcastle—essentially the county town of Northumberland—with a beautiful interior 1776 by the local architect William Newton.

Perhaps the best example of a Georgian county town is Bury St Edmunds. The plan form is totally medieval—largely laid out in the late eleventh century (page 77). After the upheaval of the Dissolution and the loss of the Abbey, the town flourished as a great marketing centre, and as a social centre for the aristocracy and gentry of East Anglia. Moderate sized, comfortable-looking Georgian town houses, faced in brick, were built individually facing the streets, interspersed with older, more modest, timber-framed houses which were often outwardly 'Georgianized' (page 58). The Athenaeum, with its ballroom of 1789 and early nineteenth century Classical front, faces the spacious Angel Hill (**42**) alongside the gentlemanly Palladian Angel Hotel of 1779. Georgian shop fronts survive in Abbeygate Street (**114**) leading up to the Market area, with Robert Adam's former Town Hall. In East Anglia the taste and outlook of the Georgian age seems to have continued well into the Victorian period, as is suggested by the Classical Corn Exchange, opened in 1862.

16
The Development of Industrial Britain, 1830–1900

The population of England and Wales grew from nine million in 1801 to 32½ million in 1901. The increase was very unevenly distributed. London expanded vastly, but it was in a corner of the country otherwise essentially rural, apart from a few coastal towns. Elsewhere, the areas where different industries had developed in the early years of industrial change (as described in Chapter Thirteen) continued to expand through the Victorian period. Large towns grew into great cities; smaller towns into large ones; a few new towns were established. Many adjoining towns consolidated, thickly or loosely, into what we now call 'conurbations'—Birmingham and the Black Country; Manchester and much of Lancashire; Leeds and the West Riding; Sheffield and South Yorkshire; Liverpool and Merseyside; Newcastle and Tyneside; Cardiff and South Wales. Teesside and the Potteries were smaller 'conurbations'; Bristol, Hull, Plymouth, Portsmouth, Nottingham and Leicester were free-standing cities which grew considerably. Otherwise, outside coalfields and a few coastal areas, Britain continued to develop mainly at a 'pre-industrial' pace. Old county capitals grew modestly; some small market towns expanded while others were static or contracted; a few isolated places grew fast, but still within modest limits, due to special causes such as the development of transport.

The transport revolution
In 1825 steam was dominant as the source of power for industrial production. But inland transport was still almost entirely related to the capacity of the horse—whether hauling barges on canals, coaches or carts on turnpike roads, or, latterly, trucks on iron railways. Richard Trevithick's experimental railway engine ran in South Wales in 1804; George Stephenson's locomotives hauled coal to Tyneside quays from 1814 onwards. Passengers were drawn by steam power on the Stockton and Darlington Railway in 1825, but for many years this was operated mainly by horses. The line was built primarily to carry coal from pits near Bishop Auckland to riverside quays at Stockton, but Stockton's capacity proved too small, and in 1831 the railway was extended to an almost uninhabited place called Middlesbrough further down the River Tees, where a new port was established, and a small town laid out—the first anywhere to owe its existence to a railway.

The opening of the Liverpool and Manchester Railway, entirely steam-operated, in 1830, initiated the railway as the primary means of transport for goods and people. The completion, by 1850, of Robert Stephenson's and John Dobson's superb High-Level Bridge over the River Tyne at Newcastle, with iron girders on stone piers (70), and of Stephenson's viaduct over the River Tweed at Berwick, together enabling trains to run from London to Edinburgh, may be said to symbolize the triumph of the railway over the canal and the turnpike road, and of the steam engine over the horse. But it must be remembered that local transport, especially in towns and cities, continued to be horse-hauled for a considerable period longer.

Apart from the viaducts, tunnels, and bridges, the architectural heritage of the railways is impressive. The façades of the more important stations were designed monumentally in various historical styles—pure classical at Huddersfield (1847), and Monkwearmouth in Sunderland (1848); Elizabethan or Jacobean in Brunel's original Temple Meads at Bristol (1841) and Stoke-on-Trent (1847); and Italianate at Chester (1848), which is the finest surviving building designed by the great Victorian station architect Francis Thompson (126), collaborator also with Robert Stephenson in the Britannia Bridge over the Menai Strait into Anglesey. By contrast, the interiors of some of the great stations were daringly of the Industrial Age, notably the great iron-arched train halls such as Newcastle (1848 on); Brunel's Paddington (1850 on); St Pancras (1868 on), behind Sir Gilbert Scott's stunning Gothic hotel building; and York (1867 on) with its superb interplay of curves. The last of the great iron-roofed stations, appropriately at Darlington, was started in 1887. Because most of the major stations were built on the edges of already established towns, they are not usually dominant features in present-day city centres. Exceptions are at Huddersfield, where the station is the centrepiece of the town square, and at Newcastle, where Robert Stephenson's railway cut ruthlessly through the heart of the medieval city, threading the castle bailey. At Stoke-on-Trent a fine urban grouping was formed, with the neo-Jacobean railway station hotel facing the station, railway workers' housing on either side and a statue of Josiah Wedgwood, the magnate of the local china industry, in the middle. To this day this is the finest urban composition by far in the amalgamation of pottery-making towns that now goes under the collective name of Stoke-on-Trent.

The railways might have been expected to stimulate the growth of the towns they served well, and to cause the retardation of others which they served badly or reached late. But, on the whole, they had less direct influence on the fortunes of cities and towns than is sometimes thought. Many historic towns well-placed on the railway system, such as Shrewsbury, Durham, Lichfield and Salisbury did

126. Chester Station, 1847–8, is the largest surviving work of Francis Thompson, railway architect. The Italianate style used here was varied with Gothic, Tudor-Jacobean and pure Classical in the major stations of the time.

not grow a great deal, while places like Sheffield, Bradford and Luton which, at least at first, were badly served, grew fast. Most of the major Victorian towns were already well-established before the railway age, apart from a few which were primarily ports or resorts, and some which owe their existence to the railways' own operations. Of the latter, the two most remarkable were Swindon and Crewe. The Great Western Railway set up its works, where most of its engines and rolling stock were made, in open country near the very small market town of Swindon. Isambard Brunel and Matthew Wyatt designed for the railway company a model community of workers' houses, with social and community buildings, most of which has been recently rehabilitated; it was 'small, modest and laid out without ingenuity' (Pevsner and Cherry: *Buildings of England: Wiltshire*). The town soon outgrew the original planned community—haphazardly—and linked with the older town. The town centre simply developed, casually, along a few of the streets which had originally been residential, and had no coherent form before recent redevelopment took place. At Crewe likewise, where the railway works were established at a convergence of routes deep in the Cheshire plain, a new railway village was first built (little now survives of it), which steadily grew, without any urban grace, into a medium-sized town.

Other railway companies set up their works in established towns like Derby, Doncaster, Darlington, Ashford and York. York, thanks initially to an enterprising but unscrupulous citizen, George Hudson ('Mek all t'railways coom t'York') gained not only railway works, but also the headquarters of the important North-Eastern Railway, housed latterly in a tall neo-Baroque building of 1900 just inside the city wall from the great station and its adjoining railway hotel. York would probably have stagnated but for the railway development. It had long since lost its pre-eminence among Yorkshire towns through the growth of Leeds, Sheffield, Bradford, Hull and even Middlesbrough, and its only other significant industry, chocolate manufacture, did not really develop until the end of the century. Derby was another old county town which became the headquarters of a major railway company, the Midland Railway. The original station by Francis Thompson, a landmark in early railway architecture, has disappeared, but the Midland Hotel of 1840, the oldest surviving railway hotel, remains, with terraces of early railwaymen's houses recently refurbished. Derby, unlike York, already had a developing industrial tradition with its silk and knitting industries.

At sea, the Transport Revolution was longer drawn-out than on land. The first steam vessel, with a Boulton and Watt engine, was tried on a Scottish canal in 1802; the first paddle steamer in regular use operated on the Hudson River in New York in 1807; the first regular British service of steamships ran from Liverpool to Glasgow in 1815. These were wooden ships; the first iron ship was launched at Birkenhead in 1834. The 'breakthrough' in shipping history—comparable to the opening of the Liverpool and Manchester line in railway history—came with the simultaneous sailing across the Atlantic of Brunel's steamship *Great Western* and its rival *Sirius* in 1838, the first from Bristol, the second from Liverpool. These were paddle steamers; the screw propellor was invented in 1836. But sailing ships continued to operate on long voyages for several decades; the *Cutty Sark* is a famous example. Carrying fuel for steamship engines was at first a major problem, gradually solved with technical improvements and the opening of 'coaling stations' around the world. It was only after 1860 that steam vessels became dominant, both in the merchant service and in the Royal Navy. The invention of the steam turbine by Charles Parsons of Newcastle, first used in a vessel in 1894, was perhaps the final triumph of the Steam Age; it facilitated the building of the great liners and battleships of the early twentieth century. The huge developments in the Royal Navy are reflected in the Dockyards, particularly at Devonport and at Portsmouth, where majestically scaled buildings in brick, stone and iron went with the warships of iron and, later, steel as surely as the older brick and timber storehouses went with the sailing ships (page 185).

By the Victorian period Liverpool had completely superseded Bristol (see Chapter Fourteen) as Britain's chief transatlantic port—for cargo, for embarkation of hundreds of thousands of often impoverished emigrants, and as the prestigious terminus of the world's busiest oceanic passenger service, that to New York. Its heyday was in the Edwardian era and up to 1914, when its tremendous waterfront took shape (127). The ten-storey Liver Building of 1908–10 named after a mythical

127. Liverpool Waterfront, from Albert Dock (103). The near building, domed, was the Docks and Harbour Board headquarters, 1907; the middle one, flat-topped, the Cunard Building, 1913; the furthest and tallest the Royal Liver Building, 1908–10. The tower on the right is the later entrance to the Mersey Tunnel.

bird which legendarily gave its name to Liverpool, was the centrepiece, adjoined by the former Cunard Building of 1913 and the former Docks Office of 1908 (too much in Liverpool today is 'former'). As they were being built, the decline of Liverpool was starting; the White Star Line transferred its largest liners to Southampton in 1907, because they could only with difficulty navigate the Mersey. Its example was followed by the Cunard Line in 1921. Southampton had declined from its medieval greatness to a small Channel port, with some reputation as a resort until the first dock was opened, after the completion of the railway from London in 1840. Southampton then developed erratically until 1892, when the docks were bought by the enterprising London and South-Western Railway, which greatly expanded them. The port's huge advantage was that there were double high tides, because of the configuration of the Solent, enabling large ships to dock at open quays, provided the channels were dredged, at any time. In other ports, like London and Liverpool, large ships had to be impounded in enclosed docks reached through lock gates.

Meanwhile the Port of London expanded proportionately; it always remained the country's largest. The first dock in London was the West India Dock, built in the Blackwall marshes at the eastern end of Tower Hamlets in 1800, followed by the London Docks at Wapping in 1802, and the East India Dock in 1805. ('East' meant the Indian sub-continent; 'West' the West Indies). Other docks followed, through to the present century. The old maritime Tower Hamlets (page 134) were transformed by the new docks, wharves and warehouses, with dense housing built between and behind them. In the early steamship age there was a thriving ship-building industry at Blackwall, but this declined after mid-century.

The ancient port of Hull was transformed by the demolition of its medieval town walls and the buildings of a series of docks outside their line, almost insulating the original town (XVII, p. 119). Later, docks were built up and down the Humber. Hull was the outlet for industrial Yorkshire and part of the Midlands, and it also became a major deep-sea fishing port. So did Grimsby, an early medieval port of some importance which later declined and was revived only with the coming of the railway. Older fishing ports of the sailing age, like Scarborough, Whitby and many in the South-West declined, at least relatively. Yarmouth retained its old importance as a herring port into the twentieth century; Lowestoft's fishing trade grew from small beginnings in Victorian times. Fleetwood, in Lancashire, was a new town originally intended to be a seaside resort, which developed instead as a fishing port.

Newcastle and Tyneside, together with Wearside, already had centuries of tradition in wooden shipbuilding, as well as in iron manufacture, and a more recent reputation in railway engineering, when the first iron ship to be built on the Tyne was launched in 1842. Thenceforth shipyards developed along the river, producing cargo ships, warships, and eventually liners. One of the most significant was Charles Palmer's, opened at Jarrow in 1852, where the organization and manufacturing methods were advanced for the time. Jarrow must then have offered the acutest contrast between the quality of the products and the sophistication of the industrial process on the one hand, and the meanness of the living environment outside the shipyard on the other. Jarrow had for long been a straggling colliery and agricultural village with a church dating from the time of the Venerable Bede (see Chapter Two). After the shipyard opened, it developed quickly into a town, with rows of minimal houses—they were no worse generally than those in other industrial and mining towns in the North-East, being simply typical of the region at the time. There was a comparable contrast between workaday Jarrow as a town, and the splendid Classical city centre of Newcastle a few miles away (101), whose building was complete when the Jarrow shipyard was opened.

In Newcastle itself, William Armstrong pioneered hydraulic cranes, first used on the local Quayside, and then, in the 1850s, rifle-barrelled artillery. This had revolutionary effects on both land and naval warfare; Armstrong soon supplied a high proportion of the governments of the world with guns. He then turned to warship building. The Armstrong engineering and shipbuilding works at Els-wick and Walker were marvels of mid-Victorian industrial enterprise. By contrast, the workers lived in tight-packed terraced houses climbing the steep slope across the Scotswood Road—famed in Victorian song—from the Elswick works. But Lord Armstrong (as he became), typically for a successful Victorian industrialist, first lived in a secluded mansion in an inner but leafy suburb, Jesmond, and then moved deep into the country. He restored for habitation the dramatically sited Bamburgh Castle, and commissioned the rising architect Norman Shaw to build, in 1870, the mansion called Cragside, in a highly picturesque (and un-Northum-brian) style, whose already rugged setting was made exotic by thick and varied planting.

Sunderland, at the mouth of the River Wear, although only a few miles from Newcastle and with similar activities (coal export; wooden then iron shipbuilding; glass-making) was always a place with its own identity, with some affinities to Scottish towns. Some of the earlier workers' houses were single-storeyed, (a Scot-tish tradition) and, as in Glasgow or Edinburgh, the Georgian tradition of middle-class housing survived nearly till the end of the nineteenth century. There are robust Victorian terraces and crescents, interspersed with greenery, in the south-western parts of the town, where the shipyard owners, the prosperous tradesmen and the ships' captains must have lived.

Hartlepool was an ancient port revived. By 1835 the old town on the headland with its superb church (page 120) had dwindled to village size. In that year a railway was opened from the mining hinterland, as a rival to the ten-year-old Stockton and Darlington line; new docks were built, after the demolition of much of the medieval town wall, and the town repopulated. In another ten years, a rival town, West Hartlepool, was founded across the harbour, connected to yet another coal-carrying railway. It was so successful that for a time it handled more trade than all the other ports of North-East England combined. An initially am-bitious plan for the new town was only partly realized, though one or two crum-bling Grecian-style buildings, and a focal parish church by the Victorian 'rogue architect' E. B. Lamb suggest a might-have-been urban character. So many new Victorian towns developed in such a way—a decent plan to start with, then sub-sequent rapid growth without any coherence or grace as also happened in nearby Middlesbrough.

Mining and manufacturing

The early coal pits in North-East England were within reach of the Rivers Tyne and Wear. Their geographical distribution widened with the development of, first, horse-drawn and, then, steam-drawn railways of which the most famous was the

Stockton and Darlington line. This, and other railways that followed, opened up the West Durham coalfield. Improvements in mining technology enabled deeper mines to be sunk later in the century, as in eastern Durham, parts of Northumberland, southern Yorkshire, and the Derbyshire-Nottinghamshire borderland. The earlier mining villages were often small and scattered, but as mines became generally larger their attendant villages were usually more substantial and more compact. The typical North-Eastern mining village of the late nineteenth and early twentieth centuries consisted of tightly grouped, often parallel, terraces of houses, dominated by the winding gear at the pit entrance and, more and more pervasively, by the ever-heightening tips of colliery waste. Most of these villages owed their existence to the mines; they were usually quite separate from the older, originally agricultural, villages which in County Durham were characteristically set around long or many-branching greens. Sometimes, where local iron ore as well as coal led to the establishment of ironworks, new settlements of town size developed, as at Spennymoor and Consett, while the old market town of Bishop Auckland grew in importance. There were comparable patterns of development in the Yorkshire and Derbyshire coalfields, where the market towns of Barnsley and Chesterfield, pre-dating the exploitation of the coalfields, grew into major focal centres for the new, widely dispersed, mining and metal-working communities.

In South Wales much of the early industrial development took place around Swansea, and at the heads of the mountain valleys, where coal and iron ore were found close together, as at Merthyr Tydfil (page 175). Before the Victorian period, Welsh coal extraction was mainly related to the local metal industries, with a little being sent out from the then small ports. The opening of railways up the valleys, beginning with the Taff Vale line in 1841, led to a huge expansion in mining, most of the output being exported, overseas or coastwise, from rapidly developing ports such as Cardiff and Newport. New villages extended along the valleys and up the lowest slopes of the enveloping hills, usually in the form of long terraces of stone-built houses. In the most developed valleys the villages simply grew into each other; in the main part of the Rhondda Valley there was continuous settlement along both sides of the valley floor. At a few focal points, especially where there were iron or other industries to supplement mining, substantial towns grew up, like Aberdare and Pontypridd, which took on the character of thriving market centres for the surrounding densely developed country. Apart from the coastal towns, almost all the settlements in the coalfield area dated from the industrial era. Only Bridgend, Neath and Caerphilly, with its tremendous castle, had any previous existence as market towns, and they were very small. Much of the incoming population presumably came from other parts of Wales or the Border (page 175); certainly the mining villages, with their chapels, became as Welsh in many ways as those of the rural parts of Wales. Most of the coastal towns—Swansea, Cardiff, Newport, even Port Talbot (formerly Aberavon)—were of ancient origin, though they were small before the industrial era. Cardiff's spectacular development into Wales' premier city is described in the next chapter.

Some of the most important technological developments in Victorian times were in steel-making. Hitherto 'steel' had meant the hard, refined iron used for knives and other blade tools, for which Sheffield was famous. Iron, wrought or cast, had been the metal used for construction and machinery. Following the invention of the Bessemer process in 1856, and the Siemens or open-hearth process in 1864,

17
Victorian Cities and Towns

During the second half of the nineteenth century in Britain there occurred, probably for the first time anywhere, a fundamental change in the nature of large cities. Hitherto the central parts of cities had been densely inhabited—dwellings were mixed with commercial premises and civic buildings. By the end of the century the centres of large British cities were predominantly devoted to commerce, entertainment, local—and sometimes national—government, and other activities we now associate with central areas. Living quarters were elsewhere—they usually began immediately beyond the edges of the central areas, and extended for increasing distances outwards. (Here it is appropriate to insert a topical observation; we hear a great deal today about 'inner cities', which people sometimes confuse with city centres. The distinction ought to be clear. City centres are the commercial and civic quarters as already defined; inner cities are the areas immediately beyond, which in Victorian times were usually densely populated, and which are often the problem areas of today.)

It was, of course, the development of public transport which made this separation of city centres and living quarters possible. Horse buses existed in early Victorian times, but their capacity was limited. Horse tramcars were introduced from about 1860; the tracks made haulage of large numbers of people practicable at low fares, enabling wage-earners to live at some distance from their work. Meanwhile, what we now call 'commuting' by train developed—it started in a small way around 1840 and rapidly increased through the century, particularly around London with its Underground network—the District and Metropolitan lines already operated, by steam, in late Victorian times. Electrification of tramways and some railways, as well as construction of the deeper 'Tube' lines of the London Underground, began about 1900, and hastened the process of dispersal further.

Centres of cities
The City of London was the first place to obtain the characteristics of a present-day city centre, populated heavily by day and hardly at all by night. In 1841 there were still 123,000 people living within the restricted boundaries of the ancient City, which had not been altered since the early Middle Ages (see Chapter Twelve). By 1939 there were fewer than 10,000 people in the same area. How and why did this dramatic decline take place?

In 1841 the City's inhabitants still normally worked, shopped, worshipped and spent most of their leisure time within, or very near, the City's boundaries. True, most of the richer merchants, bankers and businessmen by then lived outside, either in Georgian terraces or squares, or in semi-rural suburbs, reached by private or hired carriage, but many still retained *pieds à terre* on or near their business premises. Lesser merchants, shopkeepers, clerks and craftsmen generally lived near, within, or 'over' their workplaces. There were still numerous poor people within the City boundaries, particularly on the eastern and northern fringes.

During the nineteenth century the number of people engaged or employed in business in the City steadily increased, but the amount of residential accommodation greatly diminished, through conversions, public works, and commercial redevelopment. The public works included a series of new roads cut, at various times, through the dense tangles of essentially medieval streets and alleys, from which they are usually distinguished by their straightness. Such were King William Street, linking with the rebuilt London Bridge in the 1830s, and Queen Victoria Street, which in the early 1870s connected the newly-formed Embankment with the already complex junction at the Bank of England. New railways and termini displaced many poorer people, particularly at Liverpool Street in the 1870s.

In the hundred years after 1840 most of the City was rebuilt, piece by piece. Old, often multi-purpose properties, usually at least partly domestic in origin, were replaced by purpose-built commercial premises, to house banks, insurance companies and other financial and mercantile concerns as they developed along modern business lines. The new buildings followed the complexities of Victorian architectural fashions, with emphasis on styles derived from the *palazzi* of the Renaissance—especially, and appropriately, those of the mercantile heyday of Florence and Venice (130). The most favoured building material was Bath stone, buff-brown in colour, usually from the quarries of North Wiltshire rather than those nearer to Bath itself. But there was much embellishment in marble—either from Italy or from the Scottish coast near Aberdeen—and other exotic materials, especially in columns, pilasters and friezes. Gothic, Byzantine, Romanesque and other historic styles were, on the whole, less favoured in the City of London than in some other British city centres, although there were some notable examples of these styles in the City. Towards the end of the nineteenth century the national fashion for Flemish, Dutch and so-called 'Queen Anne' styles, with delicate detailing in brick, terracotta and other colourful materials was apparent in some of the new office buildings, while from the 1890s there were some inventive designs in what is broadly called 'Free Baroque'.

Until the end of the century most commercial buildings in the City were fairly small in scale, not much larger than the basically domestic buildings they often replaced. It was only after about 1900 that large numbers of monumental banks or insurance offices were built, particularly in the area around the Bank of England. By that time Portland stone had returned to favour—as the prestigious external material for commercial as well as public buildings.

One notable characteristic of Victorian and Edwardian commercial architecture was the way in which the designers exploited prominent corner sites, as if to allow their clients maximum self-advertisement. Corners were emphasized by domes, (as in Grey Street, Newcastle in the 1830s, (102)), turrets or prominent angular windows. A very successful example is the present Mappin and Webb building in the angle between Queen Victoria Street and Poultry, facing the Royal Exchange (129). This was built following the construction of Queen Victoria Street in the early 1870s, which left this sharply-angled and very prominent site. The architects, J. and J. Belcher, responded magnificently with a building, which, though modest in dimensions, asserts itself completely, with its corner dome, against the much more monumental buildings (some of them later in date) around it.

The essentially medieval street pattern, with intricate lanes and alleys (72) remained except where new streets were cut through. But the typical, basically simple, brick architecture of the post-Great Fire and Georgian City was replaced by a richer variety of densely detailed, more colourful buildings. Most of Wren's and the later Georgian City churches survived (though there were some bad losses in Victorian times) their Portland stone contrasting with the usually darker materials of the later buildings (78, 129).

The Victorian City of London was not only offices, banks and churches. There were warehouses by the river; the surviving Livery Company halls, some grandly rebuilt like those of the Fishmongers and Goldsmiths; and the specialized markets of Smithfield and Billingsgate, together with Leadenhall Market of 1880, which, with its glazed roofs, overlay a network of partly medieval alleys. The City developed as the mercantile and financial hub of the country and, to a large extent, of the world, but for shopping, entertainment and many other metropolitan activi-

129. Poultry and Queen Victoria Street, City of London. The prominent building with a circular turret, by J. and J. Belcher, 1872, makes the most of a sharp corner—as in the earlier Grey Street, Newcastle (**102**). In the background is the steeple of Wren's St Mary-le-Bow.

ties the centre of gravity had shifted to the West End.

The process of depopulation and commercial intensification took place in other Victorian city centres. Leeds is probably the best example of a major city still with a substantially Victorian centre (though with older elements, and a great deal of later redevelopment). The originally medieval market town grew a little in the seventeenth century and a great deal in the eighteenth (page 163). By 1830 warehouses and factories were concentrated along the River Aire and its interconnecting canal. Population increase was at first accommodated both through intensification and through peripheral expansion. The poor crowded into sites within, or on the fringes of, the original town, often into former yards and gardens behind buildings fronting the streets—most notably into what had been long burgage plots fronting the main street, Briggate, or into plots along the even more ancient Kirkgate. This process produced typical 'courts' of houses, usually entered through narrow passageways from the streets, such as were characteristic of other growing but old-established towns (page 59), and were so vigorously condemned by Victorian sanitary and housing reformers. At the same time new low-rent houses were built, at comparable densities, on plots that became available piecemeal on the fringes of the town. This process is described later. By contrast, the middle classes, many of whom had previously lived near their businesses, moved to the outskirts, especially the more salubrious higher ground to the north-west. At first they moved to typical late Georgian red brick town houses round Park Square or along adjoining streets (132), later to Victorian villas in semi-rural Woodhouse and Headingley beyond. But the poor remained, densely packed, in central and inner Leeds; only in the later part of the century were many of them dispersed.

The centre of Leeds developed in Victorian times in ways which were typical of many other British cities. Businesses moved into the hitherto Georgian residential areas, as the middle classes moved out. Some of the Georgian houses were converted to offices (many remain round Park Square); others were replaced by office buildings in varied styles, with a higher proportion in Gothic than in the City of London. Others, especially to the south-west, were replaced by warehouses—the most fanciful, with a Moorish façade of 1878, occupies the south side of Park Square (it is now converted into offices). As elsewhere, the older, mainly Georgian, street pattern remained while the buildings were replaced or converted.

Much more magnificent than any of the commercial buildings was the new Town Hall (131), built in 1853–8 to the design of Cuthbert Brodrick, an architect who originated in Hull. Leeds, unlike some of the other new-rich cities, such as Birmingham, Sheffield and Manchester, was an old-established borough, but like others was reconstituted, with property-owners becoming voters, under the Municipal Corporations Act of 1835. This was the first of the really great Victorian Town Halls built by such new or reformed councils. Its nearest precedents in scale were the Georgian Town Hall and the later St George's Hall in Liverpool (page 179), some of whose functions it combined. It was not primarily, as might be expected today, a base for municipal bureaucrats, since there were very few such people at the time, as compared with later times. It contained a council chamber, such offices as were needed, law courts, and a great public hall suitable for massed musical performances, particularly choirs, which were highly popular throughout the Victorian period—Town Halls like these were called 'Temples of Handel's Messiah'.

220

It is Anglicized Renaissance-Baroque, with its great fronting colonnade and massive steeple-cupola. Typically English, too, is its lack of a formal setting; it was simply built on a site which became available, with just enough open space left in front to set off the grand stepway to the colonnade. Otherwise there was, and still is, a heterogeneous collection of buildings around it. Leeds Town Hall set a precedent for municipal grandeur in varied styles at, among other places, Manchester, Halifax (137), Bolton, Portsmouth and, at the end of the century, Colchester (10) and Cardiff.

Broderick also designed one of the most extraordinary Victorian public buildings in any town, the Corn Exchange, heavily detailed and elliptical in shape, where every dimension, apart from that of the vertical walls, appears to be curving.

Briggate, the traditional main street of Leeds, became the main Victorian shop-

130. **Former National Provincial Bank, Bishopsgate**, 1865, one of the earliest and finest City banks, with Italianate detail, and a splendid interior, now converted into a Livery Hall. The architect, John Gibson, designed banks for the company (now part of the National Westminster Bank) in numerous towns, as well as Todmorden Town Hall (92).

131. **Leeds Town Hall**, 1853–8 by Cuthbert Brodrick, was the first of the really great Victorian Town Halls. It contains a concert hall and law courts with (by later standards) relatively modest municipal accommodation.

ping centre. The older buildings, usually both commercial and domestic, were replaced piecemeal by shops and other business premises, many of which extended also over the sites of slums which had accumulated in the courts behind. As in other cities, fairly large department stores appeared by the end of the nineteenth century, although the earliest nation-wide chains of shops did not generally develop until the beginning of the twentieth. In 1898 large-scale redevelopments started on the east side of Briggate, where an area, containing many of the city's worst slums, was cleared at the initiative of the City Council and rebuilt with two new thoroughfares, Queen Victoria and King Edward Streets, lined with uniform large commercial blocks with busy rooflines of turrets, gablets and cupolas, typical of the time. Uniform streets like this were most unusual in Victorian cities; earlier new city streets in the post-Georgian era were mostly developed piecemeal as soon as they were formed. The central block of this development contained the County

132. Leeds Town Hall seen from a corner of Park Square—which was built for the Georgian middle classes, and is now an office quarter (page 163).

Arcade, one of the finest among many of its kind in Britain. Shopping arcades were fashionable in Regency London—the Burlington Arcade is a survivor—and there are good Classical examples from the 1830s in Bristol (St James' Arcade) and Ryde in the Isle of Wight. Many arcades were built in Victorian times, with glazed roofs, arched or gabled, supported on light iron framework; Leeds and Cardiff have the best series. The County Arcade, opened in 1900, was designed by Frank Matcham, the leading theatre architect of the day, with fascias, upper storeys, and the bases of the intermittent roof domes faced in brown terracotta, with richly theatrical Baroque details (**134**).

Another major feature of Leeds which was typical of Victorian and Edwardian cities is the covered market hall, Kirkgate Market, originally built in 1857 to replace the open market which was first held in Briggate in the thirteenth century. There were partly covered market halls in London and elsewhere in the eighteenth and early nineteenth centuries; the finest early example surviving is Charles Fowler's recently refurbished Market at Covent Garden of 1828–30, with later iron roofs (73). Fowler also designed two splendid markets in Exeter; the neo-Classical façade of one (1838) survives. John Dobson's Grainger Market of 1835 in Newcastle, part of the Classical city centre of the time, is set behind normal street frontages. Many covered markets were built in the Victorian period, especially in Northern industrial towns, where the climate made large open markets less acceptable than further south. Often they were splendid buildings with large-scale internal iron structure and glazed roofs. Many have recently been lost through redevelopment, but fine ones remain at Bolton (1853 and later) and, especially, Halifax (1895), where the brightly painted, mosque-like, iron-framed interior (133) contrasts completely with that of the nearby Classical Piece Hall

133. Borough Market, Halifax, 1895 by Leeming and Leeming, a fantasy in iron and glass, with delicate details in brackets, girders and other steelwork brightly painted.

134. *Opposite* **County Arcade, Leeds**, 1898, by Frank Matcham (**139**). The coved, glazed, iron-framed roof has domes at intervals; the shiny decoration above the fascias is in brown faience. There were arcades in most important Victorian towns; usually several—Leeds and Cardiff have the best series.

135, *Below* **Kirkgate Market, Leeds,** built 1903, is a masterpiece of massing, and of meticulous detail building up to the skyline of domes, turrets, cupolas, chimneys and gables—a superb enlivenment, on a suitable scale, of the centre of a large city.

136. *Opposite* **Kirkgate Market, Leeds,** another fantasy in ironwork and glazing, by the same architects as the one in Halifax (**133**). Such buildings were once found in many Victorian towns, but several have recently disappeared.

(**93**). The architects of the Halifax Market Hall, locally based Leeming and Leeming, largely rebuilt the Leeds Market Hall with its present stupendous exterior in 1904, with a vibrant skyline of domes, turrets, sweeping roofs and gables (**135, 136**). Shopping arcades and market halls were both forerunners of modern 'shopping precincts', but few of the latter achieve, in modern terms, the elegance and excitement, internally or externally, of the best of their predecessors in the Victorian and Edwardian age.

Birmingham's city centre developed similarly, in many ways, to that of Leeds. There was a small medieval market town which prospered in the seventeenth century and grew greatly in the eighteenth (page 172), when new residential streets were laid out on the rising ground to the north-west. Commerce moved into this area in the early nineteenth century, as well-to-do residents moved out, especially to sylvan Edgbaston (**XXIV**, p. 243). Waterloo Street, laid out about 1830, contains the Classical Midland Bank, one of the earliest purpose-built banks. In 1832 the

present Classical Town Hall was started. As Birmingham had no town council until one was set up under the Municipal Corporations Act, 1835, it was not an administrative building, but simply an assembly and concert hall. It was, however, the starting point of an expanding series of civic and cultural buildings including the Library of 1865 (now replaced), the Council Offices of 1874 and later, and Museum and Art Gallery of 1881–5. These formed a typical (though unusually large) accumulation of ornate Victorian public buildings in varied styles round an irregular pattern of streets and spaces, without any overall formal layout. Before recent redevelopment this area had an intricate grandeur.

Birmingham's central street pattern was altered more radically than that of most major Victorian cities, thanks largely to the city administration led by Joseph Chamberlain, which in 1878–82 cut a new main street, Corporation Street, through a swathe of mainly poor property, much of which the City Council had acquired under a recent Act intended to facilitate slum clearance. The street was mainly developed privately, on sites leased by the Council, with shops, office blocks and hotels, all individually designed, and collectively with a lively, generally Gothic, skyline. Little has survived the waves of post-Second World War redevelopment,

137. Halifax Town Hall, 1859–62, by Sir Charles Barry, completed by his son. It expresses the civic pride of an ancient, but recently enriched town, and especially that of its leading manufacturers—the Crossleys (page 259) who gave the site and undertook redevelopment around.

apart from Sir Aston Webb's full-blooded brick and terracotta Law Courts of 1887–91, another symbol of civic pride. In nice contrast is the equally lively, but less domineering, College of Arts and Crafts of 1881–93 in nearby Margaret Street, by local architects Martin and Chamberlain, in artistic Gothic with rich floral decorations in terracotta.

The vast Victorian developments in the centre of Manchester cannot be adequately summarized. Their culmination was Alfred Waterhouse's Town Hall of 1868 onwards, a Gothic masterpiece which, unlike some other buildings of its kind, is said to have been exceptionally well planned internally. By this date municipal responsibilities had expanded greatly, nowhere more than in Manchester which, outside London, had the greatest urban problems. Unlike its counterparts in Leeds and Birmingham, the Town Hall is seen to good effect as the centrepiece of a large square—although few, if any, buildings of adequate quality have ever been built on the other three sides. The nearby Victorian office quarter developed, as at Leeds and Birmingham, in what had been a Georgian residential area, around King Street. Here there is a characteristic stylistic mixture varying from the magnificent neo-Classicism of Cockerell's former Bank of England branch, similar to that in Castle Street, Liverpool, to the Germanic Gothic fantasies of some of the later buildings. Among the most memorable features of Victorian Manchester, after the Town Hall, were the great cotton warehouses on the southern fringe of the central area,

138. Former Watts Warehouse, Portland Street, Manchester, 1851, the largest and most fantastic, and one of the last surviving, of numerous cotton warehouses built on the southern fringes of the city centre in Victorian times.

139. Theatre Royal, Portsmouth, built 1884, and altered, with a splendid new interior, 1900, by Frank Matcham, the leading theatre architect of the time (134). The iron arcade over the pavement is of 1884, but the storey above, with a bar, was added in 1900. The theatre has been saved through local effort after long neglect.

of which the finest surviving is the Watts Warehouse in Portland Street (138).

Manchester was a major centre for political movements and events (page 162), and it provided Engels with much of the material which helped to form his own philosophy. His famous descriptions from the 1840s portray the great contrasts between the densely inhabited streets in the area of the original medieval town, near the minute but murky River Irwell, with their horrifying sanitary conditions, and the fast-spreading villas of the bourgeoisie further south; in between was the developing city centre, parts of which were already becoming depopulated.

The City of London, and the centres of Leeds, Birmingham and Manchester illustrate features characteristic of many more large Victorian cities. Old street lines, whether medieval or later in origin, often survived the piecemeal replacement of the buildings fronting them, though some underwent widenings at times. But many new streets were cut through the older networks, often distinguishable by their straightness; normally their frontages were built up piecemeal, though quickly. Residents steadily moved out of the central areas, the well-to-do of their own accord to salubrious suburbs, the poor through commercial redevelopment, municipal slum clearance or the building of roads, railways and major public insti-

tutions. Banks and office buildings were built solidly in various styles, preferences varying from Italian Renaissance, the favourite in London, to versions of Gothic. Many were carefully designed so as to enhance the effect of corners and other prominent sites, with domes, turrets and other devices, so advertising their occupants architecturally. Municipal buildings vied with each other in magnificence, but usually did not have formal settings. Other civic buildings expressing municipal pride were law courts, libraries and museums. Covered shopping areas—arcades and market halls—sometimes brought elements of fantasy to the mundane hearts of cities. Large shops appeared towards the end of the century. Other buildings which contributed to the character of Victorian city centres included theatres (**139**), large hotels (**140**), and, of course, the ubiquitous public houses, whose architectural heyday was around 1890 and 1900. Even more than business blocks, and with less restraint, they made the most of corner sites.

Cardiff had a pattern of development different from that of any of the major English cities. It was a medieval castle town (page 34) with Roman beginnings. It hardly developed between Tudor times and the end of the eighteenth century, during which period it had a trickle of maritime trade largely orientated towards

140. Lime Street Chambers, Liverpool was originally a hotel, 1868–71, by Alfred Waterhouse, architect of Manchester Town Hall and the Natural History Museum in London. It is attached to Lime Street Station and was characteristic of the great Victorian railway-owned hotels in cities and resorts.

Bristol; it must have been something like Pembroke or Conwy still are. Swansea and Merthyr Tydfil preceded it as industrial centres. The Glamorgan Canal, opened in 1794, extending up the Taff Valley to within a few miles of Merthyr Tydfil, provided the first stimulus to its economy.

The heiress of Cardiff Castle, and of much land round about, married the first Marquis of Bute, a Scottish peer, in 1766. The second Marquis married a banking heiress, and initiated the development of the port with the building of Bute West Dock in 1839. Railway lines, penetrating the valleys of the hinterland from 1841, led to enormous development of the coalfield, much of whose output was shipped from Cardiff, where the dock facilities were steadily expanded by the Butes. Cardiff grew at first southwards, into the district called Bute Town (fictionally 'Tiger Bay'), known from the beginning of this century as a multi-national area, where foreign sailors settled. Nowadays it is largely redeveloped, but has a cluster of Victorian commercial buildings of varying grandeur, some decaying, others put to new uses, as well as the modern Welsh Maritime and Industrial Museum. Much of the early wealth of the Bute family, derived from docks, ironworks (page 175), mines and city rents, was spent on transforming the ancient, still inhabited, Castle into a Victorian fairy palace under the intensely brilliant Gothic Revival architect

141. Cardiff Castle, remodelled by the architect William Burges for Lord Bute, is a Victorian fantasy. The towers to left and right, and the skyline features, are Burges', but the octagonal tower is 15th century and the curtain wall, left, is on a Roman base—Cardiff began as a Roman fort (page 34).

William Burges (141). Meanwhile, the original walled town south of the Castle (the walls were pulled down about 1800) developed into the commercial centre, retaining the medieval street pattern but with all the buildings replaced, apart from the parish church (142), including a fascinating series of arcades.

The climax of Cardiff's development came after 1898, when Lord Bute sold to the city, on favourable terms, part of the park adjoining the Castle on condition that it was suitably laid out as a Civic Centre. The result is perhaps the finest concentration of public buildings in England or Wales outside London. The City Hall, designed by Lanchester and Rickards and finished in 1904, is a triumph of Edwardian Baroque; the adjoining Law Courts are less ebullient but very dignified; the National Museum of Wales, complementing them, was built later. Other

142. The Hayes, Cardiff. The street pattern of the small medieval town survives in the centre of the modern city, though the buildings are Victorian and later—apart from St John's Church with its tower in the Bristol tradition, built 1473 (page 94).

buildings in the Civic Centre include the inventive University College of 1903–9, by W. D. Caroe, and, in the middle of the central garden, the beautiful, shrine-like, War Memorial by the church architect Sir Ninian Comper. The layout of the Civic Centre is a simple grid; there is no symmetry between buildings—each is an entity in itself. But the total effect is monumental in the Classical sense, especially when viewed across the public gardens from the south, where the City Hall with its (from here) asymmetrical Baroque steeple is the dominating feature—but a crass City Council allowed an insensitive developer to build a high-rise tower just to the south a few years ago. The Civic Centre contrasts marvellously with the adjacent Castle in its Victorian fantasy, which is itself the 'hinge' between the Civic Centre and the commercial heart of the city with its more irregular pattern and innumerable arcades. This is the best British city centre dating in its essentials, though with earlier influences, from the period from 1840 to 1914, and one of the few cities outside London—Bath and Newcastle are others—which achieve effects of monumentality.

Victorian country towns

Agriculture prospered in the mid nineteenth century from the demands of the hugely increasing urban population. The repeal of the Corn Laws in 1846, which removed controls on the import of corn, did not at first have a serious overall effect on British farming, since imports were then only from European countries. But, after about 1870, the production of wheat on the North American prairies increased vastly, and cheap imports from there depressed British arable farming. For a while, livestock rearing continued to prosper, but the introduction of refrigerated ships before the end of the century depressed home meat production as well. Dairy-farming and market-gardening were henceforth the main forms of agriculture which continued to prosper.

All this was reflected in the development of country towns. Corn Exchanges were built, usually privately, in countless market towns in the early to middle parts of the nineteenth century, particularly in the East where arable farming prevailed. The earlier ones were usually Classical in style; that at Bishop's Stortford of 1828 is typical, and that at Bury St Edmunds of 1861 is exceptional, both for its size and its conservative style for the date. At these Exchanges, samples of corn were sold or auctioned. Between markets they were used as public halls, as many still are today. Not all Corn Exchanges were in country towns; one of the largest is in Leeds, which drew on the agriculturally rich Vale of York to the east (page 221).

The life and economy of many smaller market towns continued through the nineteenth century at much the same pace as in the eighteenth. Buildings were replaced piecemeal, usually in Classical or simple Italianate styles up to about 1870. Shopkeepers usually continued to live 'over' their shops, although the more prosperous ones often moved to villas on the outskirts in the later part of the century. Many trades based on local resources, or serving the local community, continued to flourish, such as flour and animal feed milling (whether still based on water power (**107**), or operated by steam), and tanning. Every country town had at least one brewery. Malting was more concentrated, especially in the barley-growing areas of Eastern England, from which much malt was sent to the London or Midland breweries. Groups of great maltings with their distinctive outline are, or were

143. Bliss Valley Tweed Mill, Chipping Norton, Oxfordshire, 1872. This Cotswold town had a historic textile industry which developed unexpectedly in the steam age. The architect, G. Woodhouse, came from Lancashire, and there are, or were, many mill chimneys in the North rising from as elaborately treated bases as this.

till recently, characteristic features of some towns such as Manningtree, Ware (36) and Sleaford. As agriculture became more mechanized, using steam-powered equipment, engineering firms developed in many small towns, some of which acquired wide reputations. In some towns, old-established industries continued to flourish partly on the domestic system—like glove-making in Yeovil and Martock, and net-making in Bridport. In the latter town, small steam-powered net factories were built in the backlands of some of the austerely fronted Georgian houses (6), but the more meticulous processes of net-making continued to be done in people's homes—as they are to this day. In Bedfordshire, the local cottage craft of straw-plaiting led to the establishment of straw hat making, as a domestic industry, in Dunstable and then in Luton—where it later became mechanized and caused the town's rapid growth in the later nineteenth century.

Building materials in country towns, and even in many larger cities continued, largely, to be locally-based throughout the nineteenth century. Brickmaking, mainly for local use, flourished wherever there was suitable clay. Stone continued to be the normal building material in, for instance, the Pennines (94), many parts of Wales, and the Cotswolds. There was even extension of the use of local materials in some areas—for instance flint, hitherto considered in many areas a lowly material used mainly in boundary walls, barns and humble cottages, became a great favourite of the Victorians in some chalkland districts. Many quite substantial villas and even public buildings were built of it, while churches which had hitherto been plastered over were often refaced in flint—to considerable visual effect.

Railway services were perhaps generally more important to the fortunes of smaller country towns than to larger towns. Towns which were well placed on the railway system sometimes expanded a little at the expense of others which were not. To take two pairs of examples; Framlingham in Suffolk, at the end of a branch line, declined as a market centre while Stowmarket, near the junction of main lines, throve. Bishop's Castle, at the end of a particularly picturesque but leisurely line in Shropshire, declined, while nearby Craven Arms, at an important junction, is a rare example of a new Victorian market centre developing where there had been no previous town or even a village. Markets became more specialized—corn selling went to the new Corn Exchanges; cattle dealing was often transferred from open streets or market places to enclosed auction yards. General open markets survived in many towns, and expanded considerably in a few, but, except in some market-gardening or fruit-growing areas, they dealt decreasingly with local products.

Many local crafts and small-scale industries which had flourished in country towns steadily declined, through the competition of mass-produced goods from the factories.

Public parks

The oldest English public parks were the Royal Parks in London. Hyde Park (then well outside the built-up area) and St James's Park were open to the public in the seventeenth century, and the latter was superbly remodelled in the 1830s by Nash as described in Chapter Thirteen (86). Elsewhere, town-dwellers made use of adjoining commons which, though primarily intended for communal grazing, were usually accessible for recreation and were sometimes the sites of annual events like races or fairs. The Town Moor at Newcastle is an outstanding surviving example. Many such spaces disappeared during the period of industrial expansion, following 'enclosure' through Acts of Parliament, after which they were usually built over.

Private pleasure or amusement gardens, accessible through admission fee or subscription, flourished around Georgian London. The most famous and longest-lasting were the Vauxhall Gardens, which originated as early as 1661 and closed in 1859. In their heyday they were lively and fashionable; near their end they were rowdy and, in the literal sense, popular. The Sydney Gardens were a lesser counterpart in late Georgian Bath; they survive as an open space. More sedate, privately-owned, parks with restricted access included Victoria Park in Bath, opened in 1830, and the fascinating Museum Gardens at York, laid out informally around the neo-Classical Yorkshire Museum of 1827–30, which was designed deliberately to contrast with the romantic ruins of medieval St Mary's Abbey. Both Victoria Park and Museum Gardens are now public.

The first park intended primarily as a public recreation ground in an industrial town was the Arboretum at Derby (1839–40), sponsored by Joseph Strutt, a successful and pioneering textile manufacturer of nearby Belper. It started as a small, featureless plot of land on the developing edge of the town, where the new railway station was being built. The landscapist J. C. Loudon, already famous for his private garden layouts, made the very most of the plot. He designed a central, formal, pattern of straight broad paths, lined with trees, intersecting in the middle, and, in complete contrast, a series of intricate, irregularly curving, banks of earth, planted thickly, round the edges of the site. Trees of many different species were planted, hence the title Arboretum. Paths curved between and around the banks and shrubberies, providing a seemingly lengthy walk with changing scenes. This intense and intricate landscape offset the dense housing which quickly developed in the vicinity, but which was largely hidden from the centre of the park by the mounds and planting, when mature. The Arboretum survives, but because so much of the original small-scale planting has gone, it now appears barer and more open than it did in its heyday.

The greatest Victorian park designer was Sir Joseph Paxton, who began his career as gardener to the Duke of Devonshire at Chatsworth, where he designed an early glass and iron greenhouse, now demolished. In 1842 he laid out Prince's Park in Toxteth, Liverpool, as the centrepiece of a new fashionable district of terraces and villas on the outskirts of the city (**XXII**). In 1844 he began his greatest park, Birkenhead Park, across the Mersey from Liverpool. Birkenhead started to develop after the opening of the steam ferry in 1819. Both William Laird's engineering, later shipbuilding, firm and the grand classical central square of the new town, Hamilton Square, were instituted in 1824–5. The park was intended to be for the benefit of the whole town, but it was to be financed from the sale of substantial houses on its fringes. Paxton created, out of featureless fields, a superb landscape with serpentine lake, intricate banks of earth (constructed of soil excavated for the lake), thickly planted and threaded with paths—as at Derby but on a far larger scale. Wide areas of open greensward were left in the inner parts of the park, irregularly fringed with trees, much in the tradition of Humphry Repton. Exotic features like a Swiss bridge, and lodges in various styles from Greek to Gothic, provided visual seasoning. The layout of Birkenhead Park had an important influence on the American landscapist F. L. Olmsted in his design for Central

Park, New York, perhaps the greatest urban park anywhere. Paxton's plan to ring his park with fashionable terrace houses and villas, as had been done at Prince's Park, was only partly realized at Birkenhead; most of the land originally allocated for such private development eventually became part of the park.

Paxton designed several other town parks, including that around his own Crystal Palace, when it was re-erected at Sydenham in South London, and People's Park at Halifax. The latter was promoted by the carpet manufacturer Sir Francis Crossley. Paxton made the most of a limited site, with a formal terraced promenade

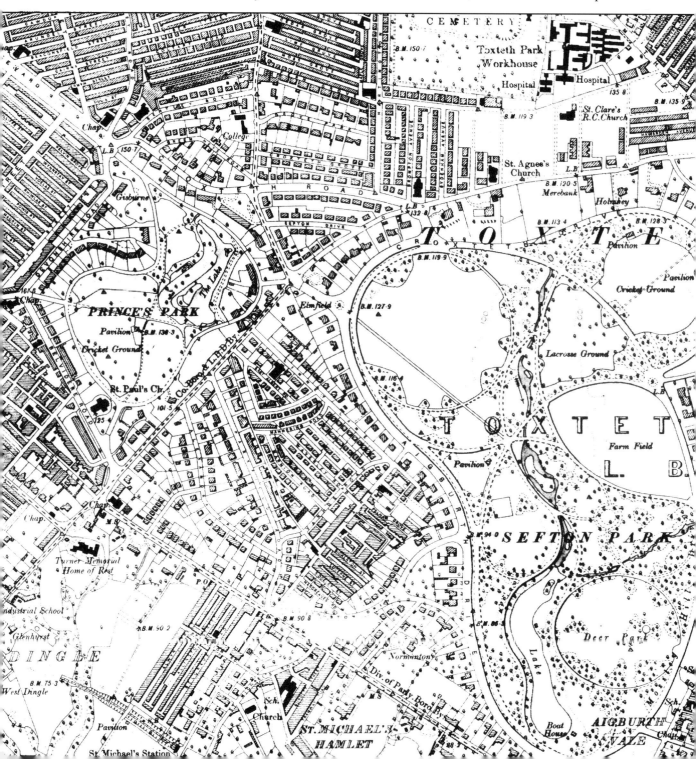

and Italianate pavilion on the higher side, which contrasted with winding paths, thickets of trees and shrubs, and a serpentine pond at the lower levels. Crossley's own house, Bellevue, now the Public Library, overlooked the park on one side, and nearby he laid out model housing, described later (page 259).

Several new parks were created in the growing districts of Victorian London, beginning with Victoria Park in the East End, opened in 1845. Battersea Park, completed by 1857, was the most successful; it had a typical combination of formal layout, with straight axial avenues, and intricate landscape, with winding paths amid trees and bushes, as well as an irregular lake. Every substantial town had at least one park by the later part of the century; examples among very many are Avenham Park in Preston, Grosvenor Park in Chester, and Jephson Park in Leamington Spa. The tradition of contrived informality which was essentially initiated by Capability Brown, and developed by Humphry Repton, reached a zenith in St James's Park (designed by Repton's one-time associate John Nash), and continued in these Victorian public parks, sometimes with elements of formality which contrasted effectively with the intensive irregularity of the rest of the landscape.

Suburbs and resorts

The depopulation of city centres and the development of purely residential areas was one phenomenon of Victorian urban Britain. Another was the widespread rejection by the middle classes of the terrace house as a desirable type of dwelling, in favour of the detached, or semi-detached, villa. However, this rejection was not universal—terrace houses of the grander sort continued to be fashionable in the extended West End of London, in Scotland, and in some resorts.

In Georgian London and Bath the upper classes had lived, even if only for parts of the year, in houses which formed parts of continuous streets, squares or, occasionally, crescents, built in the Classical tradition (83). The middle classes—merchants, industrialists and some professional people—followed suit, and moved in large numbers, during the later Georgian period, into similar, proportionately smaller, houses on the ever-expanding outskirts of London and other large towns, or in the developing resorts.

However, even in the seventeenth century, and to a much greater extent in the eighteenth, London people who could afford them had country houses or 'villas' outside the capital, where they might live for what we now now call weekends, where their families might spend longer periods, and to which they might retire (pages 134, 217). People associated with the Court, or with the literary and artistic life of the capital, might have their villas up-river, from Chelsea to Twickenham and beyond; City merchants would choose villages to north and south such as Highgate and Clapham. There was a similar pattern outside other large commercial cities, such as Bristol.

Nash's plan for Regent's Park (page 150) included detached villas, Classical and stuccoed, among the trees. Beyond the edges of the park, he also designed two clusters of houses called Park Village West and East, which were started in 1824 (144, 145). These, to some extent, carried on a tradition of romanticized rusticity which had its beginnings in eighteenth-century landscaped parks like that at Stourhead, reached a peak of intensity in Marie-Antoinette's make-believe *hameau* at Versailles, and was perfectly examplified by Nash himself in the rustic fantasy

Map XXII *Opposite* **Prince's Park and Sefton Park, Liverpool**. Princes Park, left, was laid out 1842 by Sir Joseph Paxton, with surrounding terraces and villas. Sefton Park dates from 1867. Both have typical Victorian park landscape with irregular planting, curving paths and drives, and artificial lakes. By 1890, the date of this map, tight working-class housing had developed to the west.

144. Park Village West, Regent's Park, laid out by Nash from 1824 (page 150) is a prototype of suburbia, with rustic villas, Gothic here, set informally in well-planted gardens along curving roads.

of the cottages he designed in 1811 at Blaise Hamlet outside Bristol. But the Regent's Park 'villages' were built not for make-believe peasants, as at Versailles, nor for retired estate workers, as at Blaise Hamlet, but for Londoners wishing to escape from, while not altogether leaving, the city. The houses of Park Village West—East survives only in part—are built with studied informality round a sharply curving road, each in its own garden plot, in different styles which are meant to be reminiscent, however remotely, of rural dwellings of England or their counterparts in Italy. More particularly than anywhere else, this is the prototype of the British low-density suburb.

By the 1840s, suburbs of villas in gardens were developing round the fringes of London and many other towns, in styles which varied from the Classical and the vaguely 'Italianate', to the Gothic or the romanticized rustic. Generally, those inspired by the Classical or Italianate traditions had low-pitched, slated roofs (slates from Devon and Cornwall, and, increasingly, Wales, were distributed by water or railway), while those of Gothic or rustic inspiration usually had steep-pitched roofs and prominent gables, often embellished by bargeboards. Windows were frequently large-paned, following the development of plate-glass manufacture, and were often given prominence by being brought out in massive, diagonal-sided bays.

Building materials for Victorian houses varied according to locality—the idea that they generally ceased to be of regional or local origin is erroneous. Hard Pennine stone continued to be used in towns like Halifax (**150**), and rough 'Pennant' sandstone, in colours varying from grey to brown and purple, in Bristol and the South Wales towns. The minor Victorian accretions to Bath, as well as to Trowbridge and other nearby towns, were in Bath stone. Brickworks were ubiquitous in Victorian times, though there were concentrations in some areas, as around Fareham in Hampshire, in central Sussex, and around Reading—to give examples in Southern England. Changing techniques in brickmaking, including the universal use of coal, made Victorian bricks generally harsher in appearance than their

Georgian counterparts. This is specially apparent in the products from large brick-works which supplied the industrial areas of the Midlands and North, such as those at Ruabon in North Wales and Accrington in Lancashire. In suburban villas, materials were often variegated—brickwork might be patterned in contrasting colours, and stone (often Bath stone) used for window frames—or, if this was too expensive, stucco imitating stone. An almost universal feature in a substantial villa after about 1850 was a conservatory—providing a setting for exotic plants and an additional, specially heated, room.

Ideally, each house in a villa suburb should be visually isolated from its neighbours, giving the illusion of total seclusion. Gardens were, characteristically, thickly planted on their perimeters with trees and shrubs, enclosing secluded lawns and flower beds—a style of landscaping derived, in large measure, from the works of the garden designer J. C. Loudon. The villas might be glimpsed, through contrived gaps in the planting, from the street outside. They were usually

145. Park Village West. Another view in this neo-rustic enclave; the style here is Italianate.

Map XXIII *Below* **Smethwick, near Birmingham**. The map of 1890 shows the development of an industrial area. Large factories adjoin canals and railways. Workers' terrace housing has been built sporadically; the spaces between the terraces were soon to be filled. To the south-west, a different pattern suggests the rural past. Compare nearby Edgbaston, **XXIV**.

Map XXIV Edgbaston, Birmingham. The Calthorpe family of Edgbaston Hall, with its Capability Brown park and lake (bottom of map), developed their estate as a low-density suburb from *c* 1820. The map of 1890 shows detached villas along mainly

fronted by substantial garden walls, sometimes decoratively treated, or thick hedges, with massive gateposts flanking the entrances. If the front garden were deep enough, the approach to the front door might be curving and indirect, to enhance the effect of a secluded domain. Of course, vegetation took time to mature, but many favourite Victorian plants were quick-growing.

Because of the pressures on land around fast-growing towns, suburbs could not always be as spacious or secluded as their residents might desire. The semi-detached villa was an ingenious compromise. Early pairs of such houses were usually designed so as to appear at first sight as single dwellings, their entrances being at the sides, giving the occupants of each part a high degree of privacy from their neighbours, and their visitors the illusion that they lived in a house twice as big.

Curving roads, carefully related to topography and landscaping, so that views along the roads were generally limited by the planting in the gardens on the outsides of the curves, with occasional glimpses of gables, rooftops or chimneys, could enhance the feel of suburban seclusion. There was a close analogy between the layouts of the more intricate suburbs and that of informal landscaped parks.

A notable early villa suburb was Edgbaston (**XXIV**). This was the domain of

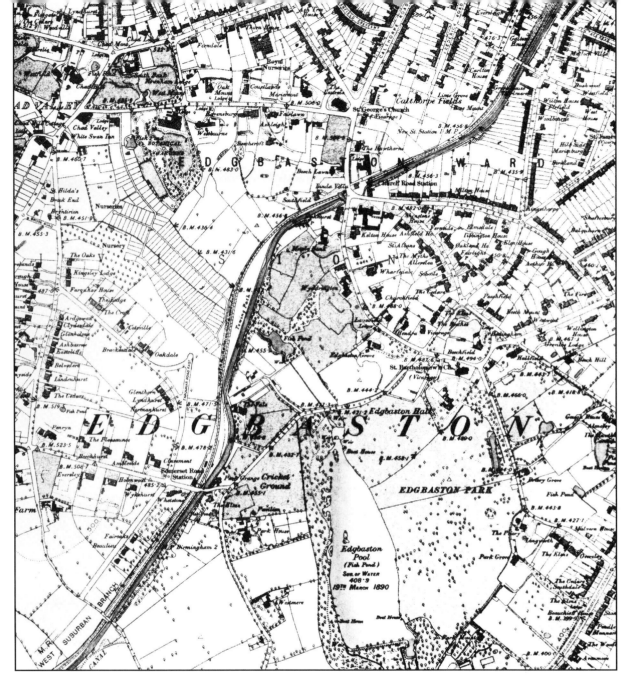

the Gough family, Viscounts Calthorpe, with a Georgian mansion and a Capability Brown park. (The park partly survives as a golf course and the mansion is its club house.) Expanding Birmingham encroached on to the estate's fringe in the early nineteenth century, at first with urban Georgian terraces. From about 1820, stuccoed Classical villas were built on plots further into the estate, in settings already sylvan before being enhanced by more planting. After about 1850 the pace of development quickened, still under careful control by the estate, with gabled Gothic villas along gently winding roads. Birmingham merchants and in-

winding roads; the canal and railway seen on the map are not conspicuous on the ground. Though mostly within a mile of the heart of Birmingham (to the north-east) the area retains its sylvan character. Compare Smethwick.

dustrialists drove in their carriages from their businesses in the smoky, congested town into this Arcadia scarcely a mile away. Despite erosion on its fringes, much of Edgbaston retains a mature, lush, Victorian suburban character to this day, in astonishing contrast to the brash twentieth-century city centre.

Most of the developing cities and towns had suburbs with some of the characteristics of Edgbaston. At Portsmouth, from 1838, a local developer and architect, T. E. Owen, laid out a large part of the seaside suburb of Southsea, inhabited by naval officers and successful town tradesmen. Owen built some terraces in his own idiosyncratic versions of the Regency tradition (147), but most of his houses were detached, or semi-detached, in rustic Gothic or Italian styles, usually along winding roads where the garden walls, overhung with greenery, are distinguishing features. Much survives; The Vale, built in the 1850s (146), is a latter-day version of Park Village West (144). In Clifton, Bristol, Vyvyan Terrace and Worcester Terrace, two of the last terraces to be built in the grand Regency tradition (page 156), in the 1840s and 1850s respectively, both face, across gardens of the Georgian square type, ranges of Gothic villas of the same dates. These combinations depict dramatically the overlap between two contrasting types of middle-class housing, the urban Georgian and the mock-rural Victorian.

North Oxford is one of the best-known of the Victorian sylvan suburbs. In this conservative city two Georgian crescents were built at Park Town, facing each other over an eye-shaped garden, as late as 1853–5. But these were quickly seen to be old-fashioned, and from that date the suburb extended with individual villas in their gardens, which, with their flowering and scented trees in season, are celebrated by Sir John Betjeman in more than one of his poems.

The Georgian tradition of urban terraces for the upper and middle classes survived longer in London than in other parts of Britain, apart from Scotland and some places near the Border, like Sunderland, and a few resorts. Belgravia was complete by about 1850; South Kensington and Bayswater developed, as further extensions of the West End, in the following two decades, with thickly detailed stuccoed streets, often punctuated by ponderous porches, and occasionally relieved by landscaped square gardens of Georgian character. Part of Notting Hill—the Ladbroke Estate—was laid out with more flair during the same period. Here, terraces and crescents front on to streets in the normal way, but they back on to strips of communal garden (restricted to occupants of the adjoining houses, as in Georgian squares) which thread the area—a nearly unique arrangement which had a smaller-scale counterpart in Victorian Folkestone. The last flourish of the Georgian tradition in urban layout, though not in Georgian design, in London was the formation of Cadogan Square and adjoining streets, from around 1880, with houses in neo-Dutch, neo-Flemish and so-called 'Queen Anne' styles, dominantly in red brick and terracotta; some are by Norman Shaw. Older parts of the West End, like the Grosvenor Estate in Mayfair were partly rebuilt in similar styles during the same period.

Although Bath ceased to be really fashionable after 1800, other inland spas flourished through the Victorian period. Cheltenham has its early Victorian terraces in stone or stucco, continuing the Regency tradition; it also has a large number of early nineteenth-century villas in sylvan settings. Leamington grew suddenly from a village into a spa town soon after 1800. The earlier parts are mostly terraced in the Georgian tradition; Lansdown Crescent and Lansdown Circus, which adjoin

146. *Left* **The Vale, Southsea, Portsmouth**, part of extensive suburban development by T. E. Owen, a local architect and speculator, for civilian middle-class and naval officers' families. The Gothic villa, 1859, is typically glimpsed amid greenery behind a garden wall, and the twisty lane is a piece of deliberate romantic planning.

147. *Below left* **Sussex Terrace, Southsea, Portsmouth**, 1854, by T. E. Owen, continues the Regency tradition in its terraced form, but with odd Italian detailing. By this date, middle-class people usually preferred to live in detached villas, as in **146**.

each other, illustrate yet again the transition from formal to informal planning. The first is a typical crescent of 1830; the second, built a few years later, has semi-detached houses following the curve.

The practice of taking annual seaside holidays became firmly established among the middle classes as the railway network was developed. Brighton, with its administratively separate neighbour Hove, continued to grow with miles of tight-packed streets, usually at right-angles to the sea-front, and generally in terraced form since there was little room for spacious villa layouts. Eastbourne, a collection of villages before the 1850s, was developed in that decade by the principal landowner, the Duke of Devonshire, in what was then a very conservative manner, with grand Italianate terraces and hotels facing the sea and broad tree-lined streets behind, rather like Kensington or Notting Hill by the sea. By contrast, Bournemouth was built in the newer fashion. There was almost nothing there at all in 1836, when the architect Benjamin Ferrey designed, for the landowner, an informal 'marine village' of detached villas on curving roads, centred on a landscaped garden where the miniature Bourne approached the sea. (Nothing survives but the road layout, the stream and the garden.) It expanded, equally spaciously, over what had been open heathlands, latterly covered with self-sown pines—which were not indigenous but quickly came to symbolize Bournemouth. Few of the villas were remarkable; the town's chief fame architecturally is for its Victorian churches. Bournemouth kept itself deliberately quiet and 'respectable', as much a retreat for retirement as a rendezvous for holidays. Victorian seaside towns, like spa towns during the period, housed thousands of people retired from industry or commerce, from service in the armed forces, or from a career in the expanding Empire (page 156).

Torquay started to develop earlier than Bournemouth, with a few Regency terraces above the original fishing village, but its major growth was in Victorian times. Big Italianate or Gothic retirement homes were built along winding roads in the hilly country to the east of the town. There was one last flourish of the Georgian tradition in Hesketh Crescent, built in 1846 by a cove in what still seems a half-wild setting—perhaps the most outlandish setting for any grand urban crescent.

Sidmouth did not grow much after early Victorian times (**90**), but Clevedon, on the Bristol Channel coast, was developed informally from a straggling village by the Eltons of medieval Clevedon Court, with villas, often gabled, in the rough local stone along curving roads on well-treed slopes, and a delicate iron pier where ships to and from South Wales used to berth.

Piers were the most extraordinary features of Victorian seaside resorts. A pier was originally simply a jetty, which might also become a place for a short bracing walk. At Brighton, the Chain Pier was built in 1823 to accommodate vessels which crossed to Dieppe, or sailed coastwise. Inevitably it became a favourite promenade, and was the focal point of the whole front, since the Pavilion was hidden inland. It was the prototype of dozens of seaside piers, which were, henceforth, usually built both for accommodating vessels and for pleasure, with the latter usually predominating in later times. Piers were places where people could promenade almost as on the decks of ships, yet be linked with land. Most outlandish of all were the theatres, concert halls, or ballrooms built in late Victorian and Edwardian times right over the sea at the ends of the piers. Brighton is still the most interesting place for piers. The Chain Pier was washed away in a storm in 1898 but was quickly replaced by the Palace Pier, still in use. The West Pier is older, originally built in 1866 but greatly enlarged in 1894, with a seaward concert hall and a smaller pavilion half-way along. Alas, it is closed as unsafe, and is at the time of writing the subject of long-drawn controversy over its future.

Traditionally, well-to-do families stayed at rented houses; in Georgian times they would take a whole house in, say, Bath, Weymouth or Brighton, and perhaps bring their own servants, for what was often a long stay. The boarding house, accommodating two or more families, was a development from this. There were hotels, as we understand the term, in Regency resorts—the oldest in Brighton was the Ship, which grew from an inn in the old fishing town. But palatial seaside hotels—like railway hotels near stations, or commercial hotels in city centres— were a Victorian development. Probably the most impressive of the period is the Grand Hotel at Scarborough, placed on a low cliff above the beach; it was designed by Cuthbert Brodrick, architect of the Town Hall and Corn Exchange at Leeds (131), the city from which, with Bradford, a high proportion of its clientele came. Scarborough is the oldest and in many ways the most dramatic British seaside resort, with its ruined castle on a headland, the old fishing town below, with its small but still lively harbour, and Regency and Victorian crescents and terraces fronting the bay. Only Llandudno among large resorts has a comparably dramatic site. This was a wholly Victorian creation, developed from about 1850 by the landowning Mostyn family in a still essentially Georgian manner, with terraces following the curve of the bay, like an architectural cliff, round to the headland of Great Orme. It makes a complete contrast to Tenby, on the South Wales coast, a much smaller resort with stuccoed terraces tight-packed into the remaining spaces of the medieval headland town, still defined by its wall on the landward side. Here the seaside function has completely superseded the old port activities.

A seaside resort which did not fulfil expectations was Saltburn, promoted on the Cleveland coast by the railway and iron dynasty of Pease in 1860 when the Stockton and Darlington Railway, which the family had first promoted, was extended to this cliff-bound site. A grand hotel was built, a pier constructed, a gully landscaped, and a new town laid out with a central square of which the handsome station façade was the centrepiece. Beyond these features nothing much of note was ever built.

Early suburbs and seaside resorts were dependent on carriages and coaches. Railways quickly hastened the growth of resorts; it took longer for them to have an appreciable influence on the development of suburbs. However, some suburban growth associated with trains took place at the very beginning of the railway age. When the first section of the London and Southampton Railway was opened through Surrey in 1838, speculators bought a farm adjoining a small station intended to serve Kingston, over a mile away. They started a new township, Surbiton, at first a mixture of short Regency-type terraces and stuccoed Classical villas, mostly semi-detached, of which a few survive. This must have been the first physically separate town (it did not become linked with London by continuous development till much later) to be dependent for its existence on travel by train to a large city a few miles away. However it is not certain how many daily travellers there would have been from Surbiton at first, as until 1848 the London terminus of the line was as far out as Nine Elms, Battersea. In that year the line was extended to Waterloo, after which there must have been steadily increasing daily 'commuting' from Surbiton, to judge from the number of villas from the 1850s and 1860s near the station today (many more have been demolished). Other towns and villages well-served by railways developed for 'commuters' from the 1850s onwards—Croydon, Bromley, Sutton, Reigate and, on another side of London, Brentwood and Broxbourne. Such places remained physically separate from London for some time. Railways serving the north, north-west and west of London were mainly interested in long-distance traffic and did not at first encourage 'commuting' from their stations near London; it was left to the railways serving south and north-east London, which had more, relatively, to gain from commuting to encourage the practice on a large scale in mid-Victorian times. The light, sandy soils of much of Surrey and north-west Kent, easy to drain, picturesque, and usually fairly high-lying, proved particularly attractive to businessmen-commuters by later Victorian times. The Chiltern country was not opened up on a large scale to daily travellers until the very end of the century.

Railway 'commuting' for the working classes was not financially possible until cheap workmen's fares were introduced on some lines from the 1870s, particularly on those leading through Tottenham and Walthamstow, opened at the same time as Liverpool Street Station (page 218), which caused those places to develop quickly as artisan suburbs. Cheap day fares to some seaside resorts were obtainable in the early days of the railway, for instance to Brighton in the 1840s. It was, however, only much later in the century that any significant numbers of working-class people were able to take periods of holiday by the seaside; this led most particularly to the development of Blackpool as a truly popular resort, benefitting from inflows of workers from Lancashire cotton towns, or places further afield, as they had their 'wakes weeks' or other equivalents—which were a curious development from medieval practice. Often they had originated as the annual festivities related to the patron saints of parish churches; by Victorian times they had simply become annual holidays for the workpeople of particular towns. Southend developed in relation to London in a way fairly comparable to Blackpool, but only at the end of the century. It was not until next century that many other resorts, originally catering for the middle classes, became, in the true sense, 'popular' as well.

The Arts and Crafts movement, which had its genesis under the influence of William Morris, Philip Webb and others who reacted against the high-handedness of some mid-Victorian architects' work, as well as against what they saw as the evil effects of industrialization, influenced the design of suburban houses from the 1870s onwards. The fashion for 'Old English' styles, derived especially from the rich vernacular traditions of Surrey, Sussex and Kent, with heavy timber-framing, tile-hanging and sometimes rough stonework as characteristic features, was favoured in the early works of Norman Shaw, and later in those of Sir Edwin Lutyens—himself born in rural Surrey. It was most appropriate in those counties, as around Godalming where so many of Lutyens' early inventive houses, as well as others by Shaw, Webb and their associates, were built. These were country retreats rather than places from which the occupants travelled daily. But the 'Old English' style became adapted by lesser architects, and developers who had little design sense, in the more suburban areas as can be seen abundantly today. There were similar tendencies under the influence of the vernacular styles of North-West England, especially Cheshire with its heavy half-timbering. Sensitive architects produced superb compositions in this revived 'vernacular' style, as did the Chester-based John Douglas, not least in the city of Chester itself. Much of Chester was rebuilt or re-fronted in latter-day variants of the local half-timbered style (1, 21); the best composition is the east side of St Werburgh's Street of 1899, designed by Douglas.

Along with the fashion for 'Old English' there developed the vogue for Flemish, Dutch and English Jacobean styles, as well as the indeterminate but often highly inventive 'Queen Anne' style, which bore little relation to anything built in England during her reign—if anything it was related to burghers' houses of the mid-late seventeenth century with flat-fronted, round-angled oriel windows like those in Sparrowe's House at Ipswich (page 52). Brick, preferably of a deep, rich red came especially into favour in reaction against both the harshness of Victorian 'industrial' bricks and the drab browns and buffs still much used in mid-century, especially in London. Brickwork was sometimes moulded or cut, as in the seventeenth century (75); terracotta, of various colours, was much used for embellishments. Gables were often prominent, whether straight-sided, or twisted in the 'Dutch' manner, and chimneys were emphasized as skyline features. Later, fashions extended towards the more sedate styles of early eighteenth-century England, with special emphasis on sash windows with thick wood framing, desirably brought out in white in contrast to the rich colour of the brick or other materials.

One of the most remarkable suburbs of the later nineteenth century was Bedford Park in Chiswick, then on the rural western fringe of London, beside a District Line station. It was developed from 1875 and was intended to house people of 'artistic' inclinations but fairly modest means. Norman Shaw was associated with the scheme and designed the 'Old English' public house and adjoining buildings, but the houses are by other architects, and are generally, though not strongly, in the 'Dutch' or 'Queen Anne' traditions. The layout is not specially interesting and derives much of its attraction from being centred on a village green or common—Acton Green—which existed already. Old hedgerow trees were preserved along road edges (so influencing the layout), until newly-planted ones reached reasonable maturity. Special emphasis was placed on garden fences bordering the roads, which were often of white-painted wood on brick bases. Gardens generally are not large, but there is enough greenery in gardens and on roadsides to offset significantly the dominance of the buildings, in the by then established tradition of the sylvan suburb. Bedford Park is sometimes thought to have initiated this tradition, but as the examples already cited, and many more, demonstrate, this is far from being the case. It stood out as a suburban oasis of good design in a period when the normal standard of design in suburban villa building had become deplorably low.

Railway-based suburbs grew round other cities, notably Manchester and Liverpool. Alderley Edge, on a Cheshire hill several miles by train from Manchester, started to grow from mid-Victorian times, while a suburb of secluded houses in varied and often fantastic styles was developed from the 1890s on the edge of the market town of Knutsford, from which businessmen commuted to Manchester. Near Liverpool the high country of the northern Wirral peninsula started to develop after the direct railway, tunnelling under the Mersey, was opened in 1886. The larger, earlier houses in 'vernacular' styles, built by shipping magnates, sometimes have settings reminiscent of their counterparts in the Surrey hills.

Spiritual and social provision

The nineteenth century was a religious age. The Church of England experienced renewed vitality, partly in counteraction to the vigorous development of Nonconformist sects, especially the Methodists. Many new Anglican churches, often called

'Commissioners' Churches', were built under an Act of 1818 which set aside a million pounds for this purpose. Most were in the developing districts of London and the growing towns of the North and Midlands. A typical series was built in 1822 in the old parish of Lambeth, which, like the later borough, extended for about four miles south from the original village on the Thames, where till then the only church stood. The four new churches were dedicated to the Evangelists, and three were deliberately sited at focal points in their growing neighbourhoods—St Matthew, Brixton; St Mark, Kennington; and St Luke, West Norwood; the fourth, St John, Waterloo, was built in an already crowded area. All these churches are Classical, with prominent porticoes. Many other Commissioners' churches were in versions of Gothic styles, usually Perpendicular, with tall pinnacled towers. The prominence of Commissioners' churches, with eye-catching porticoes or towers, was deliberate, to symbolize the ascendancy of the Established Church. Indeed, a large proportion of the fairly restricted funds available for each church under the Act was spent on imposing exteriors. Inside, these early nineteenth-century churches were frequently simple rectangles, with galleries to house the large hoped-for congregations. Where more funds than usual were available, new churches of the period would be more substantial throughout, like those of St Marylebone (1817) and St Pancras (1822, with its caryatids inspired by the Athenian originals), both replacing outgrown village churches on different sites; or like Thomas Rickman's iron-framed churches of St George, Everton and St Michael, Toxteth, both in Liverpool. None of the last-named were strictly Commissioners' churches.

The 'Low Church' of the Evangelical Revival in the Church of England was countered by the 'High Church', which sought to revive old Catholic practices in the national Church. The latter was particularly associated with the serious, often passionate, study of medieval churches which was stimulated by the fanatical Roman Catholic, Augustus Pugin. By the 1840s nearly all 'High' and most 'Low' churches were designed in what were thought to be 'correct' versions of early Gothic styles, especially those of the thirteenth-century Midlands. There were no more galleried or iron-framed interiors behind pretentious exteriors, and hardly any new Classical churches for several decades. Early and mid-Victorian church architecture was dominated by the prolific Sir Gilbert Scott and by the more brilliant and inventive George E. Street and William Butterfield; the even greater John L. Pearson belonged to a slightly later generation. At the end of the century the Perpendicular style came back into favour, with G. F. Bodley as its greatest exponent. These were national figures; there were many outstanding regional architects such as Austin and Paley of Lancaster and R. J. Johnson of Newcastle. These and many lesser architects designed innumerable new Victorian churches, and restored thousands of old ones, often excessively, all over the country. With their sometimes beautiful spires, their substantial towers or steeply gabled rooflines, they were dominating landmarks in many middle-class suburbs, like Street's St Philip and St James at North Oxford, Pearson's St Michael at Headingley, and T. E. Owen's 'incorrect' but effectively placed St Jude at Southsea. And they proliferated in poorer districts, where new churches were often paid for by wealthy people living elsewhere, or by local businessmen. Some of the grandest Anglican churches were in humdrum places; for instance Pearson's greatest masterpiece is St Augustine in Kilburn, London, never a scintillating area; Bodley's finest church is St Augustine at Pendlebury, a dim district outside Manchester; and one of R. J. Johnson's best works is St Oswald in a back part of Hartlepool. Some seaside resorts, notably Brighton and Bournemouth, have specially fine collections of Victorian churches.

There were few new Anglican churches in city centres, from which the population was moving, and only one new Victorian cathedral, at Truro. New dioceses were formed, some centred on major medieval churches in small towns, like St Albans, Southwell and Ripon, others on former parish churches in large industrial cities, ranging in scale from the collegiate church of Manchester to the moderate-sized but sophisticated St Philip's in Birmingham by Thomas Archer, architect of St John's, Smith Square, Westminster.

The Nonconformists were altogether as numerous and as vigorous as the Anglicans, and included many wealthy industrialists. Thousands of chapels were built by the various sects. The old simple, Puritan traditions of Nonconformist chapel building (14, 95, 109) survived well into the nineteenth century; many early or mid-Victorian chapels are large, simple rectangles, though often with striking Classical façades. But, from the 1840s, many Nonconformist congregations tried to compete with the Anglicans on the latter's terms, and built churches in florid Gothic styles, often with tall landmark spires. Until fairly recently many Victorian quarters of towns had skylines pierced by the steeples of rival sects, but Victorian churches, particularly Nonconformist ones, have, over the last few decades, disappeared at an increasing rate, so that such skyline effects are now much rarer—the 1960s' tower block is now more characteristic of many inner-city areas than the Victorian spire. Halifax still, at the time of writing, illustrates the old sectarian rivalry. The Anglican Akroyds, who established a large model housing estate, Akroyden, for their workers, also built All Souls' Church, with a tall spire, on a commanding site at the brow of a hill, to the design of Sir Gilbert Scott, who considered it, with good reason, one of his best works. It was the Akroyds' answer to the other leading manufacturing family, the Nonconformist Crossleys, who, just before, had built a grand new Congregational Church in the style of medieval Yorkshire abbeys, with a spire that soars above the Georgian Piece Hall nearby. Tellingly, the older, Georgian chapel was retained alongside, in a strong but simple Classical style which was characteristic of Congregational chapels of its date (1772). The recent state of both Victorian churches is all too typical; All Souls' needed a huge sum for repair; the Congregational Church, having closed, was prevented from being pulled down because it was listed; it was then fire-damaged, but the spire is retained as a landmark. St Ives in Huntingdonshire is a small town which also illustrates sectarian rivalry. The medieval church with its slender spire is at one end of the town (16); near the other end is the vigorous Gothic (1862) Congregational Church with a taller spire.

The small but devout Roman Catholic community which persisted after the Reformation was greatly augmented through Irish immigration in Victorian times. Following emancipation from severe restrictions in the early nineteenth century, numerous Catholic churches were built, often with slender resources, many designed by Augustus Pugin. Some of these churches, although usually quite modest in size, became cathedrals after the Roman Catholic hierarchy was established in England in 1850. An example is that of Newcastle, which was a modest but effective church of 1844, designed by Pugin in an early fourteenth-century style, to which a slender, lofty spire was added twenty years later by J. A. Hansom, another architect of many Catholic buildings. The one major Roman Catholic cathedral begun in the nineteenth century is that of Westminster, by J. F. Bentley, started in 1895.

The Church of England was a major force in the provision of elementary education in Victorian times. Thousands of schools were built in the middle part of the century in association with parish churches in town and country. Others were established by Nonconformists and Catholics, and a large number by the non-denominational British and Foreign School Society. But it was not until after the Education Act of 1870 that elementary education became universal. School Boards were then set up, and the still familiar 'Board Schools' built, the effect of their bulk often offset by sensitive external detailing in the neo-Dutch of 'Queen Anne' styles favoured at the end of the century (**148, 149**).

148. *Right* **Hammerton School, Sheffield**, now Kettlebridge School, was a combined infants', junior and senior school. The photograph was taken soon after it was opened, in 1904.

149. *Below right* **Hammerton School, Sheffield**, 1904, designed by W. J. Hale in an Art-Nouveau style typical of the period. The inscriptions 'Courage' and 'Courtesy' symbolize the ideals of school authorities in Edwardian times.

Most public schools, apart from Eton, Winchester and two or three in London, were essentially nineteenth-century institutions, whether they had developed out of old small-town grammar schools like Rugby, Uppingham or Berkhamsted (56), or were entirely new foundations like Marlborough or Cheltenham. Other grammar schools which had been founded in Tudor times to serve small towns such as Manchester, Birmingham and Croydon (page 98) then were, grew into prestigious day schools for their hugely expanded communities, while other similar schools for boys, and many more for girls, were newly founded in large cities and towns. Many Victorian grammar schools favoured Tudor 'collegiate' styles—Bristol Grammar School, whose earliest buildings, by the excellent and prolific local architects Foster and Wood, date from 1879, is an example. What became the King Edward VII School in Sheffield was an exception; the buildings of 1837, by the distinguished local architect William Flockton, are grandly Classical; this is perhaps explained by the fact that it was originally a Methodist foundation, while most of the more traditional grammar schools were, at least tenuously, Anglican.

England had only two universities before 1830. (Scotland had four, but they were much smaller.) Durham University was founded by the Bishop in 1832, very much under the shadow of the Cathedral, with the ancient Castle as the first college—the Bishop continued to live at his other palace in Bishop Auckland. At the same time a very different and far larger establishment was founded in London—University College, in Bloomsbury, which was strictly non-denominational. Very shortly afterwards a second college was established, King's College in the Strand, avowedly Anglican. Colleges for higher education, and medical schools, were founded in the larger cities throughout Queen Victoria's reign. Many developed, by themselves or in combination, into universities by the end of the nineteenth century or in the early part of the twentieth. The most remarkable was Owen's College, established in Manchester in 1851, which became the first part of what was called the Victoria University in 1881. Similar colleges in Liverpool and Leeds joined in 1884 and 1887 to form a federal University, which split into its component parts in 1903. All three of these first 'civic universities' have original buildings in romantic Gothic by Alfred Waterhouse, architect of Manchester Town Hall, and the Natural History Museum, London. They were located just outside the city centres, and each has now expanded over a large 'campus' where Waterhouse's turrets and Gothic windows stand in still confident contrast with the often prematurely ageing concrete structures nearby. By contrast, Birmingham University, which started in the city centre, moved to its present suburban site in 1900, when grandiose buildings by Sir Aston Webb were begun.

Many technical colleges were built in the late Victorian and Edwardian periods; some have grown into universities, others into polytechnics. A good example is at Portsmouth, where the original Municipal College (now part of the Polytechnic) was built in 1903–8 in an inventive Baroque style by the local architect G. E. Smith, grouping with the earlier Guildhall—a descendant of Leeds Town Hall in form and style, and by a Leeds architect, William Hill. Also part of the civic and cultural group was the old Public Library, designed by Smith in conjunction with the College, which is a typical example of many such institutions founded in large cities from mid-Victorian times.

Another similar group of buildings is at Stratford, in East London, started in 1898 and containing a college, a public library and a museum. The architect was

John Gibson, and his design is in the liveliest 'Free Baroque' typical of the turn of the century, bristling with turrets and other skyline features, and embellished with carved mural decorations in the Arts and Crafts tradition. These were built to serve and enlighten the inhabitants of West Ham, a once largely rural area which in the previous seventy years had developed into a densely populated industrial and dockland district on the eastern fringes of London. The Museum was founded by J. Passmore Edwards, who endowed many others like it, as well as hospitals and charitable institutions. He was one of several such benefactors in late Victorian and Edwardian Britain. One of the most prolific in his generosity was Andrew Carnegie, a Scot who made his fortune in Pittsburgh and spent much of it founding new public libraries, many of which bear his name, in towns and suburbs round Britain.

Institutions such as these were preceded in many towns by Literary and Philosophical Societies, or Literary and Scientific Institutions, which catered for the more intellectual members of the middle classes; where lectures were regularly held, and which usually had libraries and sometimes museums. A remarkable surviving example is the 'Lit and Phil' in Newcastle, housed in a Classical building of 1825 by the local architect John Green—where Robert Stephenson lectured, and the locally based Sir Joseph Swan demonstrated his pioneer electric light bulb. Mechanics' Institutes were fairly similar institutions, catering for artisans and skilled working men who were intellectually vigorous and inquiring, while many of the earliest Working Men's Clubs or Institutes, notably in mining areas, had a strong intellectual 'self-help' bias, with their reference libraries and reading rooms.

The poor, and especially the aged poor, had in some measure been provided for in medieval and later hospitals and almshouses, founded through private charity (See Chapter Eight). But these served only a proportion, varying in different places, of the people in real need. Public support for the poor started with the Poor Law of Elizabeth I which required parishes to make provision for the poor through local funds, raised largely out of rates. This might take the form of 'outdoor relief' in money or kind, to ensure a minimum level of subsistence, or residence in 'workhouses', which were originally named because they were places where the destitute were provided with work—but which might also house the aged, the incapacitated and even children. In 1835 a new Poor Law was enacted. This required that all parishes, outside large towns, be grouped together in 'unions', each being provided with a large workhouse, under the control of an appointed Board of Guardians, entry to which was to be restricted to the genuinely destitute. Conditions in these workhouses were intended to be such that no one would seek entry if it could possibly be avoided. In generally rural areas, the workhouses were normally built in the market towns, each serving several villages. Usually they were grimly but handsomely functional in appearance, in basic Classical styles (though occasionally they had Gothic trimmings, as, for instance, at Lichfield). The 'unions', as the workhouses themselves came to be popularly known, became dreaded institutions in living folklore.

There were large hospitals, in the medical sense, in Georgian times and even before. Most large towns and county towns possessed them by the end of the Georgian period, and altered and enlarged buildings of this date sometimes survive, as at Salisbury, Brighton and Exeter. Many more were founded in Victorian times, by public funds, private charity or a combination of the two. The elaborate

Gothic buildings of the Leeds Infirmary, built to a fully Gothic design by Sir Gilbert Scott in 1863–8, are fairly typical.

These descriptions can only indicate a tiny proportion of the enormous number of cultural, charitable and recreational institutions, funded from private or public money, which were established or developed during the Victorian and Edwardian periods, and which offset the usually unsatisfactory, and sometimes terrible, conditions under which a large proportion of city and town dwellers lived—which are the subject of the following section.

Housing the people

Before the Industrial Age, the poor lived in three types of accommodation. Firstly, there were traditional cottages, which in rural areas were usually set in large plots or gardens. Even in towns, particularly in the smaller ones—and on the edges of the larger ones—the humblest houses often had large plots of private ground. Secondly, old large houses, originally inhabited by people of some means, were often subdivided or simply 'multi-occupied' at high density. Finally, many poor people lived in dwellings which were packed into former yards or gardens, or on to other odd sites in built-up areas—a practice which began well before the industrial age (pages 59). Unlike traditional cottages, such 'infill' dwellings seldom had significant private spaces attached. The notorious eighteenth-century 'rookeries' of London, like St Giles-in-the-Fields, Drury Lane and parts of Whitechapel resulted from a combination of the second and third processes, subdivision and infilling.

Most of the larger industrial towns developed from older small places, and their growing proletariat was partly accommodated, at first, through the same processes of subdivision and infilling, resulting in the notorious 'courts' (courtyards) so much condemned by housing reformers. These were typically entered by narrow passageways from the streets, and often consisted of flimsy cottages crowded round tiny, usually insanitary, yards. As the population of typical industrial towns grew, more minimal houses were built, often in comparably cramped conditions, wherever suitably sited land was available (page 220). The same happened in hitherto rural areas where industries or mines were developed—although in such places the housing was often provided by the companies. In most places, apart from London and a few corporate towns, there was no control over standards of construction, housing layouts, or sanitation before the early Victorian period.

Except in dense inner parts of large towns, disposal of human waste was not generally a serious problem in pre-industrial Britain. If not used to enrich gardens or small-holdings, or cast into cesspits, rivers or the sea, it was often fairly easily disposable, like horse manure, to neighbouring farmers. With the huge expansion of densely-built urban areas, problems of disposal were compounded without, at first, the full seriousness of the consequences being understood. There was a series of reports on sanitation during the 1840s, the driving force behind which was Edwin Chadwick. These culminated in the first Public Health Act of 1848, just when a series of cholera epidemics caused widespread alarm. The Municipal Corporations Act of 1835 had resulted in old town corporations being reformed and new ones set up; some of these councils had, from the start, powers to control new building and sanitation. In other places *ad hoc* bodies had been set up to deal with such matters. The 1848 Act made it compulsory for there to be controlling authorities for sanitation and drainage in all places where the annual death rates per thousand population exceeded a prescribed figure, or where a certain percentage of ratepayers demanded such action. From then on there was overall progress, even if it was tardy or erratic in many places, towards overcoming the terrible problems relating to sanitation and water supply.

Initially, the direct relationship between contaminated water and diseases such as cholera and typhoid was not fully appreciated. Matters were even made worse for a time, when newly constructed sewers drained into rivers, including the Thames, which provided water supply. At first it was generally thought that infectious diseases were caught through breathing foul air—hence the sometimes obsessive vigour with which housing reformers advocated the virtues of providing wide spaces between buildings. However, the significance of water contamination was soon realized, and drastic measures taken—such as the prohibition from extracting water for drinking from the Thames below Teddington after 1855.

London was excluded from the provisions of the 1848 Act, but had its own body, the Metropolitan Board of Works, set up in 1855, which controlled drainage and other types of public work, including major roads, in an area stretching for several miles around the City (which never altered its medieval boundaries). This Board constructed trunk sewers north and south of the Thames, with elaborate iron-framed, brick-encased pumping stations near Stratford and Woolwich. Its most dramatic achievement was the Victoria Embankment, constructed between 1864 and 1870 on land reclaimed from the Thames, primarily to contain a sewer, but also providing a new riverside road, and an underground railway (the District Line, first operated by steam). It also assisted navigation by narrowing the river and so increasing the scouring effect of the tidal flow. Connecting with the

150. Housing at Halifax. Typical mid-19th century housing of local stone in a Pennine industrial town (page 240), although front gardens were not universal features in the North. The street retains its original paving of local 'York' stone (93).

151. Housing at Halifax. The same housing as in **150**, showing it is literally 'back-to-back'—a form that lasted long in West Yorkshire. Such close spacing would have been impossible after the Public Health Act 1875; there would have been wider, conventional, streets. Note the factory chimney.

Embankment was Queen Victoria Street, which cut through the medieval network of City lanes to the capital's financial heartland at the Bank of England (**129**).

The culmination of sanitary legislation was the Public Health Act of 1875. This required the setting up of sanitary authorities all over the country, except where municipal councils with sanitary powers existed. These authorities were required to exercise strict control over drainage, building construction, spaces between buildings, and other matters relating to new development, according to local bye-laws, all under the ultimate supervision of the central Board of Health. Henceforth, all new building reached reasonably high structural and spatial standards, resulting in the typical 'byelaw streets' of working-class housing to the newly required minimum street widths, in contrast to the cramped and usually insanitary streets or 'courts' of the earlier part of the century. In much of the North and Midlands such houses normally had only small private yards, often backing on to rear access lanes, but in the South and East, including London, the old tradition of providing back gardens even to small terrace houses largely survived. In the North-East, especially Newcastle, there was a tradition of flats in two-storeyed terraces, which

152. Model Housing at Copley, Halifax, built *c* 1850 by the Akroyd firm near one of their textile mills—earlier than their well-known housing at Akroyden. The houses were better built than most of the same rental level at the time. Separate allotments were provided as well as small private gardens.

look outwardly like normal two-floor houses except for paired entrance doors from the streets. Back-to-back housing—where one row of houses backed physically on to another, each house, apart from those at the ends, having only one outside façade—were prohibited in different places at different times. In Birmingham, for instance, where they had been numerous in earlier periods of expansion, new back-to-back housing was made illegal in the mid nineteenth century; in Leeds, astonishingly, they were permitted right into the early twentieth century, when terraces of back-to-backs, perfectly sound structurally and in their sanitary arrangements, were still built (**150, 151**).

Against the terrible general background of poor, cramped and insanitary housing for the lower-paid in the growing industrial towns, a few enlightened industrialists provided housing for their employees which was well above the normal standards of the time. Arkwright's surviving housing of the 1780s at Cromford (page 160) might come into this category. Ambrose Crowley's now vanished community near Newcastle has been mentioned (page 176). Robert Owen's community which flourished at New Lanark in Scotland at the beginning of the nineteenth century became famous throughout Britain and beyond—but more for the ways in which it was organized socially than for the nature of the housing accommodation. Butetown near Merthyr Tydfil, built from 1802, has already been described as a notable, but for its time and area quite exceptional, iron-workers' village (page 175).

The best-known mid nineteenth-century 'model' community is Saltaire, near Bradford. Sir Titus Salt moved his booming business, based on alpaca wool from South America, out of Bradford, where there was little room to expand, to a 'greenfield' site adjoining a railway and canal by the River Aire. The great mill, designed by the local architects Lockwood and Mawson, who later designed Bradford Town Hall, was finished in 1853. Beside it, Salt built a new small town, to a tight-knit pattern of terraced streets, with houses varying in size and rental, all solidly built with Italianate details. The layout was similar to that of contemporary speculative housing in many industrial towns; the quality of the houses themselves was better.

A few had small gardens; many had no more than back yards. But Salt provided two areas of allotments, available for rent to those who wanted to grow their own vegetables. He also laid out a public park on the edge of the town, in typical Victorian style, beyond which the land steadily rose towards the legendary wilderness of Ilkley Moor a few miles away. Salt also provided spiritual and social facilities; the Congregational Church—that was his denomination—stood prominently opposite the entrance to the factory. Elsewhere there were a school, notable in the days before compulsory education; an Institute, with provision for evening classes, encouraging the people to 'better themselves'; a Sunday School, which in those days could be an important agent towards literacy; and a hospital. Shops were provided, but there were no public houses—these existed in nearby Shipley, then growing from a small village into a town. Saltaire soon became well-known nationally and even internationally as an example of relatively enlightened town-planning and housing provision.

Other model housing schemes were promoted in Halifax by the rival industrial families, the Akroyds and the Crossleys (page 251). The former built Akroyden in 1859, close to the family's factory, consisting of solid stone dwellings with Gothic detailing, grouped round a large open recreational area. They varied in size; some of the larger ones were purchased by their occupants, the better-paid workers, through predecessors of present-day Building Societies. The architect employed initially was Sir Gilbert Scott, who also designed the neighbouring All Souls' Church for the Akroyds, but the scheme was taken over and completed by the locally based W. H. Crossland, who later distinguished himself in designing Rochdale Town Hall (1866–71), and the fantastic Royal Holloway College at Egham in Surrey. The Crossleys gave the site for Halifax's Town Hall (137), as well as paying for the Congregational Church, and People's Park, already described. Nearby, they built, from 1864, another group of model workers' houses. As at Akroyden, the more substantial houses are fairly elaborately Gothic, looking, with their gables, something like typical villas of the time, except that they are linked together in terraces. The cheaper houses, for Crossley's lower-paid workers, are in tight-knit terraces, but with pleasant small front gardens, footpath access at the front and vehicular access only from the back lanes—an unusual, but not unique arrangement for the time. They contrasted with nearby, slightly earlier, speculatively built housing, demolished a few years ago, which had handsome exteriors of belated Georgian character. The latter houses were back-to-back, a building form which did not survive as long in Halifax as in neighbouring Leeds.

There were other comparable model housing schemes in the middle years of the nineteenth century—including the railway development at Swindon and Derby already described (page 210), and the streets built by the Heathcoats at Tiverton (153). These model estates housed only a tiny proportion of industrial wage-earners, but they had a disproportionate influence because many of them—notably Saltaire, Akroyden and Swindon—were well-known and attracted the attention of people, of whom there was an increasing number as the century progressed, who wanted to uplift the general standards of working-class housing, and of the layout of industrial towns.

These were all new housing areas. They did nothing directly to improve conditions in existing areas of sub-standard housing. The movement to provide housing on a substantial scale in direct replacement of slums began in the 1840s when

153. St Paul Street, Tiverton, Devon. Simple handsome housing in the Georgian tradition built *c* 1850 by the Heathcoat firm to house workers at their nearby lace factory (page 170). Note the recessed rounded corner.

voluntary bodies were formed in London. One was called the Society for Improving the Condition of the Labouring Classes, with Prince Albert as patron. (The lengthy title was typical of Victorian institutions.) These bodies were organized on straightforward business lines, funded from shares, from which there would be a stated maximum possible return of five or six per cent. The rents charged were intended to be within the means of fairly low-paid workers, but to be high enough to ensure a reasonable return on capital, any surplus above the maximum dividend being re-invested. This was shown to be possible with sound but economical construction and efficient management. One notable early scheme by the Society for Improving the Condition of the Labouring Classes was built in 1849 at Streatham Street, Bloomsbury, a location that seems salubrious today, but was then on the edge of the festering slum 'rookery' of St Giles-in-the-Fields. (Most of the 'rookery' was to be swept away in subsequent decades, largely through the construction of new roads such as New Oxford Street and the far end of Shaftesbury Avenue.) The Streatham Street dwellings which survive, suitably modernized, are five storeys high, with street façades in an austere late Georgian style, and an internal courtyard with open inset balconies. These are possibly, to modern eyes, the most 'human' in outward appearance of any of the model blocks of dwellings built by the housing organizations before the end of the nineteenth century. Most of them were, and are, outwardly grim, their virtues being in their standards of construction, internal layout, sanitation and maintenance when set against those of the slums they adjoined or replaced. This is particularly true of the numerous blocks of dwellings built by the Peabody Trust, the largest and most successful, and one of the longest-lasting of the Victorian housing companies—it still exists today. It was founded in 1862 with a capital of £150,000, soon increasing to £500,000, by George Peabody, an American businessman who lived part of the time in London. Many of the Peabody blocks of dwellings were built on, or immediately adjoining, the sites of slums which had been cleared. There are typical examples of Peabody dwellings in Kemble Street, off Drury Lane, which replaced the long notorious slums which had first developed in the early seventeenth century, just before the Earl of Bedford started his monumental Covent Garden scheme to the west. Here, as elsewhere, it did not necessarily follow that the people displaced by the previous clearance were rehoused in new model dwellings. Such people could not usually afford even the modest rents charged by Peabody and the other trusts, and simply moved out to find cheap accommodation in other insalubrious areas. The dwellings would be occupied by 'respectable' tenants who could afford the rents. So the providers of dwellings of this type did not solve the worst housing problems, those of accommodating the lowest paid, the near-destitute, or people with special difficulties.

There was no previous tradition in England, unlike Scotland, of purpose-built flatted accommodation, whether for the working or the upper classes. In this respect London was very different from Paris and other Continental cities (page 137).

Early clearance of slum areas had often been carried out by municipal authorities in conjunction with road schemes, like those which eliminated the 'rookery' of St Giles-in-the-Fields, or the formation of Victoria Street, which removed the last remaining slums of the Sanctuary area of Westminster about 1850. Large-scale slum clearance together with municipal housing provision was facilitated by the Housing of the Working Classes Act, 1890, after which the newly established London County Council began their ambitious housing programmes, both of flats replacing slums in the inner areas and of would-be rural cottage estates on the outskirts.

Two housing schemes, Bournville and Port Sunlight, started in the 1890s by enlightened industrialists, the Cadburys and William Lever, later Lord Leverhulme, seemed to point the way towards providing satisfactory living conditions for factory workers. Lever moved his soap factory from Warrington to a new site on the Mersey beside which he laid out a new community for his employees, called Port Sunlight after his enormously successful product, Sunlight Soap. The Cadburys had similarly moved their factory from inner Birmingham to the city's outskirts, but, unlike Port Sunlight, the adjoining residential area of Bournville was developed by them not simply to house their workforce—they ensured that a high proportion of the population would be employed elsewhere, in order to achieve a more 'balanced' community. Consisting almost entirely of individual two-storey houses, semi-detached or in short rows, these two communities were in total contrast to the Peabody-type model dwellings, and, with their spacious private gardens to every house, they were very different too from the tight-knit terrace housing of Saltaire or the Halifax model housing schemes.

This was the period when increasing numbers of sensitive people, of the middle and upper classes, turned away in horror from the typical industrial city with its smoke-laden atmosphere, its sanitary deficiencies, (even though those were being righted); its crowded, often squalid, and usually dismal, workers' housing; its lack of adequate private spaces, or even (despite the Victorian parks) public green spaces; and the increasing distance of real country from the ever-spreading urban areas. For a few—the strict disciples of William Morris, and some of the more ardent followers of the Arts and Crafts Movement—rejection of the Industrial Age and its values was absolute; they wanted a half-imagined idealized version of a 'pre-industrial' past when workers were craftsmen with pride in their work (only a minority, in fact, were ever skilled craftsmen). Industrialists like Lever and the Cadburys, for whom industry provided the basis of wealth and success, were naturally more realistic; their factories were modern and productive, but they wanted their employees to live in settings which were to be as unlike the then urban 'norm' as possible. Hence the large private gardens, following the long-established English rural and small town tradition, round the houses in Bournville and Port Sunlight, which were made to look like improved versions of rural cottages in traditional 'vernacular' styles. Provision of parks, public greens, recreation grounds and allotments in the two communities was more than generous. Such an environment, however traditionalist its inspiration, was revolutionary for workers accustomed to the crowded conditions of typical late Victorian industrial cities. But it had strong affinities with the low-density suburbs with lush gardens to which industrialists had escaped, from the polluted inner cities since the beginning of the nineteenth century (**XXIV**, p. 243). Bournville and Port Sunlight were adaptations of the established form of Victorian middle-class suburbs to what Lever and the Cadburys considered were the needs, and to what they thought should be the aspirations, of working people.

Port Sunlight and Bournville, however well provided in so many respects, were not full towns in their own right, but appendages to factories, and to cities or 'conurbations'. At the end of the century, a new idea was formed, which owed much to these two examples, for a type of small, self-sufficient town called the 'Garden City'. This was to provide a model for living in the Industrial Age without experiencing the horrors of the then familiar industrial city. The idea was explained and defined in a book, called 'Garden Cities of Tomorrow', by Ebenezer Howard—a man who seemed outwardly unremarkable. (He was born in, of all places, the City of London, in a street which is now engulfed in the Barbican complex, which is about as different from his notion of an ideal environment as any practicable development could be.) Howard migrated, while young, to the United States and lived for a time in Chicago when it was developing into the metropolis of the Prairies, but he returned to Britain after a few years. He saw large cities as undesirable in principle, quite apart from the special shortcomings of those which had developed in the Industrial Age; he particularly deplored smoke pollution (from which we, following the demise of steam as a source of power, do not now suffer), and the inadequate provision of public or private spaces in many city areas. He regretted the increasing separation of cities from the countryside, and the decay, in his time, of most rural areas, due to the slump in British agriculture because of the competition from imported foods (page 234). Such were the feelings of many sensitive people of his time. Howard's remedy was a pattern of small, well-defined towns, with their own industries, shops, cultural facilities and generous public open space, each as nearly as possible self-sufficient, apart from dependence for certain specialized facilities on occasional larger cities. Because their size would be limited and finite through strict planning control, all parts of these towns would always be within easy reach of the countryside— which, Howard hoped, would itself be revitalized in the vicinity of such towns by supplying some of their food needs. These towns would have many of the characteristics of traditional English country towns, yet Howard conceived them as being wholly new—perhaps partly because of his background at an impressionable age in the Prairies, when the environment there was being newly formed. He seemed to take little note, in his theoretical pattern, of the tight, long-established network of small towns and villages in Britain. This is amply illustrated by the siting of Letchworth, the first attempt at realizing his theory, on a 'greenfield' site between and close to two very well-established market towns, Hitchin and Baldock, of which little account seems to have been taken.

Letchworth was inaugurated in 1903, with slender resources, by Howard and a small group of dedicated and enthusiastic colleagues. It had to be financed on the private stock market (since there was no question of Government money), with a maximum dividend of five per cent—on the principle that any returns beyond that level would be used for the benefit of the town. Whereas it was possible to find enough investors in Victorian times to finance the Peabody and similar trusts with a comparable limitation, it was not so easy with Letchworth

154. *Left* **Bird's Hill, Letchworth, Hertfordshire**, by Barry Parker and Raymond Unwin, 1906, typically set round a green.

155. *Below left* **Cottages at Rushby Mead, Letchworth**, 1911 by C. M. Crickmer, in the style of Parker and Unwin, set characteristically in large gardens. Compare these cottages—built for workers at neighbouring factories—with the housing of half a century earlier at Halifax (150, 151).

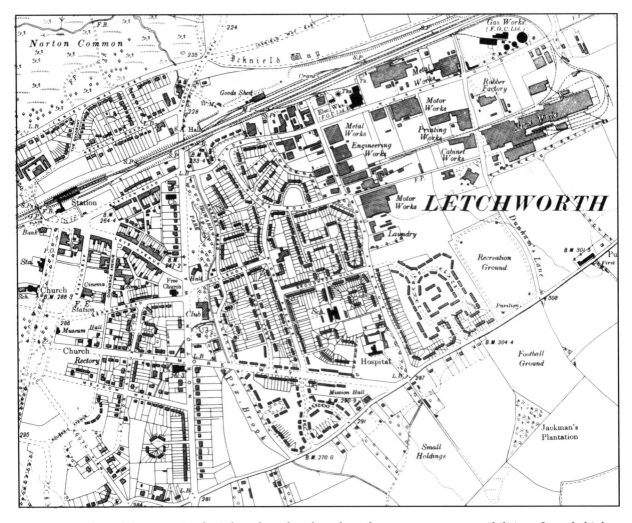

Map XXV Letchworth in 1925. The map shows the part completed twenty years after the town's inception. Houses in short terraces with large gardens are often in culs-de-sac or set round greens. They are close to the factories (Letchworth is a town, not a suburb). The town centre, on the other hand (far left), was over-ambitiously conceived and was in no more than outline at the time.

in the Edwardian decade, when there were many possibilities of much higher returns. Nevertheless the town took root and grew, though at firstly slowly. The diagrammatic 'blueprint for a Garden City', which Howard had published, was greatly modified and adapted to the gently undulating terrain with its copses and hedgerow trees, and few existing houses except in hamlets on the fringes. The overall planners, and designers of some of the buildings, were Barry Parker and, as he later became, Sir Raymond Unwin. Unwin had great influence generally on housing and housing layouts at the beginning of this century. He believed passionately that every family should have a house with a good-sized garden; his normal maximum density was twelve houses per acre, though that included a small proportion of public space. The houses he and his associates designed at Letchworth—for workers in the first, nearby, factories—are idealized versions of seventeenth- or eighteenth-century country cottages, with infinitely higher material standards inside, but looking as much as possible like their prototypes outside (**154, 155**). Unwin's cottages are usually in rows of anything up to four or five, set back behind front gardens (a rural tradition), rather than facing directly

264

on to roads (as in old towns). They are sometimes grouped round little greens, or set along culs-de-sac, which were more or less an Unwin invention. They were always carefully related to the form of the ground, and to existing trees—which Unwin always retained unless it were impossible (**XXV**).

Unwin and Parker used the same principles in designing much of Hampstead Garden Suburb—for which they are perhaps best known—from 1906 onwards, but in social terms Hampstead Garden Suburb is very different from Letchworth Garden City. The latter was intended to be a self-contained town; the former was designed frankly as a suburb, from which people would travel to London, principally by the new Underground from Golder's Green. Hampstead Garden Suburb is the culmination of the tradition of the sylvan residential area which began essentially on the edges of Regent's Park.

On the whole, Letchworth has proved a success. It is a pleasant, maturely sylvan, essentially self-contained town—in fact more people travel into work there than travel out to work elsewhere. The least successful part is what Parker and Unwin intended to be the civic centre. It was designed far too ambitiously, in deliberate formal contrast to the informality of the outer residential areas; it was never properly completed. The adjoining shopping area, however, is much more acceptable; it developed along curving roads and has almost the atmosphere of an old country town.

Howard and his associates followed the initial success of Letchworth by founding another Garden City at Welwyn in 1920, for which the master designer was Louis de Soissons. In most ways Welwyn has proved as successful as Letchworth, but it suffers from an even more grandiose central layout, very much in the then fashionable *Beaux-Arts* tradition of French derivation. Again, the formality of the town centre contrasts with the self-conscious, but usually successful, informality of the housing areas, which follow Unwin's precepts. The two Garden Cities, the self-styled Garden Suburb, the industrial 'model villages' of Port Sunlight and Bournville, and indeed the Victorian sylvan suburbs before them, were promoted in strong reaction to the shortcomings of the industrial towns of the steam age. How far they represented a dawn—or perhaps a false dawn—for a new age is discussed in the Epilogue.

Epilogue

Letchworth, Welwyn Garden City and Hampstead Garden Suburb were meant to be models for new development in the twentieth century, but much of what followed in the inter-war years was a parody of their example.

It was the age of the suburb. More of Britain was covered by new housing during those twenty-one years than in any previous period of the same length. Yet, paradoxically, it was also a period when large parts of Britain suffered acute depression. Heavy industries based on iron, steel and coal declined, in some places drastically. But new and buoyant industries developed, particularly associated with cars, or with domestic consumption. There were astonishing contrasts. Merthyr Tydfil, Jarrow, and the regions round each, suffered hopeless unemployment, while Birmingham and, still more, the ancient city of Coventry boomed with the car industry, much of which had begun literally in backyards (page 216), but which expanded in the twenties and thirties on mass-production lines. London, on the whole, was still more prosperous; a large proportion of the new industries in Britain developed on or near its outskirts. Slough in particular grew as an unbecoming, ill-controlled version of Letchworth, under the stimulus of the new factories on its Trading Estate, which attracted employees from South Wales as well as from inner parts of London.

The affluent middle classes were already in Victorian times leaving the crowded parts of cities for suburbs like Edgbaston or Wimbledon. The process continued in the twentieth century, widened geographically round London by greatly improved train services, particularly from the south and north-west. The semi-rural suburbs of Surrey and 'Metroland' now have a patina and charm which Sir John Betjeman knows best how to portray. Landscape has been allowed to dominate as far as possible—the dense but tended greenery of large gardens. The best of the houses were still influenced, even if at some remove, by the traditions of the early domestic architecture of Shaw and Lutyens (page 248).

Further into London and other cities are the thicker, though still loose-knit, inter-war suburbs which largely consist of semi-detached houses—bought with mortgages (then relatively cheap) by people with lower salaries, or higher-paid wage-earners. The character they possess is derived from their repeatedly ebullient gables, decorated with bargeboards, applied timber, or roughcast; from their ample wood-framed bay windows (the most characteristic features of inter-war suburbia); and the vegetation in their front gardens.

Finally there are the council estates. Council house building took place extensively, though erratically, through the inter-war years—mostly in sprawling estates, which were, at worst, cheaper-looking copies of private schemes or, at best, imaginatively designed layouts in the traditions of Raymond Unwin. Improved public transport—first trams, then trolleybuses and, increasingly, motor buses—reduced the disadvantages of distance from the concentrated urban facilities of the older areas from which most of the inhabitants came. But not all public housing was on peripheral estates. Many inner-city slum areas were redeveloped with blocks of flats, usually four or five storeys high—outwardly more genteel versions of the grim tenement blocks which had been built by the semi-philanthropic model housing societies of Victorian times.

What of town centres between the wars? Grand town halls were still being built, varying in style from watered-down Edwardian Baroque to impressive versions of Swedish and Dutch modern styles—like Norwich City Hall, dominating the market place, or, in London, Hornsey Town Hall, deep in Crouch End. Southampton's Civic Centre is typical, though exceptionally large, with its spreading symmetrical blocks in simplified Classical style, faced in Portland stone, and its tall and slender tower. (Southampton was a boom town of the thirties, in its heyday as a passenger port). Otherwise, city-centre planning was largely in the form of new or widened streets, occasionally achieving effects of washed-out grandeur—as in the Headrow at Leeds, where the impotence of the pretentious new buildings contrasts with the virility of the Victorian town hall at the end of the street.

The thirties were the first heyday of multiple shops. Prime parts of shopping centres were rebuilt piecemeal with threepenny and sixpenny stores, tailors of taste, and chain teashops (now nostalgically recalled), interspersed in places by banks which still maintained traditions of Victorian stolidity. New suburban 'parades' were built from the same components. The results were not inspiring. The most imaginative type of inter-war building was the cinema. Behind the fantasy foyers of Odeons and Gaumonts were Art-Deco auditoria, where people made their periodic escapes into Hollywood. By contrast, new public houses—fewer but bigger than before, because of licensing controls—were ebulliently neo-traditional. Their strident gables and overhung upper storeys were usually more than half timbered: riotous 'Tudor' was then thought by brewers to be the best background style for drinking.

Other memorable inter-war buildings in cities were the new Underground stations by Charles Holden; a few factories, such as those on the Great West Road; and, in the City of London, Lutyens' vibrant Midland Bank in Poultry, contrasting so vigorously with the other more stolid, less adventurous, banking palaces which were rising round it.

In the Second World War, the commercial centres of several cities, and much of the City of London, were devastated. Rebuilding of these places had priority after the war. In Plymouth, most badly bombed of all, the 'master planner' was Professor Patrick Abercrombie, whose plan was in a grandiose *Beaux-Arts* style— such as would have been fashionable between the wars in Britain if there had been more city-centre planning. It has a wide boulevard running north–south, pointing on the map to the Hoe and Plymouth Sound, on the ground to the brow of a hill. In fairness to Abercombie, he cannot be debited with any of the actual buildings in the city centre. Like those in other rebuilt centres of the time, such as Bristol, Swansea, Southampton, Exeter and parts of the City of London near St Paul's, they indicate the levels of dejection to which officially promoted, though largely commercially sponsored, 'architecture' had sunk.

Professor Abercrombie (later Sir Patrick) was also the author of two bold and far-seeing plans, one for London, the other for the region round. He envisaged a reduction of about a million in the population of the older parts of London, following redevelopment. He recommended that London should not grow beyond the limits of continuous development that had been reached in 1939, apart from limited rounding-off—and that the remaining country for several miles beyond should be preserved for ever as a Green Belt, apart from existing communities within it. He then suggested sites for several New Towns beyond the Green Belt, to house some of the million people displaced from London.

Abercrombie's wider plan was accepted in principle, including the Green Belt and the building of New Towns—though some were to be on different sites from those he had selected. Several New Towns were started round London by 1950, and others in the North and Wales. Most were to have populations between about 50,000 and 80,000, beyond which they would not grow; they were to be contained by permanent countryside. The best is Harlow, designed overall by Sir Frederick Gibberd, who took the greatest advantage of a gently undulating landscape, preserving most of its trees (and planting many more), and providing 'green wedges' which penetrate from the edges towards the town centre. The housing areas, designed by many different architects, vary greatly; the best are the earliest, in the traditions of Raymond Unwin.

In the 1950s there was a tremendous reaction against the low-density, mainly two-storey housing in the earlier parts of the New Towns and elsewhere. Architects, planners and, especially, architectural journalists went to the incomplete towns, saw the wide spaces which either were planned for, or were merely waiting for later development, and called it all 'prairie planning'. ('Forest planning' would have been a better term for Harlow, with all its trees.) They compared the New Towns with long-matured country towns and—this became an obsession with some architectural journalists—Italian hill-towns. More influentially, they promoted the ideals of the French architectural genius and publicist, Le Corbusier (strictly Swiss in origin).

Corbusier's urban Utopias, first illustrated in books published between the wars, included tower blocks and slab blocks—the terms have now become commonplace—standing amid and around green spaces, served by complex systems of vehicular and pedestrian access at various levels. The blocks of flats were more clearly related to Continental traditions of urban housing than to those of England. In nearly every European country flats or apartments had become established as the normal dwelling units in large towns and cities; in England and Wales (though not Scotland), houses in their own plots, or cottages in their gardens, were accepted as the desirable norm, even if not always attainable. But much closer to English ideals was the relationship of buildings to landscape envisaged by Corbusier. This is close to the pattern of Georgian squares, or that of Nash's terraces fronting Regent's Park. Unwin and Corbusier both wanted green spaces as parts of living environments. Unwin's were largely in the form of private gardens round invididual houses; Corbusier's were intended to be largely public, apart from the areas devoted to vehicles. But the admirers of Corbusier focused their vision on the high-rise blocks, taking less note of the adjoining open spaces which would have compensated for their bulk and density.

By the 1960s the spirit of Corbusier seems to have gripped not only architects, planners and journalists, but also administrators and politicians, local and national. Various arguments were used in favour of high-rise housing: it would reduce pressure on the diminishing countryside (valid, if the landscape components of Corbusier's Utopias were largely disregarded); most people liked to live in crowded surroundings (a false claim); and average journeys to work and facilities would be reduced (less important with the improvements in transportation). Public subsidies for housing were weighted in favour of multi-storey building. Every two-penny-halfpenny local authority had to have its high-rise towers in order to be worthy of the age of new pence. But the most impressive displays were provided, naturally, by the larger authorities. The London County Council, and its larger successor after 1963, the Greater London Council, developed at Roehampton— hitherto an affluent south-western suburb—a complex of mainly high-rise housing on Corbusian principles, which for many years was visited by admirers from all over the world. Here there was an ideal setting already—the maturely landscaped grounds of several very large villas, most of which were demolished (the best were preserved); the controlled wildness of Wimbledon Common on one side and Richmond Park on another. The white towers of Roehampton, when seen rising beyond the wood-fringed grasslands of Richmond Park, seemed to Corbusian idolizers the realization of what they had dreamed about for so long.

But the landscape of Roehampton was unique. From the wastelands of West Ham, of West Bromwich or of Wavertree, which were more typical settings, the grey towers appeared less enthralling (they were much more often grey than white—grey became *the* fashionable architects' colour). Most of the people who transferred to these towers had previously lived in two storeyed houses, even if subdivided, and they did not all take to living high—especially if maintenance standards were low, and children, badly provided with playing areas, turned to vandalism. Such drawbacks were becoming increasingly evident when the partial collapse of a tower-block in West Ham, after a gas explosion, focused attention on the general problems of high-rise housing.

There was a reaction in favour of two-storey housing, though at tighter densities than Raymond Unwin had advocated. The early post-war New Towns had, to their credit, continued to provide houses rather than high-rise flats, and the further New Towns designated in the 1960s, such as Runcorn and Milton Keynes, were also designed mainly for houses. The quality and form of the late 1960s' and 1970s' housing in such places varies greatly, but at its best it is pleasant and imaginative, as in the informal, contrivedly irregular scheme designed by Ralph Erskine at Eaglestone, in Milton Keynes; and on the hillslope site called The Brow at Runcorn (the most interestingly sited of all the New Towns, with its sweeping views over the Mersey). But both these towns also have housing areas which are rigidly geometrical and drearily repetitive. (There are some who say that the old town of Stony Stratford, now included in the 'new city' of Milton Keynes, is the most attractive part of the 'city'.) But perhaps there has been too much of a reaction against high-rise housing. It is not suitable, generally, for families with children, but there is a large minority of people for whom a flat, if properly maintained, is perfectly acceptable.

City centres became largely depopulated in the nineteenth century (see Chapter Seventeen). The separation between residential areas and largely commercial city centres was accepted as the norm in the new and drastically replanned towns after the war. Not all bombed city centres were as unimaginatively redeveloped as those already mentioned. The basically medieval centre of Coventry was largely destroyed in 1940—though leaving a surprisingly large number of individual medieval buildings. It was replanned in what was then a novel manner, with the central shops facing spaces devoted to pedestrians. Hitherto, almost all main shopping areas had been based on streets open to traffic, whether horse, electric or, latterly, petrol powered. It was odd that the car-producing city of Coventry should have had the first large traffic-free shopping centre in Britain, with car parks and lorry servicing areas set behind the shops and approached from perimeter roads. Coventry's early post-war buildings, apart from the new Cathedral, were banal (though some later ones are better), but in planning terms the city set a new pattern. Even the name 'Precinct', given to Coventry's new centre, became adopted as a common term, used by developers for any of the numerous traffic-free shopping centres which became so numerous from the 1960s.

Traffic planning became an obsession—not surprisingly, since the number of vehicles increased far faster than had at first been foretold. Roads were planned, and all too often built, to cater for extravagantly estimated traffic needs several decades ahead. Junctions of fantastic complexity were designed—sometimes with justification, as at 'Spaghetti Junction' on the outskirts of Birmingham, where national motorways converge, but often merely at the intersections of local routes. Wide swathes of new roadway were built across old areas of cities, sometimes only for fairly limited traffic. The corollary could be the total exclusion of through traffic from the areas bounded by the new roads, as envisaged in Sir Colin Buchanan's enormously influential *Traffic in Towns*, published in 1963, but even if this happened, the cost, in slicing up cities, could be enormous.

The 1960s and early 1970s were boom years for redevelopment. Old town centres, often with street patterns going back to the Middle Ages, and varied Victorian, Georgian and sometimes earlier buildings, were partly rebuilt as 'shopping precincts'. At first these were usually on the Coventry model, but, later, most 'precincts' were covered and air-conditioned—updated, but usually less elegant, versions of Victorian market halls and arcades. Elsewhere, even in cities as historically important as York and Bath, as well as in hundreds of attractive country towns and villages, there was steady erosion as fine or at least pleasant buildings were replaced by inferior, or positively ugly, new ones.

There was a tremendous reaction against all this. Civic and preservation societies emerged all over the country in the later 1960s, encouraged by the newly formed Civic Trust. The concept of historic Conservation Areas was established in law. More and more buildings were listed as historic, and restrictions against their demolition strengthened. The Society for the Protection of Ancient Buildings— founded by William Morris as long ago as 1877 to fight against the bad restorations of old buildings as much as against their demolition—and its descendants, the Georgian Group and the Victorian Society, were given statutory and consultative roles over historic buildings. Much has been achieved in the preservation field since this upsurge in the late sixties—both negatively, through stopping buildings being pulled down, and positively, through co-ordinated conservation schemes.

But, just beyond the prosperous, often fast-changing, centres of cities are some of the problem areas of today. The distinction between city centres and what we now call 'inner city' areas, which really began in Victorian times, is described on page 217. Victorian 'inner cities' were usually tightly built-up with factories or warehouses, and terraces of workers' housing. Today, factories in such areas have often been closed, and much of the housing redeveloped, usually in the form of flats. Reaction against such clearance, as well as against flats generally, have recently led to many remaining areas of old terrace housing being rehabilitated rather than demolished. Sometimes this rehabilitation is done comprehensively by councils, sometimes individually by owners or purchasers. This had led to what is now called 'gentrification'—a reversal of the 150-year old trend of the prosperous middle classes to move out of inner areas into suburbs. (In fact some, though by no means all, of the areas which have recently been 'gentrified' are the very areas from which the middle classes moved earlier.) Some inner districts are now, of course, known for their concentrations of immigrant or 'ethnic' population. But this is not an entirely recent process. Spitalfields was an early eighteenth-century residential area just east of the City of London. Very soon after it developed, silk-weavers who had been refugees from France, or their sons, moved in (page 215). The silk industry declined in the nineteenth century, and at the end of the century the then dilapidated Georgian and later houses were partly occupied by refugee Jews, who flooded in to escape persecution in Russia and elsewhere. Later, the Jews moved on, and by the 1960s many of the houses were occupied by immigrants from Asia. Now some of the surviving Georgian houses are being repaired, so that 'gentrification' has begun.

This Epilogue ends with two places in the early 1980s. At Milton Keynes, that 'city' of a hundred housing estates, the new shopping centre is simply a long glazed building, with shops fronting covered pedestrian ways and separate servicing accesses—efficient, effective and elegant. But is this the culmination of two thousand years of urban history? Compare a Roman forum (as far as we know what that looked like), a medieval street, a Georgian square, a Victorian market hall (with which it has some affinity), or an Edwardian city centre like Cardiff. Its exterior, its skyline and its immediate surroundings (vehicle parking areas) are all featureless, apart from trees alongside the car parks. Too many old cities have recently been disfigured by excessively tall buildings, but in Milton Keynes tall buildings are perversely proscribed. But, if there is any place in Britain which needs, above all others, tall buildings in its centre, it is Milton Keynes.

Finally, a look at Norwich. Apart from York, this is the best essentially medieval city in Britain. It suffered some bombing and insipid early post-war rebuilding, and there were bad intrusions in the early sixties, notably an eight-storey office block by an insurance company on one of the highest parts of the historic centre, overwhelming the remaining Georgian and earlier buildings nearby. But the worst threat to the city's historic character was through decay. Colegate, across the River Wensum from the city centre, was in medieval and Georgian times a wealthy district. After the collapse of the local weaving trade in the early nineteenth century (page 166), other industries developed, notably shoemaking. Factories and warehouses were built on former gardens and other spaces behind Georgian and earlier houses which, if they survived, were subdivided into either poor residential or inferior commercial accommodation. Some of the trades in these buildings in turn declined, leaving cleared spaces or decaying structures—a typical 'inner city' situation, except that a large number of the buildings were of historic interest. In the last twenty years there has been a transformation. Georgian and earlier houses have been rehabilitated, many as discreetly modernized dwellings; historic churches and chapels have been repaired, though not all as places of worship;

and cleared spaces have been filled with housing—some of it built by the council, some by private developers. Most of the housing has been sensitively designed, in self-consciously picturesque styles, related to the older restored buildings, and to the hitherto disregarded river. Through the actions of an enlightened council, private firms, and individuals a decaying inner city area of great historic character has been rescued and rehabilitated, and people have come back in significant numbers to live on the fringes of the city centre, reversing the trends of the last century and a half.

*   *   *   *   *   *   *   *   *   *

So ended the Epilogue in the first edition. What has happened to our towns and cities since 1984? Care for historic towns is very much a continuing issue—but it is part of a much wider concern which includes protection of the countryside, wildlife and the global environment. The redevelopment schemes which ravaged so many towns in the sixties and seventies are now generally unpopular. However, pressures for redevelopment in some towns have been reduced because of the trends towards huge 'out of town' shopping centres. Local authorities have been equivocal about them; certainly they take away some of the commercial pressures from the older centres, but they can also sap the vitality which often helps to keep old town centres attractive, and reduce the means for keeping notable buildings there in good order.

Lists of buildings of architectural and historic interest have been extended, and hundreds of thousands of buildings are now protected by legislation against their demolition or harmful alteration—which is restrictive but not absolute. Conservation areas in towns and cities have increased in number and extent—at least implying a presumption against harmful development in the areas they cover. Some local authorities—not all—have good records in preserving and enhancing their historic urban areas; at county level Hampshire and Essex must be specially mentioned in this respect. Against this, however, controls over the design of new developments have been drastically weakened over the last few years.

Until the 1970s a large proportion of new housing was built by public authorities. Milton Keynes is the last major monument of publicly sponsored new development. It was started during the reaction against the high-rise housing of the sixties, and all the early housing areas are of two or, occasionally, three, storeys. Many are interesting and individualistic, the houses well integrated with generous new planting. Almost all houses built in Britain since the seventies have been privately sponsored, but, sadly, the general standards of design both of individual houses (outwardly) or estates collectively have been abysmal. Considering the great tradition which developed in Britain for large-scale housing, from Georgian Bath and Bloomsbury and Victorian garden suburbs to green and spacious industrial townships like Port Sunlight and Letchworth, then on to post-war New Towns at their best and to some of the more enlightened schemes of the fifties to seventies, it is disgraceful that new housing developments are not generally pleasant and appealing and, on occasions, delightful—but, unfortunately, they are not. This is a more pessimistic note on which to end this edition than that for 1984; all the more reason to appreciate—and understand—the still plentiful townscapes from more enlightened periods.

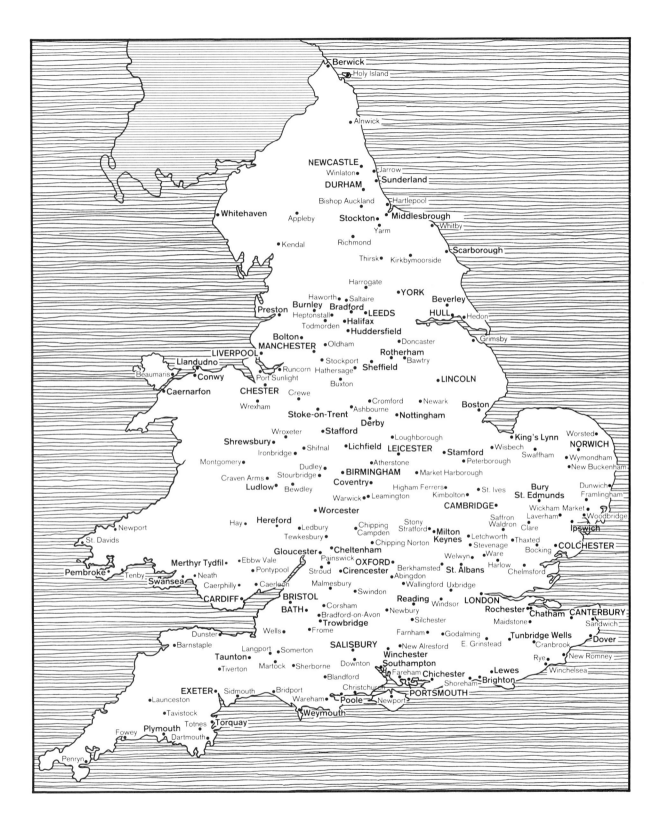

Berwick
Holy Island
Alnwick
NEWCASTLE
Winlaton   Jarrow
DURHAM   Sunderland
Bishop Auckland   Hartlepool
Whitehaven   Appleby   Stockton   Middlesbrough
Yarm   Whitby
Kendal   Richmond
Thirsk   Kirkbymoorside   Scarborough
Harrogate
Haworth   Saltaire   YORK
Burnley   Bradford   Beverley
Preston   Heptonstall   LEEDS   HULL   Hedon
Todmorden   Halifax
Huddersfield
Bolton   Oldham   Doncaster   Grimsby
MANCHESTER
LIVERPOOL   Rotherham
Llandudno   Stockport   Bawtry
Beaumaris   Conwy   Runcorn   Hathersage   Sheffield
Port Sunlight   LINCOLN
Caernarfon   CHESTER   Crewe   Buxton
Wrexham   Cromford   Newark   Boston
Stoke-on-Trent   Ashbourne
Wroxeter   Derby   Nottingham
Shrewsbury   Stafford   Loughborough   King's Lynn   Worsted
Shifnal   Lichfield   LEICESTER   Wisbech   NORWICH
Ironbridge   Stamford   Swaffham   Wymondham
Montgomery   Atherstone   Peterborough   New Buckenham
Dudley   BIRMINGHAM   Market Harborough
Craven Arms   Stourbridge   Coventry   Higham Ferrers   St. Ives   Bury   Dunwich
Ludlow   Bewdley   Warwick   Leamington   Kimbolton   St. Edmunds   Framlingham
Worcester   CAMBRIDGE   Wickham Market   Woodbridge
Hay   Hereford   Chipping   Stony   Saffron   Laverham   Ipswich
Newport   Campden   Stratford   Milton   Waldron   Clare   COLCHESTER
St. Davids   Ledbury   Keynes   Letchworth   Thaxted
Tewkesbury   Chipping Norton   Stevenage   Bocking
Merthyr Tydfil   Ebbw Vale   Cheltenham   Welwyn   Ware   Chelmsford
Gloucester   Painswick   OXFORD   Berkhamsted   St. Albans   Harlow
Pembroke   Neath   Pontypool   Stroud   Cirencester   Abingdon   Uxbridge
Tenby   Caerphilly   Caerleon   Malmesbury   Wallingford   LONDON
Swansea   Swindon   Reading   Windsor   Rochester   Chatham   CANTERBURY
CARDIFF   BRISTOL   Corsham   Newbury   Silchester   Maidstone   Sandwich
BATH   Bradford-on-Avon   Farnham   Godalming   Tunbridge Wells   Dover
Dunster   Trowbridge   New Alresford   E. Grinstead   Cranbrook
Barnstaple   Wells   Frome   SALISBURY   Rye   New Romney
Langport   Somerton   Downton   Winchester   Lewes   Winchelsea
Taunton   Martock   Sherborne   Southampton   Chichester   Brighton
Tiverton   Blandford   Fareham   Shoreham
EXETER   Sidmouth   Bridport   Christchurch   PORTSMOUTH
Launceston   Wareham   Poole   Newport
Tavistock   Weymouth
Fowey   Plymouth   Totnes   Torquay
Dartmouth
Penryn

273

Index

Illustrations are in bold type, and indexed under plate number: not page number

Bawtry, Bewdley, Boston, Cambridge, King's Lynn, Lechlade, St Ives: **16**, Ware: **35**, Yarmouth

ROADS AND TRAFFIC; Roman: Watling Street, 16, 22, 42, 65–6, **120, VII**; riding: packhorses, 42, 195; coaches: carriages, 42, 186, 195–6, 202, 208, 244; goods by road, 42, 64, 114, 119–20, 164, 173, 186, 195, 208; highway towns, 41–2, 60, 64–6, 72–3, 91, 195–6, 202, 208, **26, 33–5, 120, VII, IX, XI, XIII**; turnpikes, 186, 196, 199, 208; river-road connections, 64–5, 112, 117, 119–20, 173, 176, **16, 35–6** post-war, 270

Rochdale, 161

Rochester; Roman, 17, 26; wall, 20, 104; cathedral, 21, 26; port, 22; *see* Chatham

Romney, New; port: silting: ch. 113

Romsey; abbey, 76, 90

Rope making: dockyards, 184

Rotherham; church: chantry: school: bridge chapel, 88; iron, 176

Rothwell; Market House, 100

Ruabon; bricks, 241

Rugby; school, 96, 253

Runcorn: New Town: housing, 269

Ryde, 192–3; bows, 193; arcade, 223

Rye; port, 113; Landgate, 105

SAFFRON WALDEN; medieval houses: Sun Inn: Bridge St.: separation of town from country, 49, 52, **22**; market encroachment, 48; ch. 93; saffron, 108

ST ALBANS; pre-Roman, 15; Roman Verulamium, 16, 18–21, 25, **4**; abbey: cathedral, 19, 24–5, 76, 90, 251, **4**; martyrdom: shrine, 19, 25, 77, 91; St Michael, 18, 25; Saxon town, 25, 47, **7–8**; market place: encroachments, 25–6, 47, **7**; belfry, **7**; Fishpool St. **8–9**; houses, 51, **7–9**

St Asaph: St Davids; cathedrals, 80

St Helens; glass: canal, 180

ST IVES, Huntingdonshire; river port, 41, 54, 118, **16**; fair, 41, 118; bridge: chapel, 88, **16**; chs. 251; stone, 54

St Neots; market place, 46, **VI**; ch. 94; Eynesbury, **VI**

SALISBURY; Old Sarum, 82–3; medieval city, 46–8, 73, 82–4, **46–50**; wool, 41, 84, 107, 114; market place: encroachments, 46–8, 84, **49**; High St. **50**; Poultry Cross, 100, **49**; medieval houses, 51, 56, 84, 206, **47, 50**; bldg. materials, 56, 83–4, 191, 206, **47–50, 124**; bishops, 48, 74, 83–4, 205; cathedral, 48–9, 94, **48**; close: clergy houses, 83–4, 103, 206, **46–7, 124**; close wall: gate, 83–4, **50**; landscaping, 84, 206, **46**; link with Southampton, 114; tiles, 56, 191, **50**

Salt: early use of coal, 112, 177–8, 180

SALTAIRE; model village: Sir Titus Salt: factory: housing: ch.: institute: park, 258–9, 261

Saltburn: resort: station, 247

Sandwich; port: houses: ramparts: gate, 113; Flemish refugees, 111; Romans, 15–6

SANITATION; absence: water contamination: cholera: typhoid: Edwin Chadwick: Public Health Acts: local boards: supposed infection from foul air: sewers: pumping stations: byelaws, 255–8, 261

SCARBOROUGH; port: fishing: castle: setting, 120, 212, 247; resort, 151, 247; hotel, 247

SCHOOLS; grammar schools, 66, 68, 88, 96, 98, 253, **56**; public schools, 96, 253; assocd. with almshouses, 98, **57**; with chantries, 88, 96; charity schools, 87–8, 96, 162; church schools: British and Foreign School Society, 252; Sunday schools, 259; Education Acts: board schools, 252; early local authority schools, **148–9**; styles and materials, 96, 253, **56, 148–9**

SEASIDE; early bathing, 150–2; drinking sea water, 151; royal visits to Weymouth and Brighton, 151–5; bathing machines, 151; formal devlt: terraces: crescents: squares, 151–5, 246–7, **87, XVI**; informal devlt: villas: cottages ornées, 155, 246, **90**; bowed facades, 154, 192–3, **88–9**; hotels: boarding houses, 247; piers, 246; dramatic settings, 246–7; retirement, 246; effect of railways, 155, 245, 247–8; failed resorts, 155, 247; chs. 246, 251; fashionable clientele, 151–5, 246–7; middle-class, 245–8; popular, 155, 248

Severn, River, 33, 42, 59, 115, 117, 173, 180

Severus, Emperor, 17, 19

Seville, 125

Shaftesbury; Saxon burh, 22; abbey: destruction, 25, 90; parliamentary borough, 43

Shaw, Norman, archt., 213, 244, 248–9, 266

SHEFFIELD; cutlery, 112, 176, 214; ore import, 112, 120, 176; crucible method, 176; Sheffield plate, 176; modern steel, 214–5; railway, 210; schools, 253, **148–9**

Sherborne; Saxon cathedral, 26, 83; abbey, 90; bldg. materials, 55–6; silk, 159

Shields, North and South; shipbuilding: salt: pollution, 178

Shifnal: linear town: encroachment: ch.: chapels: workhouse: cattle market, 48, **IX**

SHIPBUILDING; sailing ships, 125, 134, 177, 184–5, 210, 212–3; Royal Navy: dockyards, 173, 184–5, 211; HMS Victory, 185; first steam vessels: first iron ships: paddle steamers: screw propellors, 210; Great Western and Sirius across Atlantic, 210; steamships, 184–5, 210–3; liners, 211–2; problem of fuelling, 210; steam turbines, 211; steel, 215

Shipley, 259

Ships, *see* Ports: Shipbuilding

Shire Halls, *see* Counties

236, 240, **92, 94–5, 100, 150–2**;
Northumberland, 177, **70, 101–2**;
marbles, 218; granite, 185; Caen
stone, 55, 89, **59**; roofing slabs, 58, **92,
100**
STONY STRATFORD; traffic: coaching, 42,
65, 202, **120**; market place: burgage
plots, 66; fire: rebuilding, 66, 202,
120; bldg. materials, 56, 202, **120–1**;
relationship with Milton Keynes, 202,
269
STOURBRIDGE; wire: nails: slitting mills,
172, 176; glass, 173
Stourhead; landscape, 101
Stourport; canal port, 173, 181
Stowmarket, 236
Stratford, near London; flour milling,
64; college: library: museum, 253–4;
pumping station, 256; name, 44
Stratford-on-Avon, 44, 53
Straw; plaiting: hats, 236
Street, G.E., archt. 250, **78**
STREETS (a) *Roman*; 15–6, **1**; **21**; **I**
(b) *Medieval*; Saxon, 22–4, 28, 46, 123,
5–6, 26, II; later medieval, 44–52, 57–
84, 105–6, 123–5, 128 *passim*; grid
patterns, 23, 44, 68, 71–2, 77–8, 82–3,
IV, XV; streets as market places, 28,
46–8, 60, 64, 68, 71–2, 202–3; notable
streets, at Appleby, 47, 68, **37–8**;
Ashbourne, 66, **XII**; Atherstone, **VII**;
Blandford Forum, 200, **V**; Bocking,
65–6; Bridport, 23, **5–6**; Chester, 15–
6, 48–9, 53, 56, **1, 21**; Chipping
Campden, 46, 59–60, **29, XI**; Dunster,
15; Durham, 78–80, **XIV**; Fareham, 59,
72, 198, **118**; Farnham, 47, 72, **XIII**;
Godalming, 74, **40–1**; Hull, **XVII**;
Kimbolton, **17, VIII**; Langport, **II**;
Ledbury, 53, 61–2, **30–2**; Lewes, 46,
26–8; Marlborough, 47–8; Oxford,
23, 46, 56, 106; Pembroke, **70–1**;
Penryn, 62; Saffron Walden, **22**;
Sandwich, 113; Stockton, 47, 202–3;
Stony Stratford, 65–6, 202, **120–1**;
Trowbridge, 46, 168, **99**; Ware, 48,
64–5, **33–4**; Yarm, 47, 59, 202–3, **122–
3**; grid plans at New Buckenham, 68;
Bury St Edmunds, 71, 77–8, 207, **43**,
114; Caernarfon, 71; Lichfield, 71, 82,
XV; Newport, Pembrokeshire, **13–4**,
IV; Newtown, Isle of Wight, 71;
Salisbury, 47–8, 51, 82–4, **50**;
Wallingford: Wareham, 23;
Winchelsea, 71; Winchester, 22–3;
encroachments on wide streets, *see*
Encroachments; towns along
highways, *see* Roads and Traffic;
survival of medieval tradition in 17th
cent. 56, **104–5**
(c) *Georgian and prototype*, 58, 129–57,
177–80, 188–90, 194–5, 198–203
passim; notable streets in Bath: Gt.
Pulteney St., 156, **81**; Bradford-on-
Avon, 168, **97**; Liverpool, 179–80;
London, 129–57 *passim*; Newcastle:
Grey St., 177–8, 218, **101–2**; streets of
medieval origin with Georgian
buildings are included in (b)
(d) *Victorian and later*, 217–34, 244,
255–61 *passim*; workers' housing, *see*

Housing; new streets in central
London, 218–9, 230–1, 244, 256–7,
260–1, **129**; Embankment, 256;
notable streets in Birmingham, 228;
Cardiff, 233–4; Chester, 248; inter-
war, 267; post-war redevelopment,
268
Stroud; wool industry, 110, 168–9
Stucco, *see* Plaster
SUBURBS; medieval, 105; city merchants'
rural villas, 128, 134, 182, 217;
Regent's Park, 150, 239, 265, **144–5**;
move from city centres, 217–8, 220,
226, 230, 234, 239–40, 243–4, 262,
266; villa suburbs, 156, 220, 230,
239–49, **90, 144–6, XXII, XXIV**; semi-
detached houses, 239, 242, 245, 247,
261, 266; styles and bldg. materials,
236, 240–1, 243–4, 247–9; seclusion,
241–2; romantic rusticity, 150, 155,
239–40, 244, 248, 262, 264, **90, 144–7,
154–5**; gardens, *see* House Plots;
planting, *see* Landscape;
conservatories, 241; bay windows,
240, 266; Edgbaston, 226, 242–4, 266,
XXIV; North Oxford, 244, 250;
Southsea, 244, 250, **146–7**; Arts and
Crafts tradition, 248–9, 261–2;
commuting, 244, 247–9, 265–6; cheap
fares, 248; Bournville: Port Sunlight,
261–2; Hampstead Gdn. Suburb, 265–
6; inter-war, 266; council housing,
261, 266; contrasting Scottish
traditions, 239, 244, 261; survival of
Georgian traditions, *see* Houses (e)
Sudbury; wool industry, 110
Sugar, 112, 126, 178, 180
SUNDERLAND; Monkwearmouth
monastery, 21; station, 209; coal, 176,
178; shipbuilding: glass, 177, 213;
Ambrose Crowley, 176; Victorian
housing; Scottish traditions, 213, 244
Surbiton; early railway suburb, 247
Swaffham, Norfolk, **X**
SWANSEA; port: Bristol links, 117, 180,
182, 214; copper: brass, 112, 174, 214,
232; post-war rebuilding, 267
Sweden; import of iron ore, 112, 176;
timber, 177, 188
Swindon; railway town: model housing:
haphazard growth, 210, 259
Sydney; Francis Greenway, 156

Taff, River, 175, 214, 232
Tanning, 187, 234
Taunton; weaving, 110; ch. 94
Technical Colleges, *see* Universities
Tees, River, 120, 202–3, 208, 215
Tenby; port, 117, 180, 247; wall, 104,
247; resort: setting, 247
Tetbury; Market House, 100, **58**
Tewkesbury; abbey, 90; burgage plots:
infilling, 51, 59; river trade, 117
Thame, 48
THAXTED; guildhall, 99; ch. 94, 100;
cutlery, 99, 112
THEATRES, 128, 130, 177–8, 223, 231,
101, 139
Thetford, 28
Thirsk; church: original settlement site,
91, **53**